Government
and
Politics in the
Twentieth
Century

Government and Politics in the Twentieth Century

THIRD EDITION

Gwendolen M. Carter
and John H. Herz

PRAEGER PUBLISHERS
New York · Washington · London

Permission for the reprinting of excerpts
adapted from MAJOR FOREIGN POWERS by
Gwendolen M. Carter and John H. Herz has
been granted by Harcourt Brace Jovanovich,
Inc.; copyright © 1949, 1952, 1957, 1962,
1967, 1972 by Harcourt Brace Jovanovich,
Inc.

PRAEGER PUBLISHERS
111 Fourth Avenue, New York, N.Y. 10003, U.S.A.
5, Cromwell Place, London SW7 2JL, England

Published in the United States of America in 1973
by Praeger Publishers, Inc.

© 1961, 1965 by Frederick A. Praeger, Inc.
© 1973 by Praeger Publishers, Inc.

This is the third edition of a book first published in 1961.
A previous revised edition was published in 1965.

Library of Congress Cataloging in Publication Data

Carter, Gwendolen Margaret, 1906–
    Government and politics in the twentieth century.

    1. Political science. I. Herz, John H., 1908–
joint author. II. Title.
JA66.C3 1973   320.3   72-83003

Printed in the United States of America.

CONTENTS

PREFACE

The systematic study of comparative government and politics has most commonly been concerned with the institutions and activities of European countries and the United States. Moreover, in those works in which the institutions of the newer countries have been examined analytically, the consideration has nearly always been either of a particular state or of several of these states compared with each other. In this Third Edition of *Government and Politics in the Twentieth Century*, we continue to seek a broader focus of comparative analysis by dealing with both developed and developing countries and by testing generalizations obtained from the study of mature states in the light of the experience of the newer states of Asia, Africa, the Middle East, and Latin America.

Accepting the theoretical dichotomy of democracy and totalitarianism, we recognize that even highly developed states do not conform exactly to the characteristic features of either system. Particularly among the newer states, there are political systems lying between democracy and totalitarianism that not only partake of the characteristics of both but also add something distinctive of their own.

This book makes no pretense at finality. Rather, we have sought to stimulate further investigation into a field that becomes increasingly suggestive as its focus is widened. We have therefore deliberately sought great breadth of scope. We have been concerned with the operation and results in different settings of what may seem to be similar institutions, with those forces that make for uniformity and those that make for diversity, with the interaction of traditional and revolutionary forces and with reactions to the strains of ideological conflict. Moreover, while continuing to emphasize the role of force in international relations, we have also examined in a wholly new chapter the impact of force on the dynamics of change in domestic conditions and regimes.

When this small volume was first published, it evoked a degree of interest both in this country and abroad (evidenced by its translation into eight foreign languages and its adoption by the British Open University) that was as exhilarating as it was unexpected. In preparing this new edition, we have made numerous, and substantial, changes in detail, necessitated by new developments and emphases. Our central purpose, however, remains the same. While putting into sharp focus the divergencies of governmental and political systems in the twentieth-century world and while not playing down the conflict situations that such divergency is bound to create, we hope to have made clear both the validity of the assumptions of democracy and the merit that can exist in systems that differ from Western models. It is in accordance with the democratic approach to grant others their right to find their own answers to their particular problems. Only thus can this "one world" become a world of neighbors.

GWENDOLEN M. CARTER
JOHN H. HERZ

PROLOGUE: ARISTOTLE'S DREAM

My dear Cleon:

Is life a dream? Is what we call our dreams our real life? The other day I had the strangest incident of my life. I pre-lived immortality. In my strangest dream, the gods showed me the future of the human race. When I awoke, they told me that I had been in torporlike sleep for almost forty hours. If every minute of my sleep corresponded to a year, I saw in that dream what happened to man, and the star on which he lives, for more than two thousand years. And what I saw, even you, who are not among the incredulous, will have a hard time believing.

I shall dwell only briefly on what happened in the times closest to our own—tempting though this would be, for we are most curious about that which is close and familiar.

Familiar yet strange was what had happened to our Hellas. For the first time, I found it united but, alas, only under the rule of alien tyrants. Those barbarians from Graecia Magna, to whom our colonies had brought the light of reason, ruled us for centuries, but there was triumph, too: In ruling us, they fell under the spell of our customs, our way of life, our art, our thoughts. And, greater triumph still, the very words and concepts of our language entered their language and their minds and, from there, those of all generations in those millennia I witnessed. In that ultimate period I lived through in my dream, men everywhere on the globe still spoke of "politics" as we speak of what happens in our *poleis;* and, while they invented a new name for the political community, they still distinguished forms and types in familiar terms: democracy, aristocracy, oligarchy, monarchy. I am embarrassed to report that to the very science and method of thought, dialectic and logic, they had given the attribute of my name.

You may be surprised to hear me speak of "men on this globe." Indeed, my friend, what some of us had suspected in the teeth of unending ridicule (and I must admit I had been one of the ridiculers), was found true: This earth is not a flat pancake but a sphere, a star among stars, revolving on its axis around the sun. And now I must tell you the unbelievable: Men, at the end of these millennia I saw, had not only penetrated to the ultimate ends of the globe but learned to thrust themselves into the universe and set foot on the moon, ready to travel to other stars. Having told you about this achievement, you will be less surprised to hear that they also had learned to fly into the air that surrounds the globe, to travel from one place to another with unbelievable speed. They also speak to each other through the air over huge distances and, by looking into an illuminated box, are able to see what happens in far, distant places. As a matter of fact, I saw many of them, and most of the very young, for most of their lives sitting in front of the box and staring at what happened elsewhere. Had they thus attained the "good life" of which we philosophers debate on end?

I must tell you, my friend, that my impression of what they had achieved was strangely ambiguous. You remember, I once wrote that slaves would become unnecessary if men should ever invent inanimate contraptions that could perform the work of slaves. Men, using what we discovered—science, the laws of nature—have fashioned them. They call them machines, and the art of using them—again borrowing our terms —they call technology. Has this made them free to live the good life? I am afraid not; for, having freed the slaves by substituting machines, they have themselves become slaves to their machines. They toil without end to make them do what they want, make them transport them hither and yon, make them even think for them, but it does not seem to me that they have freed themselves thereby for leisure and contemplation—the only pursuits worthy of humans.

Had they at least solved the problem of ruling themselves

in freedom, of living as true citizens? Alas, no. Do you remember that strange philosopher, Phaleas the Chalcedonian, who believed that all ills came from economic inequality and proposed the utopia of a society of equals, wherein class struggle would no longer occur because each had what he wanted? Over two thousand years later, a latter-day Phaleas became the prophet of a movement that made half of the people of the world accept his belief and set up communistic societies. Alas, what I had said about the Chalcedonian's theory proved true: "Since men are guilty of the greatest crimes from ambition, and not from necessity, that polity which Phaleas establishes would only be salutary to prevent little crimes." And I also had blamed him for forgetting relations with foreign nations and the ensuing danger of war. Those Phalean societies I found ruled tyrannically, and their coexistence with other countries beset by the threat of war. But what about these others? You remember that I once put my students in the Academy to work to engage in comparative politics? To compile the constitutions of all the *poleis* and to study their systems? Since latter-day men had covered the entire earth and established *polei*s (which they called states) everywhere, there was to be found an immense number of these, all with their own governments and institutions. In this letter, I cannot give you even the merest inkling of their great variety. So, I shall try to write up some of the impressions I have gained in a separate treatise.* But one thing I must say already here:

Men, in that faraway eon, would boast interminably about the "progress" mankind had made since our times (about which, by the way, they were amazingly well informed). And, considering their having reached the stars, and all the other miracles they had accomplished, one might be tempted to agree with their boastful use of that strange term. But then I looked more closely at their lives, whether under the Phalean system or whether on the huge continent of Atlantis that our descendants, the Europeans, had discovered and settled, or on

---

* See the following chapters.—The Editors.

other continents. Their much vaunted "democracy" hardly came up to the standards I had set for the form of government I had called *Politeia;* it rather amounted to ochlocracy or plutocracy. And many did not even have that. They were ruled, as are so many of our states, by tyrants. It made me very sad to see our own dear Hellas so governed. True, it had become united and was no longer in that perennial state of discord and war. But discord and war had simply been transferred to the plane of the larger units. And the means of killing and maiming and destroying in war (again, thanks to technology) had become so refined that one major strife could wipe out entire countries and civilizations.

Living forever in the shadow of destruction, men could not be happy. They would seek to divert themselves from unhappiness by staring at the illuminated box, or by traveling in high speed from place to place, or by temporarily escaping reality by swallowing intoxicating substances. It seems to me that, in their intoxication with growth and expansion, with more and more in terms of production and people, with bigness, speed—in short, with "progress"—they had lost that which we Greeks had found to be the essence of humanity: *Sophrosyne*—Measure, Moderation.* I once suggested that the right size of a manageable political community was a few thousand human beings. More becomes not only unmanageable but lifeless and mechanical, controllable only by huge organization, with its inevitable machinery of coercion. But, as human beings, we cannot forego the intimacy of personal relationship. We Greeks certainly had, and, indeed, still have, our goodly measure of strife and cruelty. But we are still at home with nature and our gods. Look at that green peninsula, our Attica, with its forests and glens, and the white temples shimmering in the sunlight. In that faraway era I dreamt of, I saw that the green of the woods had disappeared, an evil yellow fog covered Eleusis, and the brooks and the rivers and

---

* Here, as elsewhere, it becomes quite clear to what extent Aristotle, genius that he was, was yet the child of his less-enlightened times, with all their premodern prejudices.—The Editors.

even the purple sea had become discolored with slime. That Attica, the name of which they had seen fit to give to one of their most cruel prisons, had become a dream in their remembrance of times past. Would they, with all their ingenuity and inventiveness, be able to survive? They had become so many that they filled the last nook of the planet and were about to suffocate in their own wastes. Measure—lost. No *sophrosyne* as standard of behavior (although they would endlessly study "behavior"), only the hubris of the strong and the despair of the weak. Although tired from my rush through so many centuries, I was extremely curious to know more. How would they extricate themselves from the danger of annihilating themselves and everything by applying the superweapon of which they told me, and which seemed to be based on what appears of utmost illogic to a Greek: the splitting of the world's basic substance, the atom?

*　　*　　*

At that point, I suddenly woke up. My servants have since told me that there had been the most terrible thunderstorm they ever witnessed, and that I woke at the moment of the most terrifying thunderclap of all. They had believed it was the end of the world and were amazed not only to have survived but to see me come to life again.

Government
and
Politics in the
Twentieth
Century

I

GOVERNMENT IN CONTEMPORARY SOCIETY

All states participate today in a common process of "development" that is as inevitable as it is relentless. The lures of "modernity" and the fruits of affluence urge mankind forward along ways signposted by the values and findings of science and technology. Yet, all societies also seek a measure of order within which such movement can proceed. The chief agency for organizing, and in the end controlling, both development and order is government whose instrumentalities are wielded by those possessing political power. Thus, government and politics have become ever more dominant factors in determining the character of life in modern societies.

THE RISE OF THE MODERN STATE

So much have we become accustomed to the idea of government as an active, positive agent in the direction of the affairs of our communities that we often fail to realize the significance of the change that this idea represents. In the English-speaking countries particularly, the nineteenth-century view was that government should restrict itself to the basic, and somewhat negative, function of maintaining law and order, acting only, as the half-contemptuous phrase expresses it, as a "night watchman." The transformation of this concept of the state into the modern concept of the welfare or social-service state is indeed a revolution.

This transformation in the role of the state is in essence a by-product of economic and social changes that are themselves of revolutionary character. The French Revolution and the Industrial Revolution—two separate but nevertheless in-

3

escapably interrelated historical forces—gave rise to a profound change in attitudes toward the individual and his place within the community. The French Revolution preached the equality of individuals, a doctrine that directly challenged the long-existent, rigid social hierarchies of Europe; at the same time, it aroused the sentiment of nationalism, which exalts the community. Thus, the individual was freed only to be merged into the group. But, if the French Revolution provided much of the ideology and spur for social change, it was the Industrial Revolution that provided the new circumstances in which change was inevitable. Industrialism, with its new modes of production, opened the way for individual activity and permitted social mobility to a degree never before seen. Yet, while industrialism stimulated individualism, particularly in its early stages, its own inner logic was toward mass production, standardization, and vast economic units. Thus, with industrialization as with the French Revolution, the tendency was to free the individual from the restrictions of the past only to fit him into new and larger entities. Inevitably, the breakdown of traditional social and economic groupings produced the mass society characteristic of our time. This mass society is now undergoing the process of accelerated change that is called "modernization," the "scientific-technological revolution," or, in the field of economy, the "second industrial revolution," based on computerized services and planning and on automation. This process, with its array of new tasks and problems, inevitably enhances the role of the state.

In these conditions, government, as the chief agency of social and economic control, is likely to emerge as a more and more vital instrumentality of "modernization." The technological process itself is characterized by an accelerating rate of change and, in turn, produces ever more rapid changes throughout society and human affairs. Coupled with the population explosion (especially in the developing countries) and the increasingly rapid move of the masses to urban areas, it poses entirely new and, in the case of the modernizing countries, almost insuperable tasks for government. Other, equally vital tasks are created by the headlong rush toward "control of nature," through which man's natural habitat is being destroyed in favor of a synthetic environment. Here, the rate of change is particularly remarkable, and potentially dangerous. It took man thousands of years to gain insight into the nature of his environment and to evolve means of survival in his struggle with hostile forces (such as wild animals). It took only hundreds of years to discover all of the globe and to explore it. Now, man is propelling himself into the universe, reaching for the moon and beyond, and at the same time transforming the surface of the earth itself into "cultivated" areas, producing an artificial "second nature" directly and exclusively serving the maintenance of humans—indeed, one huge factory providing the necessities of life on the pattern of the synthetic environment created for the inhabitants of spacecraft.

Obviously, the ensuing problems of the preservation of resources, natural as well as human, of land and landscape, purity of water and air, the protection of physical health, endangered as it is by pollution and chemicals, and of mental health, threatened by the "modern" mechanized way of life, test the ingenuity of organized society. It is equally clear that many, perhaps most, of these tasks can no longer be performed by individuals and smaller groups but must be undertaken by the "Great Society," or even, increasingly, through the cooperation of governments acting regionally or at the global level.

Thus, the distinguishing feature of modern government is its universal recognition and acceptance as an active force in the forming of economic, social, and environmental conditions. Even the most reluctant take this process more and more for granted. While the idea that government should be only an umpire adjudicating the rules by which other forces in society compete still commands greater allegiance in the United States than it does in Great Britain or France, yet even Americans accept with little question such governmental activities as the TVA or credit controls or the increasing amount of direct government intervention to cope with such problems of modernization as facilities and transportation in vast urban complexes and the elimination of "poverty in the midst of plenty." Moreover, the United States's major political and ideological opponent, the Soviet Union, which in theory is so antagonistic and different in outlook and structure, shares fully and even enthusiastically the underlying ideal and attitude of "modernity." In fact, one of its major stated objectives is to "match and surpass" the United States technologically, scientifically, and economically—in areas that, in Communist societies, of course, are entirely the responsibility of the state.

It is an irony that the two chief theories produced during, and in consequence of, the age of industrialization, namely Marxism and liberalism, were both based on expectations in the political field that proved the opposite of what ensued in practice. The one forecast the "withering away" of the state; the other, its reduction to insignificance under conditions of *"laissez faire."* In contrast, what developed was either totalitarianism or the giant welfare state—both all too often a warfare state.

Both these nineteenth-century theories simply failed to reckon with, or even to anticipate, the incredible technological potentialities for domination in the twentieth century. Although used in a wholly negative and destructive way by such leaders as Hitler and Stalin, they can be equally used for constructive purposes. In either case, however, their effects are too far-reaching to permit them to be exercised outside the control of the state. The nuclear weapon, on one side, and "atoms for peace," on the other, are merely the current ultimates in the vast range of these powers and capabilities. There are others, frequently overlooked, that are equally, if not more, foreboding or promising. Science reveals more and more the mental and social malleability of man in mass society, and even the feasibility of biological transformation. This fact opens vistas of psychological manipulation and eugenic determination of inheritance that might change the very substance of man and mankind. If the state does—and perhaps must—control such decisive actions, who or what controls, or restrains, the state? Perhaps we already know too much for the safety of mankind. Since knowledge is power, the predominant problem becomes one of restraint, of limits and limitations. More than ever before, therefore, the problem of limited power, one of the major themes in our subsequent analysis, emerges as perhaps *the* foremost problem both of political science and of political practice.

BIG AND ACTIVE GOVERNMENT

In the new mass society, the role of government—the complex of institutions that have a monopoly of organized force in internal and external affairs—of necessity has changed. The state, the organized political community, needs a certain degree of stability in the social system in order to maintain its own equilibrium; this requires not only the adjustment of conflicting demands by different groups in the new social and economic order, but also the deliberate creation of conditions of social well-being demanded by the new doctrine of equality. Thus, government, as the agent of the state, has been forced more and more to assume positive responsibility for the creation and distribution of wealth. In so doing, it has almost universally become big government.

There are two chief problems arising from this development. In the first place, a greatly increased number of persons become government officials and, thus, peculiarly subject to the pressures of an unscrupulous regime. In some Western countries, the state pays the salaries not only of those carrying on the public administration at the local as well as national level, but also of all those engaged in public education and even—as in West Germany—collects the funds for the salaries of the clergy. Democratic countries erect safeguards, such as merit and classification systems, to protect public employees against favoritism in appointment and promotions, undue influence, or exploitation, and in France there is the highly effective Council of State. It was not difficult, however, for the Hitler regime (to take but one example) to disregard many of these protective devices and use to the full the influence afforded by the unusually large number of public employees in Germany.

More serious, under normal conditions, is the problem of concentration of power, particularly power over the economy in a highly developed state. The struggle to improve living conditions has led all advanced states to undertake a substantial amount of public regulation of the economy and an increasing degree of economic planning. It is often argued that to subject the expert planners to control by the inexpert public would destroy the value of their plans. Moreover, planning requires a firm and stable government, it is said, for no plan can be effective if its sponsors are likely to be turned out of office at any moment and their policies reversed, or even if important modifications can be made by parliamentary vote. And, while it is not difficult to point out that, in practice, democracies have erected safeguards in this field, too, such as decentralization through the public corporation, the very complexity and far-reaching character of the operations that government now undertakes can leave no one feeling entirely complacent about the degree to which popular control of public activities is possible. Add to this the almost incredible intrusions that government agencies can now make into the most intimate spheres of one's personal life—e.g., "bugging" a home or place of work through electronic devices—and one arrives at an uncomfortably close parallel of government and the Big Brother of Orwell's counterutopia, *Nineteen Eighty-four.*

Thus, keeping government responsible and yet effective places a tremendous strain both on the machinery and personnel of government and on the alertness and active concern of the public and its organs of information. In this respect, the age-old problem of responsiveness to public opinion versus manipulation of opinion has been rendered immeasurably more difficult by the growing complexity of issues inherent in the process and age of "modernization." Moreover, the public is daily confronted with (or fails to face) an increasing number of issues. And there is the growing size of the group whose attitudes and views should be taken into consideration by the policy-makers who are supposed to be responsive to the public.

From all these facts and difficulties, some observers have drawn the conclusion that an authoritarian government, able to act promptly and decisively without regard to special pressures, constitutional obstacles, or the need to conciliate mass opinion, is more efficient and far better suited to the conditions of modern government than is a democracy. We can point out, in return, that, in two world wars, democracies proved able to mobilize their resources as efficiently, if not quite as quickly, as dictatorships, and that the more mature democracies have been able to provide higher standards of living for their people than have any dictatorships, though this is partly because of the wealth of their resources and their advantage in having had an earlier start. But, as we watch the progressive industrialization of the newer countries, we must be aware that one of their greatest difficulties will be to handle their governmental machinery in such a way that it performs expertly the tasks that they ask of it and, at the same time, remains responsible and responsive to the interests of the public it serves.

Developing states whose number and variety are misleadingly cloaked by so generalized a designation have special needs that differentiate them from developed states. Developed states are by definition those that have acquired the technological and industrial capacity, as well as the sophisticated social organization, required to meet the basic needs of their populations; their overriding need is to bring about a more equitable distribution of goods, both material, and those defined in value terms. Developing states, as the very designation indicates, have much more difficult multiple tasks: to expand their range of options through material development and at the same time to provide and maintain a relatively equitable distribution of their returns. They are thus faced with far more difficult political alternatives than are developed states. Developing states must balance the urge to material development, which as we have indicated is a universal drive, against the inevitable segmenting of their previously more static and thus more harmonious societies that will result. If a valuable mineral is discovered in one part of a new country, the adjacent inhabitants secure a disproportionate return from its exploitation that cannot help but mark them off as more privileged than those in more remote areas without special resources. Even a new road tends to provide differential advantages. So does a new high school, likely, of course, to be sited near an urban center. These material distinctions inevitably exacerbate existing divisions, like those of ethnicity, which might well have been overlaid by centuries of peaceful living together.

Moreover, since government in developing, even more than in mature, states is *the* organizing instrument of the society, the possession of political power is the chief prize to be secured. Rivalry for such power or secessionist efforts to escape it prove the most divisive of all factors, leading at times to bloody civil wars, as in Nigeria, Pakistan, the Sudan, and Burundi, or to military coups and military rule seeking to provide the stability, and sometimes also the modernization, that feeble or chaotic civilian rule has failed to stimulate.

We must thus be aware, as we study different forms of rule, that we are discussing primarily the developed states that, like the United States, the nations of Western Europe, or the older Commonwealth countries, notably Canada, Australia, and New Zealand, evolved in an earlier, less complicated international milieu; or states that, like the Soviet Union, have already gone through the pangs of forced development. From time to time throughout this book, we will refer specifically to developing states, some of which, as, for example, those in Eastern Europe, have been forced into totalitarian or semi-totalitarian forms of political organization and development, while others, such as India, have maintained democratic rule, and still others have experimented voluntarily or under external pressures with a variety of political systems reflecting the difficulty of reconciling inadequate resources and skills with ever mounting aspirations. There is a very real need, therefore, in considering the manifold forms, problems, and opportunities of government and politics in the modern world, to keep in mind the differences between developed and developing states, however much both are subject to the twin pressures of development and order.

DEMOCRACY AND TOTALITARIANISM

Although all modern governments today exercise a wide range of responsibilities, there remain highly significant differences between the objectives and techniques of those states that we call democratic and those that are avowedly totalitarian, whether of the Communist or fascist type. Democracy and totalitarianism as systems are polar points on the spectrum of political alternatives. At the same time, as we have noted, there is between the two a wide range of governmental forms that do not fit neatly into either category.

In order to distinguish between, and clearly categorize, forms of polities, analysis should proceed in terms of a twofold dichotomy, depending on which one of the two most fundamental questions is posed.

The first question concerns the subject, or "bearer," of political rule: Who governs? To this the answer may be: the totality of the adult members of a particular political community, i.e., the "people." In that case, we call this form of government "democracy." If the answer is only one, or a few, or an elite, or some type of minority, we call this regime "rule from above." More specifically, it can be categorized as an absolute monarchy or a one-man dictatorship or an oligarchy, aristocracy, or authoritarian system.

Quite different are the answers to the second basic question that may be posed in regard to government, and which concerns the spheres controlled by political authority of whatever type: How wide is this sphere? Here, the two polar answers are either that political authority is exercised in principle over everything in the life of the respective people and society, in which case we refer to the regime as "totalitarian," or that government is limited, leaving certain, often large, spheres of individual and group life unregulated. If these spheres are guaranteed by law or protected by convention against government intervention, we refer to the regime as "liberal."

Definitions such as these are subject to historical change and qualification. The "people" who, in terms of Greek antiquity, constituted the bearers of a "democratic" system (Athenian democracy) today would be considered the rulers of an oligarchic system, lording it over a majority of slaves, non-citizens, and women. Most people today would refuse to characterize the rule of the white minority in South Africa as "democratic," a designation accorded it in the past; or, as far as local and state matters are concerned, to the rule exercised in Mississippi and other restrictive areas in the southern United States. Equally, to *laissez faire* liberals of the mid-nineteenth century (and to those who still echo their views), the degree of government regulation and government intervention, especially in the fields of economy and industrial relations, that obtains today in "liberal-democratic" countries such as the United States would certainly have appeared as "totalitarian." While we should be sensitive to these changes of views and of definitions at different periods of history, our task is to give them content in terms of current conditions.

How, then, do these pairs of concepts and systems correlate? Theoretically, each could correlate to any one of the others—e.g., liberalism to democracy, yet also to oligarchy or aristocracy; totalitarianism to dictatorship, yet also to democracy. Indeed, there are historical examples, if only incidentally, of such seemingly "incongruous" pairing. Especially in the initial stages of a popular revolution, democracy can tend to disregard limitations on political authority and thus be "totalitarian." Authoritarian rule may sometimes be restrained by the acceptance of limitations (which are at times even constitutional ones), as witness the early nineteenth-century monarchical-aristocratic "constitutionalism" of continental European countries, or of England before it became fully democratic.

Much more common, however, both historically and organizationally, is the pairing of the two other characteristics resulting in liberal democracy, on the one hand, and totalitarian dictatorship (or totalitarian oligarchy), on the other. Experience suggests, in fact, that totalitarian democracy, as in the French Revolution, tends to turn into small-group or one-man rule, while a liberal authoritarianism, such as existed in many earlier European regimes, tends to give way to full-fledged liberal democracy. The combination of liberalism and democracy characterized political developments in the Western countries during the era encompassing the rise of the middle classes and the first industrial revolution, i.e., roughly, the eighteenth and nineteenth centuries. In the twentieth century, the United States, Great Britain, the first overseas members of the Commonwealth—Canada, Australia and New Zealand—and most of the countries of Western Europe successfully adapted liberal democracy to new social and economic demands. Elsewhere, however, the impact of unsolved social and international problems created a reaction that turned many societies into totalitarian ones, politically controlled by dictatorship. This development reached its acme in the fascism of the German-Nazi variety and in the Stalinist version of Communism.

Between these polar-type regimes are many others that more or less approximate totalitarian dictatorship, and at least as many that more or less approximate liberal democracy. Certain regimes characterized by dictatorial or oligarchic controls may lack some or most of the characteristics of totalitarianism. In fact, the standard, traditional forms of "rule from above," as they are inherited from the predemocratic, more or less authoritarian, past, still prevail in certain countries of the developing areas.

Despite individual variants, the norms are sufficiently constant so that, in contrasting, in the following pages, democracy and totalitarianism as the chief polar opposites of political and governmental structures, we shall use our terms in the following ways: "democracy" in the sense of "liberal democracy," and "totalitarianism" in the sense of "totalitarian dictatorship" or "totalitarian oligarchy."

In making these distinctions, we have thought of them as standards that real systems and actual regimes may approximate, and do not intend any "cold war" equating of all Communist regimes with the most excessive of the fascist regimes, in particular with Nazism. While we believe the totalitarianism-democracy dichotomy is still a useful one for purposes of clarification, we recognize that concepts and definitions like these must be applied with extreme care. Both systems and concepts are "relative" ones, each differing in character not only between countries but also between stages of development. Thus, totalitarian states differ in revolutionary fervor, in type of leadership, in organization of social and economic structure, and, as has become increasingly clear in recent years, in degree of "total" or not quite total controls. On the other hand, even mature democracies sometimes exhibit, particularly in periods of crisis, some of the characteristics of totalitarianism; the far-reaching powers given to democratic executives in time of war (e.g., Great Britain in both world wars) are cases in point. But what proved the chief democratic safeguard even in such instances was the universal agreement, or consensus, that such powers were granted temporarily, and that control would be reassumed by the "people" through its customary channels and representatives as soon as the emergency was over. In cases, however, where those to whom such temporary controls are entrusted abuse them to continue their "emergency powers" indefinitely, liberal democracy degenerates into autocracy.

CHARACTERISTICS OF DEMOCRACIES

Liberal democracies are characterized institutionally by limitations on governmental action to provide safeguards for individuals and groups; by means for securing the regular, periodic, and peaceful change of their leaders; and by organs of effective popular representation. In attitude, they require tolerance for opposing opinions, flexibility, and willingness for experimentation. Limitation on governmental actions means not only that there are private spheres of life in which government must not interfere, but also that governmental agents, like private persons, must abide by the rules of law and exercise authority only to the degree the law provides; that is, that the monopoly of coercion that government possesses must be exercised within limits set by law.

Peaceful changes of representation and of leaders involve a system of elections with meaningful choice between candidates, either at the nomination or at the election level. It implies a system of nomination, and also a formulation of program, that is associated with the candidates running for office. It necessitates political organization, commonly in the form of political parties, to keep constant contact between the public and its leaders and representatives. Moreover, so that such choice may be exercised freely and public policies kept under review, political parties and other associations must have the opportunity openly to analyze issues, criticize governmental actions, and crystallize public sentiment. Organs of opinion—the press, radio, and TV—must be permitted the independent purveyance of news and formulation of judgments. Thus, freedom of speech, of association, and of assembly are essential political as well as civil rights.

To make democracy effective, however, requires not only institutions and guarantees but also attitudes. Respect for the right of the people to assert their point of view, however unpopular or seemingly wrong-headed, is fundamental to the workings of the democratic process of discussion and choice. This basic attitude is expressed in the saying, "I abhor your opinion, but I shall fight to the death for your right to express it." Nothing can exert a greater influence on the democratic character of a state than the individual citizen's tolerance of (though not indifference to) ideas, whether expressed individually or through associations, that are contrary to or challenge his own. Censorship and governmental restraint are obvious ways of creating conformism, but social pressure may be no less a force in crushing the interplay of ideas, on which democracy depends.

Democracy is characterized further by respect for minority and individual rights, by the use of discussion rather than force to settle disputes, by an acceptance of the legitimacy of the system under which the people are governed, and by the experimental method. Democracies have ideals and objectives, but they do not have fixed goals, except to maintain an "open society." Thus, they proceed through trial and error, changing their programs in response to popular need and present circumstance. All states are limited by their past and by their environment, but democracies believe that they are not restricted by any inevitable process of history, and that there exist opportunities for experiment and choice of alternatives.

The Nature of Totalitarianism

In contrast to the conscious efforts of democracies to maintain diversity, open discussion, freedom of choice among ideas and leaders, and open-mindedness on future programs, totalitarianism is characterized by a persistent drive to enforce uniformity by the crushing of opposition and by a leadership that claims superior, if not infallible, knowledge of how policy should be directed and exercises power through a self-perpetuating elite. Behind these actions lies an ideology or doctrine that justifies the concentration of power—and whatever restrictions on individual and group liberties this involves—as the means necessary to attain some ultimate and fixed goal or certain end toward which nature or history is said to strive.

Communist Totalitarianism

Thus, Communism, not only as seen from outside but even more in its self-interpretation, is very different from simple rule by force or autocracy. Because everything that happens now is meant to be merely a transitional stage on history's inexorable path toward a future depicted as one of complete human emancipation and freedom, everything, be it ever so coercive, partakes of the nature of a necessary but minor evil to attain this end. Opinion has to be controlled and censorship instituted; but this is only because portions of the public are still "backward" in their "social consciousness," and therefore have to be "educated" by a "vanguard" possessing full consciousness of history and the things to come. This same vanguard has to exercise controls and accumulate powers that, to the uninitiated, look excessive and dictatorial; but the holders of power consider themselves the agents of a movement that fulfills the deepest yearnings of the masses of the people, and therefore purport to act "democratically" in a more profound way than do the people's representatives in the democracies, who, according to this view, are merely self-seeking agents or stooges of business and other "interests."

Thus, Communist leaders, in their own view, are performing the historic task of social and general reconstruction, a task that ennobles whatever shortcomings the current Eastern-style "democracies" may still embody. If East Berlin, for instance, appears somewhat shoddy to a Western visitor who contrasts it with West Berlin, it does not seem so to a person steeped in the "right" philosophy; to the latter, any building or enterprise owned "by the people" is intrinsically superior to the glittering façade of a structure that, because capitalist-owned, symbolizes the degeneracy of the capitalist system. Moreover, the first is bound, in due course, to surpass the second, even in aesthetic terms, and thus will attain the beauty of the "higher system" that the true believer already discerns in what is defective at present.

It is a basic characteristic of Communism that it makes

social change a major objective, and that it mobilizes all the instruments of the modern industrialized state—technology, education, communications media—to accelerate this process. In doing so, it has a twofold objective: to move as rapidly as possible toward the transcendent goals formulated by its leaders, and to keep the society so mobile that nonparty groups have little chance to stabilize and thus exercise effective influence on its character. Thus, what is often called "permanent revolution" characterizes these regimes. The early Soviet Five-Year Plans were major instruments of social and economic revolution backed by fear, force, and measurable, though often unattainable, production goals. Moreover, in the background of all totalitarian regimes—and sometimes in the foreground—is the purge: a technique of government with its own positive as well as negative features.

The purge promotes specific policies at the same time that it removes those who oppose them. It may eliminate, displace, or undercut the power of those against whom it is aimed. It acts against those considered a danger to the ruling elite either because they hold different social objectives (as was true of sizable groups in the early days of fascist and Communist regimes), or because they endorse different techniques for moving toward the common goal (as did those in the Soviet Union who, in the 1920's and again in early post-Stalinist days, emphasized the need for consumers' goods rather than concentration on heavy industry), or because they threaten to establish the predominant influence of a nonparty group (as in Hitler's purges of the military).

Fascist Totalitarianism

It may, perhaps, be questioned whether the Nazi system, though totalitarian in its use of the purge and in its total interference—in theory as well as practice—with all spheres of life and society, also shared the other characteristic of Communist totalitarian regimes: their social and economic dynamism. Initially, the Hitler regime did not affect such established institutions as business enterprises and private prop-

erty; through steadily increasing control of economic as well
as all other matters, it tended more and more, however, to
deprive such institutions of their usual functions. Of what use
were private holdings, in practice, when all discretion of the
holder to plan production, employ labor, and determine wage
and price policies was taken away through over-all control by
planning agencies, which, in turn, were dependent on the
varying policies of the political leadership? And, particularly,
of what use were they when the holder, like any other individual, might at any time disappear in a concentration camp
in case he failed to comply? Hitler himself once commented
that there was no need to socialize the means through which
business and commerce were carried on, since "we socialize
human beings." In addition, Nazism showed signs in its later
stages of carrying through a more radical transformation of
the economic and social structure, and it may be doubted
whether capitalism—or any other traditional system or structure—could have endured if the Nazi system itself had lasted.

Nazism provides the most extreme case of fascist totalitarianism. In comparison with Nazism, other fascist regimes,
including the one that furnished its name, Italian Fascism,
were, or are, not only less "totalitarian" in their intended or
actual control of spheres of life and society, but frequently
less dynamic also. Italian Fascism, as one of its early critics
put it, had risen as a "counterrevolution against a revolution
that never took place"; throughout its tenure, it seemed intent on preserving basic institutions of the economy and society. Indeed, it did not even destroy such traditional political
institutions as the monarchy, powerless though it rendered it.
Other fascist, or protofascist, regimes, such as those in Spain
and Portugal, have proved even more conservative and traditionalist. In some instances, as in the case of Franco Spain,
the dictator officially proclaims his rule as a regency for a vanished or to-be-re-established monarchy. Such versions of totalitarianism or dictatorship thus actually came close to what
Marxian interpretation says of any and all "fascism": that it
constitutes the rule of traditional forces such as "monopoly

capitalism." In reality, however, this type of dictatorship is more frequently powered by non–middle class groups, such as the church and landed aristocracy, which oppose liberal democracy for fear the latter will prove too weak to withstand the onslaught of revolutionary proletarian forces.

Such regimes, then, may turn out to be replicas of traditional, predemocratic "authoritarian" regimes, not unlike traditional Latin American military or civilian juntas. They strive to maintain one-man or oligarchic control in a community without basically changing its structure; rather they tend to preserve the traditional social structure and to work through established lines of authority. As a means of maintaining their dominance, they aim at preserving a climate of internal tranquillity quite unlike the climate of permanent change and dynamic transformation prevailing in the full-fledged totalitarian regimes. While it was going too far to speak of General Charles de Gaulle's administration in the Fifth French Republic as being such a system, its aim certainly was similar, namely, to reduce tensions, prevent social revolution, and establish governmental stability. One over-all problem facing such regimes is whether their political conservatism can withstand the "winds of change" that development carries with it. A predemocratic climate of attitudes, especially in the relationship between governors and governed, is ill suited to the antipaternalistic tendencies of "modern" man in the modernized, technically oriented machine world.

DEVELOPING STATES BETWEEN DEMOCRACY AND TOTALITARIANISM

In contrast to more or less genuinely reactionary regimes, rapid social and economic change is the objective not only of totalitarian states but also of many of the new, developing countries of Asia, Africa, and the Middle East that are striving to achieve modernity in record time. Their leaders face the obvious temptation to adopt totalitarian techniques to achieve this difficult purpose. Yet, the appeals of totalitarianism are counterbalanced by its price. Totalitarianism demands a radical reorganization of society, which has its heaviest impact on the landed peasantry, the base of all developing countries. It tends to make the power structure rigid at a time when new national leaders seek to give their people a feeling of participation in the exercise of authority and thereby to legitimize their claims to supersede traditional authorities. It limits their opportunities to secure aid from the West as well as the East when most of them prefer to remain uncommitted to either.

For these reasons, the leaders of developing countries often attempt to combine features of both democratic and totalitarian systems. They organize state-directed community action at the same time that they foster individual enterprise. They favor one-party regimes without, however, crushing opportunities for individual or group opposition to particular programs or techniques. They sometimes incorporate the opposition, as in Senegal and Kenya, rather than eliminate it by force. They attempt to secure majority or even universal support by the popularity of their efforts to promote national growth and international recognition. As in India, they maintain the flexibility and experimental approach that are characteristically democratic at the same time that they race ahead with far-reaching economic projects.

No one can say with assurance which of the developing states will succeed in transforming traditional societies through persuasion rather than compulsion; whether they will be able to maintain a framework of stability at the same time that modernization and its customary concomitant, industrialization, enlarge the choices available to their societies and the variety of roles their people may fill; whether, finally, they will establish the modern norms of efficiency and objectivity that underpin the authority of administrators. Many people deny that democracy is suitable, or even feasible, for societies with low levels of literacy, minimal standards of living for the bulk of their people, and few economic resources. These comments can be better evaluated after the more careful study of systems of government and the workings of institutions to which much of this book is devoted. It is nevertheless worth noting that the leaders of many of the developing countries believe that their states are and can remain democratic, and they are working with this conviction.

Is Democracy Adequate for Modern Conditions?

While some people believe that only mature countries like Great Britain, the United States, Canada, and Sweden can maintain democracy under current conditions of international strain and competition from totalitarian states, others question whether democracy is a workable system even for the Anglo-Saxon and European states that have been most successful in practicing it in the past. They contend that its machinery is inadequate to modern needs. They assert that democracy's assumptions about tolerance, free discussion, responsible leadership, and willingness to experiment are based on an unrealistic expectation of rationality and maturity on the part of ordinary individuals and, more particularly, of their leaders. And they affirm further that the totalitarian ideology has a more compelling attraction than has democracy in the relatively rootless, industrialized, and urbanized society of today. These criticisms of, and doubts about, democracy thus fall into three categories: the adequacy of its machinery; the assumptions it makes about human capacities; and the strength of its appeal in an age of uncertainty and tension. In addition, these same people query democracy's capacity to deal effectively with foreign affairs in the nuclear age, a problem that will be taken up later on.

Is Its Machinery Suitable?

As to the machinery of democracy, it is questioned whether executives can be kept accountable to the public when the issues they deal with affect such all-important questions as national security, and the means at their disposal are so enormously effective. Alternatively, are democratic leaders apt to be too much influenced by passing currents of opinion or by the desire for popularity? In addition, can the public be trusted to select for the chief offices of state persons possessing judgment and capacities of leadership? In other words, is there not a basic inconsistency in the notion that efficiency can be combined with accountability? If it is said, in reply, that elected leaders provide the responsible element in a democracy, while professional administrators carry out the technical tasks of government, the comment might well be made that this association of elected amateurs with permanent professionals may mean, in practice, that the latter make the decisions and the former provide only a façade. Others may answer that there is still more danger that the amateurs will disregard the experience and advice of their permanent advisers to the detriment of public-minded policies.

Further questions are raised by the critics of democracy about the adequacy of representative institutions to provide a link between the public and the possessors of political power. Is the right to cast a ballot once every year, or every five years, a meaningful form of political participation? they ask. Even those who work hard within a party organization may find themselves without influence on policy, it is said, since parties are run from behind the scenes by cliques or "bosses" for their own interests. Moreover, it is charged that pressure groups, far from broadening the concern of public figures with community interests, merely focus attention on particular and frequently only self-seeking demands, to the detriment of the public at large. Under such circumstances, legislatures are said to be mere conglomerations of warring interests, each seeking to secure the largest slice of public moneys for itself. In any case, it is sometimes questioned whether one man can ever represent the interests and thinking of another, and whether, therefore, the whole notion of representative government is not based on a false premise. To this is added the charge that the information on which the citizen depends both for his judgments on public policy and for making his choice of representatives is apt to be distorted to their own interests by those who control the media of communication: the press, radio, and TV.

Can People Respond to Its Requirements?

The next level of doubts about democracy concerns the capacity of ordinary human beings to make judgments on the complex issues of a modern state. On the one hand, it is pointed out that more and more of the responsibilities of government are technical in character, whether they are concerned with giant roads and bridges or with nuclear power. Moreover, many of the issues that must be decided affect the allocation of resources. But, in addition to questioning the adequacy of average people to make decisions on the affairs and personnel of a government concerned with such matters, there is the nagging uncertainty about whether people can retain that sense of detachment that permits them to separate public needs from their own private and selfish interests, whether they can listen judiciously to both sides of an argument, and whether they will refrain from violence when unpopular programs are put into effect.

How Strong Is Its Appeal?

Finally, in what may well be the deepest of all challenges, it is questioned whether democracy, with its lack of assured programs and goals, can answer as successfully as can ideological totalitarianism the need of people for a faith or cause.

This is an age when transcendental religion has lost its hold on many people, and yet it is one in which strains and uncertainties create a particular need for spiritual reinforcement. Fascist or Communist ideologies, with their popular symbols and their certainty about their goals, offer the appeal of a new religion to many who are living in a spiritual vacuum. Even if democracy may be said to satisfy its mature adherents, there are many who doubt that it can equal the attraction of a totalitarian faith either to those within Western countries who find themselves disadvantaged in the competition for the good things of life, or, more especially, to the still underdeveloped, oftentimes hungry and suffering majority of the world's people, whether in Asia, Africa, or Latin America.

Such an indictment of democracy as has been made brings to the surface some of the commonplaces of political comment; it does little to test their validity. It provides a background, however, against which much of the rest of this book can examine the workings of institutions of mature democracies as well as of developing states and of modern fascist and Communist dictatorships. Politics has the right to be ranked as a science only insofar as its processes are analyzed with the same care as is given to the data of what are commonly called the experimental sciences. This book makes no pretensions to cover all issues, but it does attempt to examine the workings of different types of political systems, to evaluate their consequences in the light of such information as we now possess, and to stimulate discussion on the validity of the questions we have raised.

II

THREE MAJOR PATTERNS OF TWENTIETH-CENTURY GOVERNMENT

Within the dichotomy of democracy and totalitarianism there are, as we have seen, all kinds of subtypes, gradations, and transitions that render the spectrum of political regimes extremely varied and colorful. To deal meaningfully with them, it is necessary to select a few patterns of twentieth-century government that appear especially significant, partly because they are characteristic of the political and governmental structures that prevail in major powers, such as the Soviet Union and China, on the one hand, and the United States and Great Britain, on the other, but partly also because they now constitute the standard forms, as it were, likely to be imitated by new countries as well as by older ones when in the process of changing their institutions. These patterns have emerged partly out of history, partly out of force, and partly out of example.

We concentrate on three of these patterns: one of these characterizes totalitarianism wherever it has arisen in the twentieth century; and two markedly different structures are found among liberal democratic systems. The first is *dictatorship* based on *one-party* rule—with the official, or "state," party in turn representing the "movement" and its basic philosophy. This form has been the predominant feature of Communist as well as fascist totalitarianism. Democracy, on the other hand, though exhibiting greater variety, has traditionally operated through either of two distinctive patterns, which have been continued from the eighteenth and nineteenth centuries into the twentieth: the *parliamentary* pattern of

Great Britain and the older Commonwealth nations as well as the somewhat different parliamentary systems of West and North European countries; and the *presidential* system of the United States.

The chief difference between the two democratic patterns is that the parliamentary one is based on an interlocking between the legislative and executive branches of government, whereas the presidential system is characterized by the "separation," or, more accurately, the independence, of these branches, or "powers." As we shall see when we discuss these systems in greater detail, the parliamentary system, in particular, varies in many details, the most important being the distinction between a structure in which the executive more or less dominates the legislature and one where the legislature dominates the executive. The former relationship is characteristic of the British parliamentary system; the latter was embodied in the traditional French parliamentary structure before the Fifth Republic, and is still characteristic of Italy. What characterizes both of these structures and stands in contrast to the separation-of-powers system is the close interaction—sometimes spoken of as fusion—of the executive and legislative branches of government.

To a large extent, these three systems, one-party dictatorship, parliamentary democracy, and the presidential system, have been adopted by—or imposed upon—many if not most of the countries of the present-day world. It is particularly important, therefore, to understand their basic features.

THE ONE-PARTY DICTATORSHIP

The simplest of all modern political forms is the one-party dictatorship. Its concentration of political authority in the hands of the executive and administration is underpinned by the all-pervasive influence of a highly organized political party that can scarcely be distinguished from the governmental machinery it operates. Although representative organs are commonly a part of the structure of modern one-party dictatorships, their purpose is not to provide control but rather to serve as a sounding board for political pronouncements. Law and the courts do not operate as separate independent entities authorized to decide disputes concerning the operations of other governmental organs, but act to reinforce the norms of behavior laid down by the party leadership and ratified by the executive and administration. This remains true even when these norms are radically changed in response to new objectives. Thus, it is characteristic of one-party dictatorships that all the organs of government—executive, administrative, legislative, and judicial—find their overriding purpose in the objectives of the regime, and that these objectives are formulated by the leaders of the one political party that infiltrates and directs not only political but also economic, social, and, in principle, even highly personal affairs.

The Soviet Union

The Soviet Union has had by far the longest history of any of the modern one-party dictatorships, and it is possible in its case to identify eras of development. There are three major eras so far, each shaped by its dominant figure or figures as well as by the particular conditions and demands of the time.

The first era, under Lenin (and for a short while after his death in the 1920's), was characterized by revolutionary fervor. Although rule was exercised from the top level of the party, the system made some appeal for popular support, or at least for support by, and even a certain feeling of responsibility to, the broader party membership. There followed the culmination of one-man control under Stalin, a regime under which centralized authority backed by brutality, police-terror, and unending purges forced a social and economic revolution in order to create a powerful industrial-military structure.

In the third, post-Stalin, era, the Soviet Union still remains a one-party, totalitarian dictatorship; but, compared with the Stalinist period, there have been significant changes. The party, still the dominant institution in the political structure, continues to maintain its hold over every aspect of life and society. The early effort after "de-Stalinization" to substitute collective leadership for personal rule did not succeed. But Khrushchev's attempt to establish a personal dictatorship, coupled with his unpredictability and policy failures, ultimately led to his ouster and subsequent reduction to the status of an "unperson." Khrushchev's departure marked the first instance in modern Russian history of the peaceful transfer of power through the "retirement," rather than death, of the incumbent, through voting, albeit by a small, elite body of the Party. Moreover, while Brezhnev's primacy among the collective leadership is becoming increasingly apparent, major policy decisions continue to be made by the Politburo, which observes some accountability toward other Party bodies, particularly the Central Committee.

The open terror of the Stalin era has disappeared, and, in the economic sphere, the totalitarian character of the Soviet regime is being gradually mitigated by concessions to initiative. Yet, at the same time, what freedom of expression and creativity was allowed in science, literature, and the arts during the early part of the post-Stalin period is now being increasingly curtailed; the Soviet system is thus still dictatorial, with strongly totalitarian attitudes, as, particularly, in the areas of opinion-making, culture, and education. Nevertheless, it seems possible that the impact of modernization, of the scientific-technological revolution, and of more harmonious relations with the West may, in the long run, encourage the leadership to adopt less doctrinaire and restrictive policies.

The People's Republic of China

The second great example of Communist totalitarianism is China. An ancient, highly cultured, and traditionally bureaucratic society, China was long humiliated by unequal treaties forced on it by Western countries avid for trade. Deep internal divisions culminated in the post–World War II civil war, and the victory of Mao Tse-tung's Communist Party over Chiang Kai-shek's Kuomintang coincided with the rise of modern mass nationalism in China. Long years of warlordism and Nationalist revolution, followed by eight years of Japanese occupation and four years of civil war, had created in the Chinese people a longing for peace, order, unity, and centralized control and leadership. But permeating and ultimately dominating the new Party-government structure that reached deep into communities as well as the new nationwide mass organizations was Mao's dynamic philosophy directed at reconditioning and redirecting Chinese thinking and behavior. "Brainwash" is a Chinese slang term. And, in a very real sense, Mao has sought and in the main succeeded, through the dual stimuli of idealism and terror, in replacing traditional family and religious loyalties and values with new attitudes and concepts exalting both individual responsibility and devotion to the Party's leadership.

Until the Cultural Revolution, from 1966 to 1969, the Chinese Communist Party exercised unquestioned political dominance throughout mainland China and carried through massive programs of change. By early 1953, the nationwide land reform program started less than three years before had been completed. By mid-1956, the collectivization instituted in 1953 had enrolled 90 per cent of the peasantry in agricultural producers' cooperatives. The first Five-Year Plan for 1953–57 subordinated agriculture to industry, which, under forced draft, grew faster than that of any other underdeveloped Asian country. But the completion of "socialist transformation" had not increased China's agricultural production. Hence the Great Leap Forward proclaimed in 1958 to transform both agriculture and industry simultaneously, the former through mass mobilization of the peasantry in communes formed by amalgamating collective farms under decentralized management. The results proved disastrous. Lack of experience, planning, and management skills, plus economic errors on a gigantic scale, led to years of serious economic dislocation and to disillusionment and disaffection on the part of the masses.

Expectations had been created far faster than they could be realized. Moreover, the highly centralized Party-government-army structure of power was, in practice, an elite organization, highly status- and security-conscious, and largely impervious to pressures from below. Fearing for his "permanent revolution," Mao instituted a vast new effort, the Cultural Revolution, which mobilized non-Party agencies, notably the Red Guard youth, for a public purge of the Party. *Quotations from Chairman Mao Tse-tung,* with axioms like "The revolution must rely on the masses of the people, on everybody's taking a hand," became the bible of the Cultural Revolution. For the first time in the history of one-party states, the Party leadership turned against the Party itself.

Civil strife ensued. The Party establishment fought against the new revolutionary committees, but finally ceased to function. Schools and universities were closed and intellectuals attacked. In 1968, millions of students, along with members of the urban bureaucracy and unemployed, were sent to the rural communes. In 1969, the Ninth Party Congress, whose members had been carefully screened by the center, adopted a new party constitution and elected a new Central Committee, which then chose the Politburo and its standing committee of five. This Congress selected Lin Piao, the Defense Minister, to become Mao's successor, thereby tacitly acknowledging that power resided in the military leaders, the only component of the former governing structure still largely intact. Subsequently, however, Lin Piao disappeared, and Chou En-lai, who had retained his position as Premier throughout these changes, re-emerged as the spokesman of the regime, with Mao's thought its official ideology.

Other Communist Regimes

As in China, Communism was also established in the Eastern European countries after World War II. That these countries resemble the Soviet Union more closely than they do China is partly because of continued Soviet influence, but also because they had attained a higher degree of development (apart from cultural achievements) prior to their "communization." But, since their value systems and traditions, as well as the general sophistication of their people, had made them, more or less, a part of the West, the introduction of Communism, while in some ways "progressive" with respect to agrarian, industrial, and welfare matters, became for them, both politically and culturally, a retrogression. For the dictatorships that emerged in Eastern Europe initially imposed total control over the life and thought of their people, often resorting to brutal force; they were "Stalinist" not only in their methods but in their complete submission to Stalin's will. Only Yugoslavia, by retaining its independence from the Soviet Union, could afford less stringent controls.

With Stalin, and Stalinism, gone from the Soviet Union, much of Eastern Europe sought to substitute a more lenient type of control, whether by popularly induced changes of leadership (as twice in Poland), by an assertion of political and economic independence (as in Rumania), or by democratic reforms (as in Czechoslovakia). But the "clamping down" on Czechoslovakia by Soviet force in 1968, in the name of what has since come to be known as the "Brezhnev doctrine," made clear the limits on freedom of discussion, cultural experimentation, and even the right to criticism that still exist within the Soviet security sphere. However, some degree of liberalization is still possible, as demonstrated, strangely enough, in Hungary, where the regime that had crushed the 1956 revolution subsequently became one of the least restrictive within the Eastern bloc.

So far, it remains true that, despite great differences in their use of power and even in the distribution of authority, there has been relatively little variation among these regimes in the political structure itself. To this point, all of them have remained, or returned to, one-party systems based on control from the top level of the party, which organizes and dominates the state even where it decentralizes certain functions and allows some leeway to individual and group activities. The key still remains the concentration of power in a single party and its leadership, whose influence permeates society without becoming accountable to any representative institution. This type of regime still provides the most powerful means of centralized and pervasive rule that has as yet been developed.

THE PARLIAMENTARY PATTERN

The pattern of dictatorship is a relatively simple one; the forms of democratic states have endless variety. They revolve around various methods of attempting to secure those purposes of which we spoke when discussing democracy: an effective representation of the electorate; a relation between the organs of representation and the executive that permits effective leadership and, at the same time, keeps it in constant touch with the elected representatives of the people; and limits on arbitrary use of power by government and its officials. The methods adopted by particular states arise out of historical evolution (particularly obvious in relation to Great Britain); or out of concepts modified by evolution (as in the United States); or out of attempts to correct past inadequacies (as in the Fifth French Republic, with its great strengthening of the executive to avoid the legislative omnipotence and executive instability of the Fourth and even Third French Republics, or as in West Germany); or out of transfer of institutions to former dependent territories (as in the Commonwealth); or out of a combination of these factors. Within the wide range of democratic forms of government, the most common is the parliamentary pattern, partly because of the influence of British parliamentary experience, but more particularly because of its relative simplicity of organization and apparent ease of operation.

The prime characteristic of the parliamentary form of government is the so-called fusion of the executive and legislature. The executive becomes the governing group not because of a direct vote by the electorate, as in the presidential system, but because it comprises the leaders of one or several parties represented in the legislature that are able to command sufficient support within that body to pass the legislation embodied in their program. In a two-party system, there is no question about which party commands a majority in

the legislature; its leaders assume the executive role as soon
as an election has made this clear. In a multiparty system,
there may well be more difficulty about determining which
combination of leaders shall assume the role of the executive.
In either case, however, there is an interaction between executive and legislature that keeps them constantly interrelated
and dependent on each other but, at the same time, fulfilling
different functions. The executive prepares the program,
pushes it through the legislature by personal and direct
leadership, and supervises the administration. The members
of the legislature consider the details of the program, enact
what they decide to approve, criticize or support the executive's and the administration's handling of their responsibilities, and keep alert to the comments of their constituents and
to the general reactions of the country to governmental policy. Within the parliamentary system, therefore, there is an
intimate association of the executive and legislature, combined with differentiation of function; there is effective government (at least where the parliamentary majority is clear),
combined with opportunities—as through the daily question
period in the British parliamentary system—for making the
executive justify its actions.

Technically, the parliamentary system revolves around the
institution of (and procedures for expressing or denying)
"confidence" in the executive. Where parliament can force
the government (in the sense of the executive) to resign by
voting "nonconfidence" in it—or at least compel the executive
to dissolve parliament in such a case and appeal to the electorate—the parliamentary system is operating in its classic
form. Systems, such as those of present-day France and West
Germany, that render such expression of confidence or nonconfidence difficult, if not impossible, are thus of doubtful
parliamentary nature; rather, as we suggested earlier, they
have aspects of authoritarianism (though one that is limited
in time, due to legally required periodic elections). Even in
Great Britain, the expense of fighting elections, the strictness
of party disciplines, and general sentiments against too fre-

quent overthrows of a government act against unrestricted use of votes of confidence. In the end, responsiveness to comment and criticism and tolerance of opposition views may elicit "confidence" without the mechanism of the kind of vote on which the survival of an executive technically depends.

The close working together of executive and legislature within the framework of the parliamentary system contrasts with the nonpolitical nature of the judiciary. Judicial independence, which is essential for the maintenance of limitations on political and administrative actions, must be a principle of government in a democratic state; it is reinforced by the fact that judges are chosen from a particular profession (in Great Britain from senior barristers, i.e., those who plead cases in the law courts; in the United States also from the legal profession; and in France, and other European countries, from persons trained for this particular career), and that they have permanent tenure. In Great Britain and France, courts of law do not pass on the constitutionality of legislative acts, but in some parliamentary systems, like those of Canada, Australia, West Germany, and Austria, cases can be taken to a supreme court to determine the constitutionality of legislation in the light of the basic constitutional document. In all democratic systems, however, one court or another can make judgments on the legality of administrative acts by testing them against the statute or ordinance under which the action was taken.

The British Parliamentary System

The British parliamentary system, often looked on as a model of effective yet responsible government, evolved out of two processes operating at different periods of time. The first was one of differentiation of functions that had originally emanated from the person of the monarch, and subsequently was one of limitations on his power. This long process led to the separate jurisdiction of the courts of law, and to documents—notably Magna Carta in 1215, the Petition of Rights in 1628, and the Bill of Rights in 1689—that attempted to prevent the monarch from acting in what was looked on as an arbitrary fashion destructive of customary rights. In the seventeenth century, the House of Commons, with its twofold influence—as a grantor of money and as a representative body —assumed the leading role in attempting to limit the monarch, while the execution of Charles I and the deposition of James II made it quite clear that royal power could never again be supreme. The second process began in the mid-eighteenth century, when the king began to select his chief advisers, or ministers, from persons who had the confidence and support of a majority of the members in the House of Commons. As this principle became established, the reasons for limiting the powers of the Crown disappeared. Thus, the British Cabinet, which now wields the powers of the Crown, possesses a wide measure of independent executive authority, as well as the power it secures through its leadership of the legislative body.

This leadership, in contrast to what we may call the older "French" type of parliamentarism (i.e., of the Third and Fourth French Republics), or to that in Italy, issues not only from the traditional British two-party system, which ordinarily guarantees majority party control in the House of Commons, but also from the established right of the Crown (now exercised by the Prime Minister) to dissolve Parliament. The nonexistence, or nonexercise, of such a right in the earlier practices of the "French" system, on the other hand, coupled with a poorly disciplined multiparty structure, accounted for the weakness of the executive and the predominance of the legislature in the working of the latter system.

The party system that operates the British parliamentary structure ordinarily provides a strong majority for one major party or the other and thus effective direction and control. But this control is exercised in response to long-established political conventions. Although the British Cabinet is one of the most powerful executive bodies in the democratic world because of its control of the House of Commons, it nevertheless accepts its responsibility to act for the country as a whole, and not merely as the organ of the majority party. It is kept on the *qui vive* by the constant probing and questioning of the opposition party and by the publicity given to governmental actions and policies by the more responsible portions of the press and by radio and TV. In a somewhat similar combination of freedom for, and restraint on, governmental action, the courts in Great Britain do not question the validity of an act of Parliament, but, in handling a case in which it is relevant, they proceed from the premise that legislation is meant to be reasonable in intent, that is, to deal fairly and equally with all people. Coupled with the bias toward individual freedom of the common law, out of which have come many of the basic rules of procedure and precedents that mold the workings and judgments of the courts, this "rule of reason" reinforces the civil liberties of which the British are justly proud.

The Parliamentary System in the Commonwealth

The British parliamentary system evolved out of history and through a process extending over centuries. All the more remarkable, therefore, has been the extension of British parliamentary institutions into the countries of the British Empire and thus into the Commonwealth of Nations. Rarely have institutions resembled so closely the parent stock as those of Canada, Australia, and New Zealand. In each of these countries can be found the system of cabinet responsibility, the parliamentary concentration of power, and what is in essence the two-party system so characteristic of Great Britain.

Yet, history and environment have added individual features of major importance in each of these countries. Thus, Canada and Australia are federal systems in which the territorial division of power strains constantly against the unifying pressures of parliamentary rule; moreover, judicial review has played a far greater role in their development than it could in the unitary states of Great Britain and New Zealand, in which the territorial division of functions has no constitutional guarantee. As far as party systems are concerned, Canada follows the American pattern more than it does the British, with both its major parties, the Liberals and Progressive Conservatives, functioning as great holding companies of diverse interests, and only the minority NDP (New Democratic Party) unified by a social program somewhat comparable to that of the Labour parties of Great Britain, Australia, and New Zealand. When we look at policies, we find that Australia and New Zealand took the lead in early and radical experiments with state ownership and with compulsory arbitration of industrial disputes.

But, whatever their divergence from British forms, Canada, Australia, and New Zealand have a basic similarity to Great Britain in political tradition and constitutional attitudes that is far more significant. Underlying this similarity there is not only a common intellectual and political heritage—kept strong by ties of blood constantly refreshed by immigration and by allegiance to a common Crown—there are also the virtually ideal conditions for democracy possessed by these overseas parts of the Commonwealth. Notable among these conditions are a middle-class structure (so important, as Aristotle pointed out long ago, for the harmonious working of a constitution), widespread economic prosperity, a high degree of social mobility, and a workable balance between industry and agriculture.

Far more remarkable than finding British institutions and parliamentary traditions operating in the older parts of the Commonwealth overseas is to find them also in several of the newer Commonwealth members: India, Malaysia, and Jamaica. Here, the rate of literacy is low, the middle class is a small if dominant minority, and poverty is widespread. Yet, despite such handicaps, these countries have had considerable success so far in holding democratic elections (using symbols on the ballots, since the overwhelming proportion of voters cannot read), in operating parliamentary institutions, and even in handling that part of the government most difficult for the inexperienced—administration.

The most important of postwar parliamentary systems

within the Commonwealth and the most populous of functioning democracies is India. A republic since 1950, with a President elected for a five-year term by an electoral college composed of the elected members of the central and state legislatures, political power resides in the lower house of the central legislature, Lok Sabha, the House of the People, and the Cabinet, drawn from the ruling Congress party and headed, since 1966, by Prime Minister Indira Gandhi. India's federal system provides for an elaborately defined division of power between its nineteen states, many of which have a linguistic base of differentiation, and the central body, with the latter possessing residual powers, as in Canada but in contrast to the United States. Indeed, India is sometimes described as a "federal state with subsidiary unitary features": The President, on the advice of the Prime Minister, appoints state governors; there is one civil service for the whole country; judgments of the supreme court are binding throughout the judicial system; and the central government can take over states, as it did from 1968 to 1969 in four areas where coalition rule threatened instability. India's Constitution also includes a long and detailed Bill of Rights (not operative in any area where martial law is in effect), and its supreme court has power of judicial review. Thus, India has blended institutions found in many countries into a workable system powered by a dominant political party.

The African states that have achieved independence and Commonwealth membership exhibit a variety of political forms. Botswana and Gambia have what are essentially two-party systems, with small additional minority groups. Tanzania, always a democratic one-party state, has developed competitive elections at the constituency level and is promoting decentralization of governing functions. Kenya and Zambia are virtually one-party states, the latter now officially so by law. Several of the African states are under military rule, including Nigeria, the most populous of them, Uganda, and, since early 1972, Ghana, which had laboriously re-established civilian rule and a democratic framework after Nkrumah's ouster in 1966. Sierra Leone has moved in and out of military rule. What is apparent is that none of the new African members of the Commonwealth has the favorable conditions, such as natural resources and freedom from external pressures, that the earlier "British" overseas members of the Commonwealth enjoyed. Equally important, none of them, except possibly Tanzania and Botswana, has yet developed an overriding loyalty to the interests of the state as a whole to supersede the loyalty given to an ethnic group or religion. Thus, they are subject to divisive internal pressures and consequent instability—the major reasons, along with economic discontent, why military regimes have taken over in so many countries.

The Parliamentary System in Western Europe

The British pattern is only one facet of what is still the most widespread form of democratic political organization today: the parliamentary system. Although, in general, that system is characterized by the dependence of the executive on the confidence of the legislature, there can be wide differences in executive-legislative relations. In the British form of parliamentary government, the executive dominates the legislature, partly because, with rare exceptions, it is not parliament but the people, through their votes, who, in practice, choose the executive. In a sense, therefore, the legislature in British countries acts like an electoral college, as far as the creation of cabinets is concerned, though, unlike other electoral colleges, it continues in existence, discussing, criticizing, and passing upon the policies of the government. In the earlier French system, on the other hand, the legislature dominated the executive because it had created it and also because it could not be dissolved by it. A net result of these and other differences is that, while Great Britain has a strong, stable cabinet, France used to have a weak, unstable one.

France. What we have called the traditional and earlier French system is that of the pre–World War II Third Republic and of the Fourth Republic, which was created at the end of World War II and replaced in 1958. The Third, and even more so the Fourth, Republic provided obvious examples of the problems that arise when a too-powerful legislature, torn by a multiparty system (in which, after World War II, both the extreme left—the Communists—and, from time to time, also the extreme right were antidemocratic), results in an unstable executive incapable of providing consistent and effective leadership. The Constitution of the Fifth French Republic was designed to correct such imbalance; this has been accomplished, in practice, to such a degree that France, since 1958, has been governed by what is less a parliamentary regime than a mixture of authoritarianism and technocracy, with technical experts directing administration under the general supervision of the Cabinet (of which they are important members) and of the President, originally General Charles de Gaulle and, after his resignation in 1969, Georges Pompidou. Former French-controlled African territories from Senegal to Gabon have adopted this pattern of the dominant executive with the additional device of turning their countries into single constituencies in which the winning party takes all the seats.

The French President is no longer selected by the votes of the National Assembly and Senate meeting jointly, as under the Fourth Republic (on one occasion, the crippling force of party divisions necessitated more than one hundred ballots). Under the original Gaullist Constitution, the President was chosen by elected local office holders throughout the country. But by an amendment adopted in 1962, under procedures of doubtful constitutionality, the President is selected by direct popular election, a plebiscitary device traditionally distrusted by Frenchmen ever since the two Napoleons employed it to legitimate their supreme power. This process was meant to bestow on future presidents the kind of prestige de Gaulle possessed because of his own mystique. In any case, the President of the Fifth Republic possesses substantial reserve powers under which he can act if the Cabinet should ever cease to provide effective executive control; beyond this, de Gaulle and Pompidou have kept under their own personal direction substantial areas, including foreign policy, that in the British parliamentary system would be controlled by the Cabinet. Under the Fifth Republic, no Cabinet member may also be a member of the National Assembly, as all members were in the Fourth Republic, though he can appear before that body to direct discussions and explain policy. Moreover, the Cabinet has specific independent powers that it did not previously possess, while the Assembly, no longer omnipotent, is limited in its periods of meeting and restricted in debate.

The unique characteristic of the government of the Fifth Republic is that presidential and parliamentary institutions and functions must be kept in gear for the system to work smoothly. The President selects the Premier, who then appoints his own Cabinet. But the Premier and Cabinet must retain the support of the National Assembly for passage of most legislation, for there are provisions for votes of confidence and of censure, which in 1962 led to the resignation of a ministry and new elections.

The key to the functioning of this hybrid system has been the unprecedented control of the National Assembly by a single party, the UDR (*Union pour la Défense de la République*) whose cohesion and success, originally provided by loyalty to de Gaulle, have been maintained by the advantages of political office. Whether the President and Premier could intermesh their governing roles effectively without such party support is open to question.

West Germany. To some degree the Fifth French Republic is typical of regimes lying between parliamentarianism and new-style authoritarianism. What has emerged in West Germany since World War II shows similar trends toward such a form. As in the case of France, Germany's earlier experience with the instability of extreme parliamentarianism—during the pre–Nazi Weimar Republic—strongly influenced the drafters of the Bonn Constitution. Consequently, they devised built-in guarantees of executive stability, such as the so-called constructive vote of nonconfidence, which makes it necessary for a party or parties desiring to overthrow the incumbent Chancellor to present a candidate backed by a new majority *before* the incumbent can be forced to resign.

Since, in other respects, the Federal Assembly constitutionally enjoys the customary rights and privileges of a parliament in a full-fledged parliamentary democracy, this stipulation might not have been so important had not other factors combined to strengthen the executive at the expense of the powers and prestige of parliament. Under any circumstances, a country like Germany, not accustomed in the past to the habits of government by discussion and consent, would have had a hard time growing into such ways of political life. As it happened, the fourteen-year rule of Chancellor Konrad Adenauer, who was the prototype of the German statesman interested in *having things done* rather than in *how* they are done, molded the reconstruction of West Germany after the Nazi breakdown and defeat. By good luck and management, this reconstruction period proved to be one of unexcelled economic prosperity as well as unequalled rise to eminence in the foreign field, thereby greatly contributing to the reputation of his government. To Germans, habitually looking to the expert leader in political, executive, and administrative affairs to handle matters without much participation and initiative on their part, Adenauer's regime provided a chance to see efficiency combined with representative government. But the latter was bound to suffer. Adenauer lost no time in establishing the principle that ministers, far from being coresponsible members of the Cabinet and separately responsible to Parliament, were his own aides exclusively. In addition, many fields, such as foreign affairs, were for long periods eliminated from parliamentary purview, and the prestige and standing of the Bundestag therefore declined in public esteem.

In the 1960's, however, the major opposition party, the Social Democrats (SDP), with their strong support from labor, began to outstrip the CDU, the middle-class Christian Democrats, in vitality if not in votes. In 1959, the SPD had renounced its residual Marxist socialism and, in its Godesberg program, affirmed its goal of moderate reform on the pattern of the British Labor Party. Widespread dissatisfaction with the autocratic actions of the Adenauer Cabinet and the fumbling of his successor, Ludwig Erhard, after the aged leader had resigned, as well as with a leadership crisis following Erhard's forced resignation, left the CDU in disarray. In an unexpected move, the SPD entered into coalition with the CDU, providing the country with three years of stable government but depriving it of any effective opposition within the legislature; for, under this "grand coalition" of the two major parties, the executive, though no longer under one-man control, came to prevail more than ever over the legislature.

Then things changed. Having acquired a new respectability through its performance as junior partner in the "grand coalition" without losing its popularity with labor, the SDP altered its tactics after the election of 1969. It forced the CDU into opposition by forming a coalition with the FDP, the Free Democratic Party, which was one of several minor political groups whose balancing role had given them disproportionate influence over the making of coalition governments. By 1969, it was the only one still represented in parliament. Together with his Foreign Minister, Walter Scheel, leader of the FDP, Chancellor Willy Brandt initiated an imaginative and courageous foreign policy, involving a new orientation toward the East (*Ostpolitik*) to match West Germany's well-established postwar *rapprochement* with France, which had led to joint membership in the Common Market and close association with the United States. In the summer of 1972, the Brandt-Scheel government lost its bare majority through defections over its *Ostpolitik*. In consequence it felt compelled to call for new elections that it won handily, obtaining a clear mandate for both its foreign and domestic policies.

The last few years have thus seen the revival of a genuine parliamentary regime in West Germany, in which the legislature has recaptured the center of the political stage. The relative evenness of the political strength of the two major parties, the SDP and CDU, continues to provide the third party with disproportionate influence in the formation and functioning of a government; to this degree, therefore, West Germany still fails to operate on the same basis as the two-party systems of Great Britain and the United States. Yet, in the broader sense of liberal democratic regimes in which two major parties appeal with moderate yet distinctly different programs to a broad spectrum of the electorate, West Germany now corresponds very nearly to Great Britain and other parliamentary two-party systems.

Italy. There remains only one other major country in Continental Europe—Italy—where the traditional parliamentary system still holds sway. But the numerous falls and crises of government that it has suffered since the end of the war remind one of the Third and Fourth French Republics as well as of its own pre-Fascist history. The jockeying among nine major political parties and several minor ones has led to a variety of coalitions, of which the center-left has had the longest tenure of office. The center party, the Christian Democrats, which polls the largest percentage of the popular vote and holds the largest number, though not a majority, of the seats in the Chamber of Deputies, is itself composed of a wide range of views. Up to 1956, the Socialists allied themselves with the Communists, but they gradually extended support to the center on the basis of a reformist program and, in 1963, entered into the center-left coalition. This coalition was marked by increasing instability, and Italy, as a consequence, suffered a series of crises over its inability to secure a government effective enough to carry through needed economic and social legislation. Following upon another dissolution of Parliament and new elections in 1972, the Christian Democrats formed a government without the Socialists, backed only by minor middle parties. Thus, their political base shrunk to a bare minimum.

Where the British system stands at one end of the parliamentary spectrum, with its leadership firmly, and responsibly, in control of the legislature, the Italian system stands at the other, exhibiting the serious weaknesses of parliamentary government when no party or stable coalition can provide effective leadership of the legislature and the executive has no independent legal authority through which to act. France and, to a lesser degree, West Germany have built-in safeguards against such continued executive instability. Other European parliamentary systems have, both by convention and by practice, developed workable means of balancing multiparty representation with executive leadership and thus function better, and are more stable, than Italy's.

The Netherlands and Scandinavia. In the Netherlands, Sweden, and Norway, the executive is weaker than it is in Great Britain, but much more stable than it was in France's Fourth Republic. In the Netherlands, for example, there are about fifteen parties represented in Parliament, which obviously makes the formation of a government coalition a complex business; occasionally, there are Cabinet crises lasting several months before a ministry is formed. But, once chosen, the Cabinet, and even more the Prime Minister, tend to retain office for relatively long periods of time. This can be explained partly by two characteristics of these parliamentary systems: Cabinet and legislature are separated more from each other than in Great Britain or West Germany, yet there is far more give-and-take between the two in hammering out the legislative program.

These West European countries thus have a very different view from the British of the relation between the executive and the legislature. The executive in the Scandinavian countries and in the Netherlands tends both to bargain more and to be more flexible. To have the legislature reject an important part of the Cabinet's program is not looked on as a major defeat, as it would be in Great Britain. On the contrary, when the executive proposes a project, it anticipates that this project will not only be carefully considered in the legislature, as is true in Great Britain, but possibly also modified. It accepts this situation. Thus, these countries tread a middle way between the possible "cabinet dictatorship" of the British parliamentary system (which, in Britain itself, is avoided by the self-restraint of the Cabinet), and the executive instability of the Fourth French Republic and of contemporary Italy. The result is a system marked by compromise and a genuine executive-legislative partnership in the making of law.

Switzerland. The relation between Parliament and executive in Switzerland deviates from the usual parliamentary pattern to such an extent that some students of comparative government consider the "Swiss system" to be a third type, distinguished from either the normal parliamentary or the presidential system. Once elected by Parliament, the federal councilors who make up the seven-member Swiss executive never resign over any issue of policy that divides them, individually or as a body, from a parliamentary majority. They continue to preside over their departments, following the instructions of Parliament. Since, furthermore, Parliament cannot be dissolved under the Swiss system, the political interplay between legislature and executive that is characteristic of other parliamentary systems, and which may lead to resignations, dissolutions, and new elections in the wake of votes of nonconfidence, does not exist in Switzerland. Thus, the Swiss executive might be considered a top-level bureaucracy rather than a policy-making, issue-resolving separate "power." Issues are resolved either in Parliament or by popular vote (initiative and referendum), a typical Swiss institution. Since Switzerland's permanent neutrality prejudges most of its foreign-policy problems, and since many domestic problems are handled on the cantonal level, issues tend to be less serious and numerous than in other West European democracies.

The bureaucratic nature of the Swiss executive is further apparent from the usually long tenure of individual councilors, extending frequently over many parliamentary terms. These re-elections are possible because—in another deviation from the usual parliamentary pattern—the Federal Council comprises representatives of all the major parties, regardless

of election results, though not on a proportionate basis. Moreover, the body functions as a truly collegiate group. There is
nobody who might be compared to a Prime Minister, not
even as "first among equals." This is because the Swiss executive does not provide political leadership. In a way, therefore,
Switzerland has perhaps the truest "parliamentary" system of
all, since Parliament is in charge of all important decisions and
the executive is a mere committee of that body, without political ambitions of its own. There, the system has been highly
successful in combining democratic responsibility and representation with stability of government. But it is questionable
whether it could function equally well in larger and more
divided nations lacking the broad constitutional and general
consensus with which the closely knit Swiss community is
blessed.

Japan. Earlier, we described one important Asian parliamentary democracy, India, whose background experience was
as a member of the British Empire. The second important
parliamentary democracy in Asia is Japan. Although, in this
case, the strongest external influence had been that of the
United States, Japan's postwar constitution of 1947 transformed its former semiparliamentary, but largely authoritarian system, into a full-fledged constitutional one on the British
pattern. This became true also for the position of the monarchy. Legislative and fiscal power is vested in a bicameral
Parliament headed by a civilian Cabinet drawn from the
majority party in the lower chamber, the House of Representatives. The conservative and business-minded Liberal
Democratic Party has consistently secured an absolute majority of seats and thus maintained political office. But the
opposition parties are vigorous, and there is thus a functioning parliamentary system. Moreover, the military, which so
long intervened in civilian affairs, no longer threatens democratic government.

Japan's constitutional Bill of Rights includes compulsory
education, nondiscrimination, and a minimum standard of
living. Its appointive supreme court has powers of judicial

review. With an unparalleled cohesion built during centuries of isolation through its common language, traditions, and religion, and with an economic expansion hardly equalled even in West Germany's early postwar years, Japan is and will remain one of the world's most important powers.

What is apparent from such a survey is that the parliamentary system is infinitely flexible in adapting to local situations and traditions. By ensuring close executive-legislative relations, this system makes it imperative that the leadership be responsive to the representative institutions; at the same time, it ensures that the latter have continuous guidance from the executive center of power. These dual objectives have been paramount in the decision of mature states like Japan and Israel to adopt the parliamentary system. The newly independent states of the former British and French empires adopted it in one form or another largely because of their familiarity with it but also because of its presumed adaptability to their needs. In an earlier generation, the newly independent states of Latin America, and also Liberia, adopted the other great type of representative government, the presidential system of the United States, and it is that form to which we now turn.

THE PRESIDENTIAL PATTERN

The distinctive feature of the presidential pattern of government is that the chief executive holds office for a predetermined period, whether or not he is supported by the majority of the legislature. As the 1968 and 1972 U.S. elections demonstrated, the voters may even elect a Republican President at the same moment that they send a Democratic majority to both houses of Congress. These circumstances furnish an extreme example of the constant give-and-take between executive and legislature that characterizes Continental parliamentary systems like those of Norway and the Netherlands. Even when the American President's party dominates the legislature, the President has less assurance of control over the passage of laws than even a weak British Prime Minister.

Yet, at the same time, there are great resources at the disposal of an American President. He is the leader of his party, he controls the administration, and he can appeal directly to the people to support his program. Underwriting these sources of power is his guaranteed possession of office for four years, twice the term of office of the lower house.

As with the British parliamentary system, the characteristic features of the American presidential system are founded in history. It is important to remember that the American Constitution was drafted not in 1776, at the moment of proclaiming independence from Great Britain, when reaction against executive power was at its height, but in 1787, more than a decade later, when the balance had swung sharply, and many of the framers of the Constitution thought dangerously, in favor of powerful legislatures within the states, which were enacting radical economic measures in response to the pressures of popular majorities. The Constitution was thus designed to erect a strong national government able to curb the excesses of the states in the interests of financial stability, and within that national government to establish effective checks on the power of the lower house, the most direct agent of the people.

Hence, it provided for the establishment of a strong second chamber, the Senate, whose members were originally appointed by state legislatures, and who are still elected, one-third every two years, for six-year terms, in contrast to the two-year terms of representatives in the lower house. Hence, too, it reinforced the independent position of the chief executive, the President, by selection through an electoral college that was intended to make him only indirectly responsible to the people and by a four-year term, renewable now only once, that completes the pattern of staggered elections. The President was given the power to veto laws, to nominate officials, and to command the army. Moreover, although his veto of laws can be overridden by a two-thirds majority of the members of both the Senate and the House of Representatives, the Constitution provides for the so-called pocket veto, which makes it impossible to override a presidential veto of measures passed at the end of a congressional session.

Lastly, the pattern of checks and balances within the national government is completed by the strong position of the federal judiciary, whose members are appointed for life by the President with the consent of the Senate, and, in particular, of the Supreme Court. Whether the framers of the Constitution intended the Supreme Court to have the power of judicial review is still disputed, but, in practice, the Court has exercised that power since Chief Justice John Marshall claimed it in *Marbury* v. *Madison* in 1803. Moreover, his decision, in 1819, in *McCulloch* v. *Maryland* opened the way to a continuous broadening of the powers and functions of the national government by asserting that the Constitution provides implied as well as explicitly delegated powers. This means that Congress may choose whatever means it considers appropriate for carrying out its legitimate purposes, as long as these means are not specifically prohibited. No less significant, the judgment reaffirmed the precedent that it is the Supreme Court that determines whether an act of Congress is constitutional, i.e., has binding force because it is enacted within Congress's legally possessed powers.

The American presidential system is characterized not only by the *functional* division of national power, maintained by the checks and balances among the three, specifically separated, branches—the executive, legislature, and judiciary—but also by the *territorial* division of power between the Federal Government and those of the states. It would have been impossible to establish a national government in 1787 without leaving a considerable amount of power in the hands of the state units, which had been exercising independent authority since the Declaration of Independence. Federalism was also looked on as a further application of the theory of checks and balances by which rash acts on the part of individual states or the national government could be restrained.

Some of the obviously restrictive features of the original Constitution have been changed by formal amendment. Since

1913, Senators have been elected directly by the voters of their states; the franchise has been broadened; and constitutional provisions forbid discrimination on grounds of sex or race (though the country still faces serious problems in preventing either). But, by far, the greatest changes have come through what may be called the "unwritten constitution," which has grown up alongside the formal Constitution. Party activities, nominating conventions, the President's Cabinet are all part of the unwritten constitution, which has arisen out of usage, judicial decisions, and legislation. The popular control that keeps both executive and legislature in the national and state spheres responsive to public pressure is almost solely the result of an evolution that has gone on both inside and outside the formal Constitution.

Despite this evolution and its basic responsiveness to popular sentiment, built-in restraints and the balance of powers remain the characteristics of the American presidential system. While the machinery of government can act swiftly in response to a national emergency, such as that posed by war or depression, the constitutional provisions for dividing authority—separation of powers, bicameralism (of two more or less equally powerful chambers), and judicial review—combine to prevent or impede major changes in policy until public pressures have built up on a broad scale. Whereas the parliamentary system responds quickly to popular majorities, the American presidential system reinforces the position of powerful and organized minorities, e.g., of Midwestern farm interests and of white Southerners through their disproportionately high representation (in proportion to population) in the Senate, and on committees of the House of Representatives and Senate concerned with issues in which they have particular interest.

It is at the committee level that the power structure within Congress has so much effect. In contrast to the Cabinet's constant control of legislation and the budget in the British parliamentary system, specialized committees of Congress determine the fate not only of legislation proposed by their own members but also of proposals for legislative and budgetary measures emanating from the chief executive. Woodrow Wilson once characterized the American system as a "government by the chairmen of the standing committees of Congress." Under the traditional seniority rule, committee chairmen secure and maintain their positions through being on a committee longer than any other member of the party that holds a majority in that chamber. This provides a strong advantage to those states or districts that re-elect their representatives over and over again: among the Republicans, this advantage accrues to some of the Northern areas; among the Democrats, to the South. Since party cohesion and discipline are far less strong in Congress than they are in the great majority of parliamentary systems, these provisions (which are based on convention and are not necessarily a part of the congressional-presidential system) reinforce the power position of certain local, sectional, or economic interests.

Those who believe strongly in majority rule and want a system that will smoothly and swiftly translate majority wishes into legislation will favor the parliamentary system over the presidential. Those, on the other hand, who are concerned about the dangers of impulsive popular pressures and about the protection of vested groups and interests may well favor the presidential-congressional, or separation-of-powers, system. It is obvious that each has its own particular problems and requires a particular type of restraint and experience to operate in such a fashion as to secure effective results in needed legislation without degenerating into irresponsible majority rule.

Like the British parliamentary system of government, the American presidential system has provided a model for the government of many states. As noted above, the republics of Latin America copied, to a greater or lesser extent, the structure devised by the American Constitution. Except in rare instances, this was done of their own accord and not through any American tutelage comparable to British and French efforts to guide their colonies toward self-government through the progressive handing-over of responsibility for operating their institutions. For better or, in some cases, for worse, Latin American countries, and in earlier times Liberia, had to struggle largely unaided to make their American-type institutions operate. In a considerable number of situations the results bear litle resemblance to the parent model. This is sometimes true also in regard to those newer countries that have adopted the parliamentary system, or some variant of it. Thus, we may well ask: How deep does Western influence go among the developing countries of Latin America, Africa, the Middle East, and Asia?

How Deep Does Western Influence Go?

Taking into account the degree of imitation of the governmental forms of Great Britain, France, the United States, and the Soviet Union, we might be tempted to say that the ideas of Locke and Harrington, Montesquieu and Rousseau, Bentham and Mill, and Hegel and Marx have by and large been the determinants of the modern world. But to what degree has this been more than a surface influence? Is it not possible that the few centuries in which these ideas and their attendant institutions have flourished constitute, at least for the non-Western world, what an Indian author has called the "Vasco da Gama age"? In other words, has this perhaps been merely a transitory period of superficial Western influence over a non-Western world whose background and conditions of life are so essentially dissimilar to those of the middle-class democracies of the United States, Great Britain, Canada, Australia, and New Zealand? Is the developing third world again shaping its own destinies? If so, along what lines?

Latin America

Latin America is at one and the same time the least developed part of the Western world and the most advanced of the developing areas. Although colonialism had a deeper influence, culturally, linguistically, and demographically, in that area than it had in Africa or Asia, it was a colonialism of an early period and by two countries, Spain and Portugal, which at the time of their greatest impact on South America could themselves hardly be called Western. Persistent economic and political pressures on Latin American countries from the United States can be compared to the aggressive colonialism and mercantilism of Western Europe in Africa and Asia in the late nineteenth and early twentieth centuries and, as with the latter, have been, except in Argentina, largely an overlay. Today, Latin America, with the highest rate of population growth and mobility found anywhere in the world, is seeking, like other developing areas, its own distinctive answers to social and economic imperatives.

Over 50 per cent of Latin America's total population of some 290 million already live in cities, and urbanization continues to spread. The need for employment, which translates into the need for development in the industrial and service sectors of society, has powered popular demands for social and economic equity between and within the varied population strains of their peoples, and for regimes that will provide such equity. The new nationalism springing from this populist thrust has led to a variety of political experiments within Latin America. While all designations are suspect, one recent writer tentatively identifies the "politics of national revolution" in Mexico and Bolivia; the "politics of Marxist socialism" in Chile and Cuba: the former democratic, the latter authoritarian; the "politics of constitutional democracy" in Costa Rica, Venezuela, and Colombia; and military regimes promoting modernization in Peru, Panama, and Brazil.* Unlike the last two, Peru demonstrates an unusual combination of military control and socially progressive policies. Argentina, one of the most developed Latin American states, has for decades been alternating between authoritarian controls and very unstable parliamentary institutions. While the course of development in certain other states is not clear, all but the most conservative, like Nicaragua, Paraguay, and Guatemala

* Ben S. Stephansky, *Latin America Toward a New Nationalism*, Headline Series, no. 211 (June, 1972), 42–43.

and, in the Caribbean, Haiti and the Dominican Republic, are responding to new populist pressures for representation and reform.

Mexico, which had its Revolution in 1910, has been administered since 1929 by the Institutional Revolutionary Party (PRI), its dominating political party. The PRI has achieved Latin America's most successful integration of the Indian population into a full participating role in society, established a modern social welfare system, nationalized basic resources, and developed industry. A federal republic, with a President elected for a nonrenewable, six-year term, its bicameral legislature and judiciary are also elected by universal franchise. Neither the senators, who have six-year terms, nor the deputies, with three-year spans, are eligible for re-election until at least one term intervenes, a practice that keeps the legislature constantly renewed with fresh personnel. In comparison to this long-established and relatively stable situation, Bolivia, which is pursuing the same objectives of nationalizing basic resources, notably tin, and integrating its Indians into the national life, has moved in and out of military rule—a fairly common stage in developing countries seeking the combination of social and economic reform and firm and unified governmental control.

Among Latin American countries, the three attracting most attention are Cuba, Chile, and Brazil. Fidel Castro's Cuba is a highly authoritarian regime based, however, less on Soviet, Chinese, or Eastern European models than on Castro's own view of what a socialist state should be, as well as on his personal charisma. The economy has been completely nationalized, agriculture reorganized, and education transformed and extended; also, progressive social services have been established. Since industrialization has not advanced, however, Cuba remains dependent on exports of primary products, notably sugar, tobacco, and minerals, which are now sent mainly to the Soviet Union. Unlike other Communist countries, Cuba has no representative institutions to provide at least the appearance of regular popular participation in government, and Castro depends, apparently fairly successfully, on public support whipped up through massive rallies called at his own discretion. His regime represents what might be called a "wildcat" variety of Communism, experimental and without adherence to traditional loyalties and ideologies.

Chile, also dedicated to Marxist socialism, is operating within a political system very different from Cuba's. Its freely elected Marxist President, Salvador Allende, is leader of one of the six groups in the governing coalition, the Socialist Party, whose ideology is to the left of the participating Communists—who, in contrast to those in Cuba, are old liners both in habits of mind and in allegiance. Pledged to working within Chile's well-established constitutional system, Allende has accelerated and expanded the reform programs of the previous Christian Democratic regime. He has provoked American anger by nationalizing the copper mines without compensation, although this action follows the pattern of expropriation of foreign-owned holdings throughout Latin America: of Gulf Oil properties and U.S. Steel zinc mines by Bolivia in 1969–70; of an affiliate of International Telegraph and Telephone by Ecuador the same year; of the International Petroleum Company by Peru in 1968; and of Alcan Aluminum (Canadian) by Guyana in 1971. Whether Allende can continue his program of incorporating the peasantry and urban unemployed into Chile's political, economic, and social system without incurring the opposition of Chile's strong trade unions, and also keep Chile's economy afloat without more substantial international aid, may determine the future course of this first Marxist leader to acquire power through the ballot box.

It remains to consider Brazil, Latin America's most populous state and potentially a world power. The military coup of 1964, made in the interests of the landed middle class, halted far-reaching social and economic changes which were aimed at securing working-class and peasant support for the former regime, and were palatable as well to business and industrial interests. But the military government, under a succession of generals, has also impelled Brazil along a dynamic and largely successful program of gigantic public works and industrialization. Yet, at the same time, it has restricted freedom of speech, censored the press, dismissed many university teachers, and permitted the use of torture against presumed adversaries, including priests and nuns. What direction this army regime will take in the future is problematic, since it has wavered so often in the past between protecting of conservative landed interests and advocating measures appealing to both labor and industry.

Africa and the Middle East

The military have long played an important role within Latin American countries, and their frequent interventions have shaped the stereotype of political instability in that area. The same process was not anticipated in newly independent African states. The latter acquired formal independence in the late 1950's and early 1960's after short periods of tutelage and transition supervised by their imperial powers, Great Britain, France, and Belgium. The final transition from colonial status to full sovereignty came through negotiation, not revolution. Only the Belgian Congo (now Zaïre) erupted immediately into violence. The others struggled earnestly to cope with the divisive pressures of ethnic, linguistic, and regional diversity, the lowest levels of economic development of any area in the world, and the inflated expectations of their people.

The responses to these strains and challenges have differed widely among the more than forty independent African-controlled countries on that Continent. In sub-Saharan Africa, Tanzania, skillfully guided by an experienced, talented, and popular leader, Julius Nyerere, favors equalitarian development in both rural and urban areas. The Ivory Coast, Senegal, Kenya, Zambia, and Botswana, also under experienced and popular leaders, seek to promote capitalistic inputs and expansion. But the relative political stability in these countries has not been matched by the situation in many of the others. Ethnic antagonisms intensified by the lure of power; lack of administrative experience and skill, such as the British had successfully fostered for generations on the Indian sub-continent; and the growing gap between indigeneous haves and have-nots created situations in many parts of the continent in which, in the mid-1960's, in a rapidly spreading series of coups, a previously apolitical military seized the reins of power usually for the avowed purpose of providing stability under which these ills could be effectively handled.

Characteristic of many army takeovers in African countries has been their avowed intention of remaining only temporarily in control until stable civilian rule could be re-established. Thus, in almost all cases, the administrative structure remained relatively unchanged, pursuing its customary tasks, though also responding to new imperatives. But, however sincere army leaders have been in stating that their objective is to encourage an ultimate handing back of power to soundly based, popularly elected civilian regimes, this aim has so far only rarely been achieved. Ghana, which went through a long-drawn-out process to re-establish civilian rule, willingly turned back to military control early in 1972, when inefficient administration and unpopular economic policies combined to undercut confidence in the Busia government. The Sudan, whose first military coup occurred in 1958, two years after independence, has had several alternations of army and civilian rule, and only ended its seventeen-year-long civil war in 1972 under a military regime.

Where military rule provides a stable basis for economic reconstruction, a measure of popular representation may develop and become part of the political system. A prime example of this process is Egypt, where Colonel Gamal Abdel Nasser directed a remarkably successful economic and social revolution from 1954 on and, in 1964, promulgated a constitution that defines the country as a "democratic socialist state." The single, officially recognized political party, the Arab Socialist Union, functions through a complex of territorially defined units that interact with each other and controls the National Assembly, for which nationwide elections, with universal suffrage, were held in 1969. The President, who is officially nominated by the National Assembly and confirmed by a national plebiscite (in practice, selected by the Arab Socialist Union), is head both of the state and of the party and, in effect, also of the army. Thus, the Egyptian political system is a one-party regime incorporating substantial but well-disciplined popular representation. This type of system is sometimes termed "tutelary democracy." Some observers suggest that it may also be the direction in which Major General Joseph Mobutu is moving Zaïre.

Turkey provides a still more outstanding example of an "educational" dictatorship that stimulated rapid modernization and thus laid a basis for subsequent, more democratic developments. In the 1920's and 1930's, Kemal Atatürk, followed by his associate, Ismet Inönü, Westernized the people by means of a dictatorship operating through a one-party system. It is questionable whether it would have been possible without a dictatorship to transform Turkey from a typically Oriental, Islamic, traditionalist country into a modern nation —considering that this involved not only profound political and economic changes, but also the destruction of deeply rooted customs, such as the abolition of the harem, the veil, and the caliphate, and the introduction of the Western alphabet, script, and calendar. A gradual transformation followed this stage, although the 1960 military coup and subsequent instability after civilian rule was re-established in 1961 suggest that the political foundation was less firmly established than had been thought.

In some other situations, the old feudal interests or those of foreign capital have turned to their own purposes apparently democratic institutions, in particular parliaments that are controlled or have been bought by them. This was the situation in Egypt before its national revolution in 1953. It was also the case in Iran, where the feudal landowning interests dominated parliament, until the ruler himself, the Shah, emerged as the leader of a movement to reshape the socioeconomic structure of the nation through agrarian reform. More often, however, the movement toward change comes from below and, in the name of economic and social reform (and often with an anti-Western or anti-"Yankee" slant), establishes a "Kemalist" type of regime.

If economic, social, and cultural reforms lead toward eventual political democratization, then military rule or even dictatorship may turn out to have been a blessing in disguise. But it is also true that both have used procedures that may of themselves create that corruption and cynicism that is so dangerous to the evolution of genuine democracy. Ballot-box stuffing and manipulation of election results are not unique to regimes in the so-called educational period of transition, but where they occur they undermine whatever efforts are being made to establish a sense of legitimacy for representative institutions.

The Role of the Military in the Political Process of Developing States

Historically, the military's primary purpose has been to preserve the territorial integrity of the state and, where demanded, to implement its expansionist foreign policies. The military has also long functioned as the ultimate arbiter in extreme cases of civil strife. What has become apparent particularly since World War II, however, is that the military has increasingly become the key decision-making element in the developing countries. To a large degree the military and civilian governments appear to seek the same goals: stability, order, national unity, and rapid modernization. Why then has there been such a high incidence of extralegal military intervention in the political process? And what has been its effect in terms of such long range goals?

Some of the reasons for the extensive military intervention in Africa, Asia, and Latin America have been the blatant corruption, or visible internal squabbling, of civilian governments, their inability (or presumed inability) to control domestic violence or to avoid stalemate in the drive to achieve national goals. Threats to the needs and aspirations of the military and growth in the political aspirations of their leaders have also played a role. When a phenomena is so widespread, contagion is likely. The chances are, therefore, that the military will continue to play a major, if not *the* major, role in any developing state which does not possess what is all too rare: purposive civilian leadership supported by broadly representative political organization.

Widespread extralegal military intervention in developing states has only rarely led to a redesigned allocation of national resources that would place the national economy on a sounder basis for supporting its own economic development by stressing infrastructure and capital accumulation rather than consumption. Where the military does not simply pursue much the same economic policies as the civilian government it superseded, it is likely to engage in showy economic projects, as in Brazil, or take a larger share of resources for its own satisfaction, legitimate or otherwise, as in Nigeria, or underwrite a more dominant role in foreign affairs, as in Libya. Military rule generally has its most decisive impact on the political process. Political stability is likely to be achieved, as with Mobutu in Zaïre, and this of itself may encourage economic growth or at least prevent further disintegration. But military involvement in the political process almost inevitably results in the atrophy of participatory politics. Thus it delays, if it does not prevent, the growth of a viable set of acceptable and accepted rules for combining political participation with political stability. Only rarely does an imposed set of such rules and framework prove lasting.

A military government does commonly perform what may be called a homogenizing role, weakening ethnic and regional loyalties, attitudes, and orientations and replacing them with a sense of national loyalty and with values that aid assimilation into the modern sectors of society. To this degree it may well aid national integration. There is a danger, however, that the military may insist on focusing national loyalties on itself and become intolerant of activities by other groups and of competing objectives. If these attitudes should combine with disillusionment and distrust of the military's objectives and achievements, the long-run impact of its role in relation to political stability and national integration may nullify its original short range success. The ultimate effect of military intervention in the political process of developing states is directly related, therefore, to the degree to which its power is used to achieve objectives of lasting and national value like those sought by Kemal Pasha and Nasser in the formative years of their regimes.

THE EXTENT OF DIVERSITY

From what has been said so far, it is clear that, in addition to similar patterns among governmental systems, there is also a colorful (and sometimes dismaying) diversity, one that seems constantly increasing as more and more countries acquire independence. Fifty years ago, there were fewer than 50 sovereign nations; today, there are nearly 150, with still more to come. Some of these countries are still in the earliest stage of development, with nomadic forms of life and rudimentary or traditional and autocratic institutions. Even within one region such as the Middle East, countries of this type, like Saudi Arabia and Yemen, lie close to advanced countries like Lebanon, with its sophisticated, commercial population, and Israel, with its high degree of organization in every aspect of life. Moreover, the degree of control may range all the way from government regulation and organization of almost everything to a bare minimum of government and administration in the operational sense.

THE TREND TOWARD UNIFORMITY

But, despite all this, we should not exaggerate the factor of diversity. Behind the impression of great variety is a trend toward greater uniformity. Even though the impact of Western ideas and institutions has not (or not yet) been able to "modernize" (in Western terms) the actual political structure and life of many countries that have adopted an outwardly

Western constitution or similar façade, most of them are beginning to modernize their economic structure, in particular to industrialize themselves in order to attain higher standards of living. This is part of that scientific-technological revolution, with its attendant rapid and accelerating change in all fields of life, that, as we emphasized at the beginning, forms perhaps the overarching, most decisive new feature of the twentieth-century world. In the face of this all-important development, we may even question whether the great diversity of political patterns and systems, including that of the polar opposites—totalitarianism and democracy—will in the future be as significant as the increasing underlying similarity of living conditions and "ways of life." Indeed, there are those adherents of the theory of convergence who profess to discern a growing likeness of such conditions and even attitudes, at least among the "common people" of such political opposites as the United States and the Soviet Union. They point out, for example, that the people in the United States are getting used to more and more planning of their lives by big government and other "big" organizations and institutions, while the people in the most modernized Communist countries (not only the Soviet Union but also such former "satellites" as Hungary and Poland), though accustomed to such inclusion in the big apparatus, are beginning to exercise some "liberal" discretion in a number of areas. The fact that First Secretary Leonid Brezhnev and President Nixon negotiated directly in Moscow in 1972 on economic and disarmament issues reflected common interests and needs.

In the face of this trend toward modernization, the more traditionalist types of governments, such as feudal and absolutist monarchies, inevitably decline. Traditionalism, even of the tribal type, is bound to give way when the "revolution of rising expectations," with its demands for the better life promised by scientific thought and industrial technology, penetrates areas in which fatalism hitherto made people shun ideas of change and transformation. Once the expectation of rapid change is aroused, it cannot be stopped by inherited political institutions. Nothing, perhaps, distinguishes our age more sharply from preceding ages than the rate at which change is taking place. While populations are increasing at a fantastic rate and the number of independent countries is still growing, there is, at the same time, an ever increasing interdependence among nations, arising out of mutual exploitation of resources, threats to the environment, growing specialization of functions and, perhaps above all, the awareness that all countries, even the most powerful, are at the mercy of the appalling destructiveness of atomic and hydrogen weapons.

While it is obvious that traditional and feudal forms of government will steadily be overborne by economic change, and particularly by industrialism, it is far from certain that this development will lead these countries toward more democratic forms of government. There was a time when it was taken for granted that an advanced industrial country would be a democracy, but the interwar and postwar periods have undermined this belief. Totalitarianism, fascist or Communist, made deep inroads into regions where democracy seemed firmly established, or at least seemed to have a chance.

This means that the trend toward uniformity, which is particularly strong in the field of technology and, consequently, in areas of industrial and general organization of life, economy, and society, has not, or has not yet, been so strong in the area of political systems and governmental structures. There, the trend is not toward a single model or blueprint for political organization; rather, it is still toward either of the two opposing models that we have distinguished—the democratic or the dictatorial—or toward one or the other of those less easily characterized middle forms that lean toward one or the other. It is now time, therefore, to examine with some care the framework of limited government, the channels of political action, the role of executives, administration, and pressure groups, and the impact of belief systems and of international relations before we can come to more general conclusions about the prospects of democracy in an increasingly integrating and yet deeply divided world.

III

THE FRAMEWORK OF
LIMITED GOVERNMENT

ORIGINS AND FUNCTIONS OF CONSTITUTIONS

Constitutions define, and thereby limit, public power. The distinctive characteristics of a totalitarian dictatorship, as we have indicated above, are that the power exercised by its governing group is unlimited and unrestrained and that, in principle, the authority of the regime extends into every aspect of the public and private life of the individual—religious, cultural, economic, and social. In contrast, the exercise of political power in a liberal democracy is limited by a constitutional framework that protects certain areas of personal and group life from governmental interference and provides that governmental powers shall be exercised in accordance with known procedures. The distinction between the two forms of government is basically that between limited and unlimited government.

Genuine constitutions determining these limitations can therefore exist only in nontotalitarian countries. Formal appearances notwithstanding, totalitarian regimes do not have them. At best, such regimes may enjoy merely a self-limitation on the part of the ruling group. And, in any case, whatever rules exist are provisional, changeable, and revocable; they do not have the nature of generality, reliability, and thus calculability that the rules of law possess elsewhere. Genuine constitutionalism is likewise absent when constitutions are constantly being made and remade, changed and abolished, so as to fit the political needs of the respective power-holders.

There were times, in premodern ages, when constitutional

rules delimiting the power of rulers were likewise absent. Yet such rule, even when it was presumed to be by divine right, was not totalitarian, since rulers avowedly operated under a religious, moral, or natural law that was binding on ruler and ruled alike. Thus, the problems of political theory and practice were both personal and declaratory: How to educate the prince, for instance, so that he would govern for the common good; and how to maintain compliance by the ruler with traditional principles of justice, as witness Magna Carta. With the rise of the modern territorial state, however, and its impersonal and bureaucratic ordering of ever more spheres of life, government became too complicated to depend on the personal equation. Reliance had then to be put on the formulation, and formalization, of rules.

This does not imply that a constitution is always a written document, adopted at a particular moment in history as a comprehensive regulation of governmental life. The British Constitution developed gradually and—apart from the great charters—largely in the form of custom. Yet, what made the result of this process a constitution in the modern sense of the word was not only that it defined but that it also *limited* the power of the governing agencies. In the absence of this limiting function, the collections of rules and customs that during this same period (later Middle Ages and early modern era) defined the arrangements of other political units, did not form constitutions in this same sense.

Modern written constitutions arose in the past either from "pact" or from "compact." They arose from *pact* where, as in Continental Europe, they resulted from the contest between popular movements and royal absolutism over a share in political power. Thus, in the typical case of the Continental "constitutional monarch" of the nineteenth century, a written constitution would formalize a compromise between the crown and the people, or between the crown and the estates, under which the previously unlimited power of the crown was now formally restrained. They arose from *compact* where, as in the United States, Canada, and Australia, nations were established under commonly agreed-upon rules—the "higher law" under which the people now vowed to live.

Even to this day, most constitutions reflect one or the other of these origins. In the case of pact, the chief function of a constitution is likely to be the delimitation of the spheres controlled by social classes, economic groups, castes, or other groups. In the case of compact, the constitution is the symbol of unity, since it integrated the nation into one political unit. The delimitation of the spheres of power in this latter type of situation is between institutions that perform distinctive tasks —e.g., legislative and judicial—rather than between historically entrenched groups. The delimitation may also be between territorial units and the nation—i.e., federalism—but this division rests likewise on the original and basic agreement of the whole people or their original constituent units on how they are to be governed.

Sometimes, constitutions having their origin in pact turn into compact, as in the case of Great Britain, where the original Constitution (in this case, a mixture of written and unwritten but accepted rules) first determined the partition of power between the King and nobles, and then between Crown and Parliament, but finally came to reflect the consensus under which the British people rule themselves. In this case, the sense for constitutionalism, i.e., abiding by rules that determine the allocations and use of political power, is joined to the sense of national unity. On the other hand, where, as in France or Germany, the basis for the original pact has disappeared and later constitutions have failed to attain the symbolic character of the Constitution in the United States, constitutionalism remains fragile. This is even more the case with a number of the developing countries that have not yet achieved a national sentiment of unity, and which are more concerned with accelerating economic and social development than with establishing or enforcing constitutional limits on the use of political power.

The wide variations in the origins, functions, and strengths of constitutionalism can be illustrated by considering two of its most common and crucial characteristics: the system of fundamental rights and liberties, which embodies some of the most important substantive limitations on power; and constitutional jurisdiction, i.e., action through the courts to secure the observance of the rules of a constitution.

Basic Rights and Liberties Today

The American Bill of Rights is an outstanding early statement of the fundamental rights and liberties of the individual. So are the still earlier English Bill of Rights (1689) and the French Declaration of the Rights of Man and of the Citizen (1789). But these and similar lists of rights have, at times, been criticized in this century as being too individualistic, too little concerned with the needs of groups, and too negative, in the sense of emphasizing "freedom from" rather than "freedom to." This last charge reflects the feeling that free speech and protection against arbitrary search and seizure are small comfort to men who are denied the chance to earn a living and to improve their existence. Whether the order of values implicit in such a charge is as self-evident today, when we have again become more sensitive to the supreme value of individual liberty, as it seemed in the interwar period so beset by economic depression, is perhaps open to question. But, in any case, since World War I there have been more sweeping statements of fundamental rights not only to restrict arbitrary governmental action but, positively, to affirm the right to work and to decent payment for work, to a basic standard of living, to social security and education, and to other rights characteristic of the welfare state. Such provisions have been inserted not only in spurious documents like the Stalin Constitution but also in democratic constitutions, e.g., those of Weimar Germany, India, and the Fourth French Republic, confirmed by that of the Fifth. Indeed, the worldwide demand for such rights is shown by the headway made by the United Nations to codify them, as well as the "classical" types of rights, into binding universal conventions. Even the older

U.N. Declaration on Human Rights of 1948, and especially its anticolonialist stipulations, is increasingly being cited as valid international law. More and more, the "material" spheres of economic, social, and ecological needs assume the character of global, universal demands.

These latter rights express the aspirations of underprivileged groups or classes or of developing countries and, as such, can become the clarion calls of political movements. Their political impact, therefore, may be greater than that of the "old-fashioned" freedoms. Asian, African, and Latin American masses are often said to be more interested in freedom from want than in traditional concepts like freedom of expression; yet, even if this is partially true, there is considerable awareness of the interdependence between the two.

Classic individual rights and freedoms gain new luster when people have had the bitter experience of living under totalitarian or dictatorial rule. Totalitarian lawlessness teaches people anew the importance of basic personal freedoms, particularly that of legal security in its most elementary sense of protection from arbitrary arrest and detention. Thus, the Bonn Constitution does not list all the economic and social rights enumerated in the Weimar Constitution, but has given the traditional bill of rights new emphasis. So, too, has the post–Fascist Constitution of Italy.

There are also some new aspects to the classic freedoms themselves. It is not surprising that, in an age of mass society, emphasis should shift somewhat from traditional political rights to those affecting personal development and cultural expression. Since individuals in a mass society must conform to the standards of mass organization and inevitably have less influence over policy decisions, the meaning of freedom is now also related to the right to nonconformity in those areas of life that have not yet been invaded by the state or by other huge, impersonal organizations. Thus, in developed constitutional systems there is increasing concern with the rights of creative expression in literature and the arts; the right to be protected against the noise of one's environment;

the right of audiences to refuse to become "captive" victims of advertising; and the right of the citizen, in a shrinking and integrated world, to move freely not only within his own country but abroad, i.e., freely to leave and re-enter his country.

But the chief field of basic rights remains that of "the mother of them all," the English Bill of Rights. It is bills of rights that not only established the basic boundary lines of freedom, but also continue to constitute a bridge between liberalism and democracy; for, without guarantees of some fundamental civil and political rights—the right to vote, freedom of speech, association, assembly, and the press—genuine democracy, in the sense of rule by the people, would be impossible. What is the present status of these rights in the major countries?

In the Soviet Union, up to and throughout the Stalin era, individual rights were not protected against the state and its pervasive terror machine, not, that is, in the sense in which one understands the words "rights" and "protection." The Bill of Rights of the Stalin Constitution, for example, was merely a fig leaf, used by a dictatorship that, like other modern nondemocratic regimes, adopted pseudodemocratic trappings. But of what avail were formulations of classical freedoms if they could be exercised only "in conformity with the interests of the working people"—a "conformity" defined exclusively by the ruling political group?

For the post-Stalinist period, however, the judgment should not be quite so negative. There is no longer widespread arbitrariness, complete with legally unchecked secret police, although there is still little evidence of genuine guarantees of political rights. For one thing, detention in labor camps and, even worse, in insane asylums continues to be the punishment meted out to critics, who, with great courage, make open appeals, even if so far fruitlessly, to the personal rights "guaranteed" in the Soviet Bill of Rights. On the other hand, the picture is more encouraging with regard to the social and economic "rights" enumerated in the Constitution. With advancing economic development and time, such practices as free education, free health services, and the like, have to all intents and purposes become irrevocable. Thus, even under dictatorships, lip-service and paper promises may turn into restraints on rulers who become reluctant to disregard the expectations of their people, at least in areas not threatening to their exercise of authority.

On the face of it, the protection of individual rights and liberties in the United States lies at the opposite pole. Even as compared with other liberal democratic systems, the American system of rights is more fully defined and seems more securely implemented and protected. Rights and liberties are written into both federal and state constitutions, which enjoy the aura of a "higher law." They are protected not only against executive but also against legislative infringement; and independent courts function so as to make observation and enforcement real.

But, even in the United States, reality does not always rise to these ideals and potentialities. First of all, there are areas— in the geographical as well as the personal sense—where the enforcement machinery of the state turns against the individual to be protected instead of protecting him, and the courts are unavailable or ineffective in the face of such abuse. One must, of course, reckon with a certain amount of abuse or neglect under any system, even a liberal-democratic one, but in the United States the incidence is higher than in other democracies, and local and state police authorities and even courts have often been woefully inadequate in the protection of individual and group rights and liberties, not only in reference to the most obvious case, its black citizens.

Moreover, under the impact, first, of the cold war and, subsequently, of the U.S. involvement in the seemingly unending Indochina war, serious erosion of liberties has taken place in various ways. In the 1950's, under McCarthyism, threats came from both the investigating powers of legislatures and from the executive. "Loyalty" investigations, with ensuing dismissals from jobs, boycotts, and ostracisms, affected not only public officials (most conspicuously, members of the foreign service) but also citizens at large (again conspicuously, in the entertainment industry). From the 1950's to this day, there have been instances of extralegal social pressures for conformity, occasionally leading to mob action, against alleged "disloyals" or even mere dissenters. Not showing the flag, for instance, or even sporting long hair and a beard, may become sufficient cause for such reaction on the part of a self-styled "silent majority." With the Vietnam war and the attendant domestic ills (race riots and a white "backlash," crime, drug addiction), there have been new threats to liberties. Corruption, especially within law-enforcement agencies, has become widespread. But we shall deal more fully with corruption of public officials in another chapter. Suffice it to say here that individuals, above all among the "underclass" in the black ghettos, are frequently left without police protection, and victims of crimes are intimidated so that they dare not accuse criminals, while criminals of the professional type enjoy protection from prosecution.

In still another area—the basic and elementary area of the protection of life as such—the line between "police states" and democracies tends to get blurred. Perhaps, with brutality constantly displayed on the television screen and the widespread and almost unrestricted distribution of firearms among the population, human life tends to become cheap. "Killed while trying to escape" was the standard explanation of Nazi authorities after doing away with an "undesirable" person. A democratic system is distinguished from such "informal" and arbitrary procedure by surrounding the imposition of capital punishment, if it exists, by all the safeguards of due process—permitting the accused to defend himself, having a judge or jury sift the evidence, with careful reference made to the applicable law, and so forth. But if, as has happened, police are permitted to shoot indiscriminately into a crowd of demonstrators, or if an unarmed suspect is shot and killed while trying to escape, the limits that a liberal democracy places on authorities, as well as on private individuals, are being dangerously overstepped. It is possible that the wanton killing in Vietnam has also had an effect on the incidence of violence on the domestic scene.

Technological progress, especially in the area of electronic devices, adds to the insecurity of the citizen. Here, the United States is perhaps merely the pace-setter for all developed societies. The danger is chiefly in the invasion of privacy.* There is the ubiquitous use of the polygraph (lie detector), not only by law-enforcement agents in the prosecution of crimes but also by business in job applications, and on other occasions. There are, above all, easy ways of accumulating, storing, and retrieving data on everything concerning an individual's life history, as well as electronic means of information-gathering and surveillance from afar. All of these imply the potentiality and, increasingly, the actuality of massive invasion of privacy. Anyone (including, we discover, members of the political elite, such as Congressmen) is liable to come under the surveillance of one or another of the innumerable authorities —the FBI, Army, Navy, and Air Force intelligence; the Department of Housing and Transportation; the "Secret Service" protecting the President; the Civil Service Commission; the Internal Revenue Service; as well as a variety of police and other agencies on the state and local level—that vie with each other in setting up computerized data banks, occasionally, in their mutual competition, spying even upon each other! This hypertrophic zeal means that an individual, whether he knows it or (more probably) not, may be stamped for the rest of his life by apparently innocuous "data." A youthful participant in, say, a student protest rally may remain a suspect red "radical"; a conviction for use of marijuana may stamp one a "narcotic"; and so forth. "Big Brother," predicted for 1984 by George Orwell in 1948, can become a reality, and this *not only* in totalitarian dictatorships.

Fortunately, however, this development is not inevitable.

* For an exhaustive survey of the vast variety of potential threats in this area, see Alan F. Westin, *Privacy and Freedom* (New York: Atheneum, 1967).

Although fear and pressure for conformism have threatened basic rights in some quarters in the United States, there is increased awareness of the danger they present to the functioning of American democracy—or any democracy. Moreover, Great Britain continues to offer encouraging evidence that respect for freedom is itself the best guarantee of basic rights. While Parliament, by legislation, or the Cabinet, by delegated power, clearly has the power to tamper with personal rights, there is little danger that either would do so more than temporarily, and then only during genuine emergencies. The preservation of traditional liberties in that country, through the application of the rule of law, provides a prime illustration of the force of tradition and the prevailing spirit of a nation, as contrasted with the impact of formal rules and institutions. Nonetheless, since Britain, too, is experiencing pressures to conformity, many Englishmen now believe that to specify basic rights in a document like the American Bill of Rights would be an important additional safeguard.

Britain's frailties have always been more noticeable abroad than at home. Basic rights have been looked on as the rights of Englishmen rather than the rights of man. Although the native populations of Britain's colonies received genuine blessings, like the extension of the common law, impartial standards of administration, and sound rules of hygiene and health, they did not often enjoy, until late in their development, either the political rights or the common tolerance of unpopular opinions that have been among Britain's most distinguished attributes at home. At one point, moreover, such distasteful measures as detention and internment without trial, coupled with at least psychological torture of suspects, were introduced inside the boundaries of the United Kingdom itself in the effort to quell violence in Northern Ireland.

In contrast to the British, the French have since the Age of the Enlightenment and the Revolution of 1789 raised the battle cry of the "rights of man" rather than merely the rights of Frenchmen. But the trouble is that it has been the battle cry of only one group of Frenchmen in the perennial French conflict of opposing ideologies. Many a glorious legal and political battle has been fought over these rights and their protection, and some of them have been decisive for the liberal democratic development of the country—as witness the Dreyfus affair, where a long and ultimately successful fight was waged at the turn of the century to clear the name of an unjustly convicted Jewish army officer. But it can hardly be said that these rights are anchored as safely in France as they are in Britain. The French system is at its best in the protection of individual liberties that it offers through its system of administrative jurisdiction, but these procedures protect personal rights, such as those of property, against an entrenched and solid bureaucracy, rather than political freedoms. Recent violent demonstrations, notably the abortive student-led "revolution" of 1968, and unpopular Maoist-minded groups have received rough handling.

In Germany, as in France, liberalism has not been unsuccessful in the realm of personal security and property rights; these were clearly protected by that peculiar Central European marriage between freedom and authoritarianism known as the *Rechtsstaat*. But political rights and liberties prior to the Weimar Republic meant little more than the ventilation of grievances in the press or in Parliament, to which the ruling powers paid scant attention. If the Weimar regime distinguished—and perhaps extinguished—itself through an overbroad grant of political freedoms, the Bonn Constitution also experiments in two novel and interesting ways: first, by declaring that certain basic rights are unamendable (Article 79), a provision that raises the difficult problem of whether there can and should be limits to the power of constitutional amendment; and second, by setting out limits upon the exercise of political rights when used "in order to attack the liberal-democratic order" (Articles 18, 21). It was under these latter provisions that neo-Nazis and the Communist Party were suppressed in West Germany. In a country such as Germany, where authoritarianism has a long history, there is always danger of a relapse into illiberalism, but the experience of

Nazi oppression seems to have impressed upon the German people the perils inherent in even the beginnings of arbitrariness. Some cautious hope may therefore be drawn from the public outrage over the arrest of the publishers and editors of a news magazine, *Der Spiegel,* in 1962, on the charge of having revealed military "secrets" that were, in fact, widely known and even publicly discussed at the time. Since then, German authorities have been more careful in dealing with the press.

The suppression of the Communist Party in certain countries brings sharply into focus a problem troubling many democratic states: how to deal with the organized activity of groups and movements deemed hostile to the state. The Communists, of course, have been foremost among these groups, but there are also rightist and, more recently, non-Communist leftist radicals. The range of reactions to these groups goes all the way from toleration to outlawry. The dilemma is whether to grant freedom to those who might use it to destroy the freedom of others or to restrict freedom and thereby risk possibly far-reaching curtailment of liberties in general. Nothing has proved more easy and more tempting than to use provisions supposedly directed against a specific group or movement, such as Communism, for attacking any unwanted, nonconformist, or merely opposition group, party, or opinion.

In Italy and France, of course, the Communist Party is not only legal but able to attract large numbers of votes; it also retains a strong, even dominant, influence in the trade unions. Particularly in France, however, some extreme leftist and a few rightist groups have received harsh treatment. In Great Britain, no one would suggest action against the small Communist Party, which continues, election after election, to put up candidates, though with conspicuous lack of success. There has been much more concern about the pervasive Communist influence within some British trade unions, but the unions themselves have ultimately succeeded in limiting the scope of Communist influence. Interesting in this regard is the experience of Australia, where a Liberal administration was returned to office in 1951 with a platform of outlawing the Communist

Party because of its dominance within powerful trade unions. The legislation passed for this purpose was declared unconstitutional by the courts, and the effort was subsequently abandoned. As in Great Britain, however, the Australian unions thereafter made a massive and largely successful effort to rid themselves of Communist control.

More direct attacks on local Communist parties have been carried out in Canada, the United States, and South Africa. Canada outlawed its Communist Party in the early 1930's but has not acted against the small Labour Progressive Party that has taken its place. In Quebec, Canada's populous and largely French-speaking province, the notorious Padlock Law of 1937 was used to prevent the holding of meetings suspected of being Communist-oriented, until the law was declared *ultra vires* by the Canadian Supreme Court in 1957. The most serious crisis occurred in October, 1970, when the French-Canadian separatist *Front de Libération du Québec* kidnapped a provincial cabinet minister (later murdered) and the British Trade Commissioner ostensibly to secure the release of colleagues held by the police. Prime Minister Pierre Trudeau reacted by declaring a state of "apprehended insurrection," and invoked the War Measures Act, under which the FLQ was outlawed and hundreds of suspects were held without trial. Although the Trade Commissioner was released unharmed in December, in a deal permitting his kidnappers to fly to Cuba, most of the emergency regulations remained in force until the end of April, 1971.

The United States used the Smith Act of 1940 to prosecute successfully more than one hundred prominent Communist Party officials on the charge of advocating the overthrow of the government by force. Moreover, the Communist Control Act of 1954 prevents the Communist Party from operating, at least in the federal sphere, as a legal entity, i.e., from putting candidates on a ballot or suing in court, although it has not been formally outlawed and now is tacitly permitted to operate quite freely.

Most far-reaching of such measures is South Africa's Suppression of Communism Act (1950), which defines Communism not only as the doctrine of Marxian socialism as expounded by Lenin or Trotsky, or any other doctrine that seeks to establish a one-party state based on the dictatorship of the proletariat, but also as any scheme that "aims at bringing about any political, industrial, social or economic change within the Union by the promotion of disturbances or disorder, by unlawful acts or omissions." This provision was used to convict the leaders of the nonwhite passive-disobedience campaign in 1952, the judge terming their offense "statutory Communism." Thus, it is all too apparent how broadly such provisions can be interpreted. Two white members of Parliament, elected by the small African electorate in Cape Province as their representatives (since 1960, Africans no longer have even this type of representation in the national Parliament), lost their seats, and another former Communist was prevented from running for office. Numerous trade-union leaders have been removed from their office, and almost all the articulate black leaders have been placed under ban (if not in prison or exile). A Nobel Prize winner, ex-Chief Albert J. Luthuli, was restricted to a small area during his last years; and like many others alive or dead, may not be quoted in any South African publication. Few situations point up more clearly the dangers implicit in such broadly worded statutes. Nor is there much evidence here, or elsewhere, that such a law does much more than drive opposition underground, as evidenced by the continuous series of trials held in South Africa.

Such a survey as this underlines the fact with which we started: The response to Communist infiltration or to terrorist activities, as in Brazil, or to any kind of opposition to the discriminatory system of a country as fearful as South Africa may threaten to erode all fundamental civil and political rights. Even in the United States, in spite of the formal guarantees of the Bill of Rights, individuals have been convicted and imprisoned on the basis of what they are said to have advocated, rather than because of specific acts committed by them. To safeguard individual rights in the light of such pressures requires not only restraint on the part of government but also constant alertness by the governed.

CONSTITUTIONAL JURISDICTION

It is common in democratic countries to look upon the courts not only as protectors of individual rights but also as the agency which ensures that state action will not transgress constitutional limits. "Constitutional jurisdiction," as we have said, means court action to secure the observance of the rules of a constitution. As such, it may attain a political importance far beyond that of any other judicial action.

It is hardly surprising that constitutional jurisdiction has been particularly important in countries with a federal structure, such as the United States, Canada, Australia, Switzerland, West Germany, Austria and India. Delimiting the powers of member units in relation to those of the federal (national) unit is vital for the functioning of such a system. It took a civil war in the United States to establish the principle that a judicial organ of the Federal Government rather than an individual state (or states) is the final arbiter. As resistance to the Supreme Court decision in the school segregation cases and the long series of supplementary judgments point up, this principle has to be re-established again and again. Ultimately, history has shown that such delimitations of power depend not only on judicial interpretation but also on acquiescence by the most powerful forces in a community in the decisions that have been made.

The different ways in which constitutional jurisdiction functions can be illustrated by the experience of three countries where such jurisdiction has assumed major importance: Switzerland, West Germany, and the United States. There are three chief areas in which courts* may undertake to guarantee the functioning of a constitutional system, and each of

---

* Whether constitutional jurisdiction is exercised by the general courts of a country (as in the United States and in Switzerland) or by a special and separate "constitutional tribunal" (as in Germany, Austria, and Italy) is immaterial in this connection.

the countries mentioned illustrates one of them. In the first place, the courts may act to uphold the individual or group rights and liberties that a constitution protects. A second important sphere is the relation between ordinary legislation and the law of the constitution. The third is keeping in balance both the powers of, and the relations between, organs of government, e.g., the spheres of the legislature and executive, the rights of majorities and minorities in a parliament, or the jurisdiction of the federal government and the member states. Accordingly, constitutional jurisdiction may deal with any or all of the following: (a) conflicts between the state and individuals or groups wherein the latter contend there has been a violation of basic rights or liberties; (b) judicial review of the constitutionality of laws; (c) "organ conflicts," i.e., conflicts between the organs of the state or government.

The Swiss system implements chiefly point *a* above. Swiss courts do not deal with organ conflicts, and there is no judicial review of federal (in contrast to cantonal) statutes. The chief function of Swiss constitutional jurisdiction, therefore, is the broad protection of individual and group rights in cases concerned with the "constitutional complaint" of citizens. This function reflects a profound concern with the maintenance of a sphere of individual freedom from state interference. In contrast, the distinctive function of the American judicial system (though not, to be sure, its only function, since that system is also concerned with the protection of rights and liberties) is judicial review (point *b* above), i.e., the maintenance of the superiority of the Constitution over all state action, including ordinary lawmaking. This position reflects an ingrained American feeling that the Constitution is the higher law, to be preserved against the changing and possibly transitory will of the people.

The new German system, finally, is perhaps most interesting in providing for a legal settlement of organ conflicts (point *c*). The idea of offering political groups and government authorities a chance to fight out constitutional conflicts legally reflects a typically German legalistic approach to political problems that is rooted in the nineteenth-century origin of Continental constitutions in the crown-versus-people compromise. Provision for the resolution of certain types of organ conflicts existed even under the German Empire (when the Bundesrat, the upper chamber, had jurisdiction), and later under Weimar (when a constitutional tribunal was established). But only now has full "juridification" of the system been attained, with the Bonn Constitution allotting to the Federal Constitutional Court the power to decide even those constitutional conflicts that arise among the highest federal organs and agencies, such as, for instance, between the government and a parliamentary opposition group over the enactment of a law. Here, as well as in the protection of rights and liberties and through judicial review, the new German Constitutional Court has vigorously asserted itself. For a country with strong authoritarian traditions, this is an important new venture.

What about constitutional jurisdiction in other countries and systems? Totalitarian regimes, of course, cannot permit procedures for the effective limitation of power; they avoid even the outward appearance of such jurisdictions, asserting that to give courts powers of judicial review, for instance, would hamstring the sovereign legislature. While, in totalitarian systems, this attitude simply reflects the determination to keep all power in the hands of the ruling group—the party —it is also true that the French make the same argument on the basis of democratic theory. The French believe that sovereignty rests inalienably in the people and its elected assembly and thus reject the idea of a higher law of the Constitution. Nonetheless, the Fifth Republic has established a Constitutional Council that gives advisory, though not binding, rulings on the meaning and relevance of constitutional provisions. The French unitary system leaves no room for federal-state conflicts.

But it would be strange, indeed, to find no institutional protection of individual rights in the very country of the *droits de l'homme et du citoyen,* and such protection exists through the system of administrative jurisdiction, headed by the Conseil d'État (Council of State), which takes infinite care to protect and indemnify individuals injured by unjust or unfair acts committed by government officials or in the name of the state. Before World War II, it was difficult for private citizens to secure comparable compensation in the United States and Great Britain, but procedures for so doing were established in the United States in 1946 through the Federal Tort Claims Act and in Great Britain the following year by the Crown Proceedings Act.

The British system of parliamentary supremacy, like the French system, operates without judicial review or judicial settlement of organ conflicts. It is typically British in avoiding the use of special institutions to perform particular judicial functions relying, instead, on such general rules and traditions as the rule of law, the recognition of implied restraints upon state power, and the application of the rule of reason to any and all of the system's manifestations. Thus again, Great Britain illustrates the importance, beyond constitutional procedures and institutional devices, of national tradition for the maintenance of a constitutionalism that is nowhere more safely anchored than in that country.

This may be the place to mention an institution—the office of the *ombudsman*—that does not, strictly speaking, belong in a discussion of constitutional jurisdiction (it is hard to fit it into any one system), but which is illustrative of the inventiveness and ingenuity of democracies in seeking effectively to protect individual and group rights and liberties against administrative arbitrariness or neglect. First developed in Sweden, this institution spread from there to other Scandinavian countries and, more recently, to New Zealand, Canada, Great Britain (where the *ombudsman* is called Parliamentary Commissioner for Administration), and West Germany (where the jurisdiction is limited, so far, to the protection of enlisted men against abuse in the armed forces). This institution has been proposed as a safeguard against "administrative lawlessness" even in the United States, a mark of the "ombudsmania" sweeping the Western world.

The *ombudsman* is elected by Parliament but is expected to be independent of parties or other political influence. He deals by various means with complaints against arbitrary government actions made by the public (in Britain, they must be transmitted through an MP). Publicity is commonly the most effective of these means, but in Sweden the *ombudsman* may also "institute proceedings before the competent courts against those who, in the execution of their official duties . . . committed an unlawful act or neglected to perform their official duties properly." In the light of the vast and continuous increase of administrative activities and powers, the office of *ombudsman,* if not unduly circumscribed, may be a significant means of protecting the rights of private persons.

INDEPENDENCE OF THE JUDICIARY

Constitutional jurisdiction is not the only device for safeguarding constitutionalism. There is also an essential relationship between constitutionalism and the judicial function in general. The decisive factor here is judicial independence, whose general importance for the maintenance of a democratic system we have already noted. In contrast to police states, where the courts are looked on as instruments of the regime in carrying out its political and general purposes, courts in constitutional systems are separate, independent agencies, bound by their own rules of procedure and determining cases according to publicly known law.

It is through judicial independence (usually guaranteed by the appointment of judges for life, or until a certain age, and by their irremovability except for moral causes) that Montesquieu's device for the limitation of power has found its last redoubt in countries like Great Britain and France, where little else remains of the separation of powers. Under modern conditions of the welfare state and of government regulation, the separation between the lawmaking and the executive branches may no longer be as feasible or even as desirable as it used to be; but the separation of an independent judiciary from both seems to be the irreducible minimum required for an effective system of limitation of power. The more modern government interferes, administers, regulates, and allocates, the more urgent is the need to preserve a check on the way these activities affect individuals and groups. The helplessness of the individual in the absence of such control is all too obvious in systems where the judiciary is either dependent or powerless, whether they be premodern systems with their *lettres de cachet* or modern totalitarian systems with their knock on the door in the dead of night.

Modern tyranny has given a new perspective to the old charges that bourgeois countries are liable to dispense class justice. British socialists, for instance, used to argue that the British judicial system and the common law itself gave particular advantages to the claims of property. But today such charges are rarely heard. For one thing, British courts placed no impediments in the way of Labor's nationalization and social welfare programs after 1945. But far more important has been the terrifying example of those trials in Nazi Germany, the Soviet Union, and Soviet satellites in which the law was deliberately twisted to entrap the defendant and in which judges acted as prosecutors and executioners rather than as impartial umpires. In the face of such experience, the independence of the judiciary, known processes of law, and the continuity of principles underlying legal decisions have taken on new importance.

Democracies, nevertheless, still have their problems. Equal justice under law must, after all, be dispensed by men. The government of laws must forever be government by people applying and interpreting the laws. And human beings, however strong their feeling of independence and security, inevitably have preferred ideals and predilections, and even preconceived ideas and prejudices. An aging judiciary may be behind the times; a judiciary drawn from certain strata or classes may well reflect some caste or class bias. To some extent, and in the long run, even the U.S. Supreme Court "follows the election returns," and while this may be reasonable if it means no more than paying attention in a general way to what the majority of the people want, it must not be forgotten that courts exist also to protect minority rights and individual liberties. Legislation will inevitably reflect class interest where there is class rule, economic interests where such interests prevail in a given society, religious interests where particular denominations or churches predominate. The remedy here, if one is desired, is not a change in the judicial system but a change in the laws through democratic processes. As for class, personal, or any other bias of the judicial personnel, the remedy is not to render the judiciary more dependent, but constantly to bring about reforms that make such shortcomings less likely, for example, by selecting the German and even the British judiciary from a less narrow class base and by protecting the American judiciary, especially on the state level, from undue party influence, such as is apt to result from the election of judges for limited terms.

Recruitment of judicial personnel poses particularly important political problems. Especially where, as in France and Germany, judges (and frequently also prosecutors) are members of a bureaucracy appointed for life-time service or lengthy terms of office (something which, as we have seen, is necessary to ensure judicial independence), the judicial approach to matters that come up throughout entire half-centuries is liable to be predetermined by the original appointments. And where, as in the highest courts of the United States and certain other countries, these matters constitute the general trends in an economy, or an educational system, or a system of crime prevention, the political power and responsibility involved in those who determine recruitment is obvious. High courts of last appeal or ultimate jurisdiction in such far-reaching decisions thus come to be characterized as "liberal," "progressive," "conservative," or "reactionary," depending on the patterns of opinions and decisions of their majorities. An entirely new branch of political science, "jurimetrics," tries through quantitative methods to predict behavior on the basis of antecedent voting patterns. But in such an all-important tribunal as the U.S. Supreme Court, an unexpected attitude change on the part of a single judge may throw such predictions into confusion.

What, then, we may ask, is the best method of selecting judicial personnel, if one single appointment (or selection) may be so politically influential for decades to come? Americans hardly need to be reminded of the risks inherent in a system that confers on the President appointive powers that are limited only by the Senate's right to concur. The striking change in the Supreme Court's complexion (from the "liberal" Warren Court to the present conservative, if not reactionary, one) came through President Nixon's unique opportunity to appoint no fewer than four new judges during a single term of office.

There used to be a tradition of appointing to the Supreme Court persons who, to be sure, fitted the President's political predilections, but also possessed the legal and personal qualifications for such high office. Lately (beginning, really, with President Truman's appointments), this latter requirement has all too frequently been neglected. Thus, one may ask whether selection of judges for the highest court by parliamentary bodies, or by boards composed of members of such bodies and of ministers (e.g., in federal systems, the state ministers in the respective field), or by selected members of the judiciary, might not be preferable to the presidential appointive system. While cooptation by colleagues involves the danger of caste considerations, the middle alternative has proved quite successful in West Germany, where appointment had traditionally favored conservatism, if not authoritarianism, in the judiciary. Members of the highest federal courts, including the Constitutional Court, are now elected by special parliamentary committees (including some ministers) that, while reflecting parties and their respective strength, have acted on the basis of reasonable compromise and consideration of personal qualifications. (In the election of Constitutional Court judges, the requirement of a qualified majority has prevented any single party from giving too much party coloration to the Court.)

Entrusting courts with the authority to limit the use of power by other governmental agencies also creates particular types of problems. Difficulties arise, for instance, where courts are entrusted with overpolitical tasks. When, as in the United States, courts are called upon to decide broad issues involving free enterprise versus governmental regulation or racial segregation versus integration through the interpretation of constitutional norms containing general terms like "due process of law" or "equal protection of the law," decisions are bound to go beyond the realm of ordinary interpretation and to involve elements of policy-making. Recognizing this fact, many countries consider certain political questions (such as particular foreign-policy issues in American practice, or *actes de gouvernement* in France) as nonjusticiable, i.e., as falling outside the jurisdiction of the courts. Of course, decisions in such cases have to be made somewhere. Whether ultimate control is given to a judicial body or to the more political part of the government that is in charge of the particular field seems to be a matter of tradition and convenience. There are problems and advantages, whichever way the matter is handled. Allowing an independent judiciary to settle such issues may create the danger of rendering the judiciary open to charges of being political; but it may offer protection against the concentration or abuse of power elsewhere. Leaving the decision to the executive or to parliament provides more concentration of authority; but it may be argued that this is the more democratic method, especially where the executive or assembly has a direct mandate from the electorate.

Another problem arises when constitutions undertake to render any and all constitutional conflicts justiciable, i.e., to be settled by the courts. The more encompassing the range of what is considered justiciable, the greater the danger that, in a conflict involving basic issues of policy or fundamentally opposed forces in state and society, normative judgments will prove unenforceable. It is during those crises of a regime or country that test the very bases of its institutions that constitutionalism is put to its vital test. Only a civil war, and not the Supreme Court, was able to resolve the issues of slavery and of state sovereignty in the United States. The Constitutional Court of Weimar Germany was equally unable to enforce its verdict (compromise decision though it was) when antidemocratic forces undertook to destroy the last stronghold of Weimar democracy. In such cases, everything depends on whether judicial bodies are backed up by sufficiently strong public determination to uphold the rule of law in this broader sense.

The crucial importance of a sense of restraint on the part of governing groups is well illustrated by the highly complex situation that developed in South Africa over the Nationalist Government's attempts to place male colored (mixed blood), in Cape Province—the last nonwhites who were still permitted to vote for the same candidates as were whites—on a separate voting roll. The Nationalists at first tried to achieve this purpose through ordinary legislation, though the South African Constitution in one of its two entrenched provisions—i.e., protected by special procedures—provided that the voting rights of nonwhites in the Cape Province should not be changed except by a two-thirds majority of both chambers meeting in joint session. When the South African Court of Appeals declared the legislation invalid, the Nationalists refused to accept the verdict as a final settlement of the issue and, again by a simple majority, passed an act providing for a High Court of Parliament, consisting of the entire membership of Parliament, which was to take over the power to review legislation from the Court of Appeal. In effect, this meant that Parliament assumed the right to validate its own legislation. The appellate court declared this act to be invalid also, since it was clearly designed to serve the purpose of the earlier legislation.

The Nationalists proceeded to make the "sovereignty of Parliament" and the "interference" of the courts issues in the

1953 general election, in which they secured a larger parliamentary majority. Still unable, however, to win the necessary two-thirds majority in the House of Assembly and Senate, they then moved to more stringent measures. Five new judges were added to the Court of Appeal, and soon afterward a new measure raised the quorum to eleven whenever the Court considers the validity of an act of Parliament. More decisive, in 1955 a new Senate Act increased the size of the second chamber and made provincial representation dependent not on proportionate legislative strength, as before, but on majority vote. Under these provisions, the Nationalists controlled 77 votes in the new Senate, as compared with 30 in the old chamber. These additions finally enabled them, in mid-1956, to pass their constitutional amendment, despite widespread demonstrations against it.

It became obvious in this situation that the South African National Party had no basic sense of constitutionality, such as sparked the vigorous American opposition to the relatively mild "court-packing" proposal of President Roosevelt in 1937, which would have added another judge to the Supreme Court whenever one of those already serving reached the age of seventy-five. Even though he had achieved a remarkable electoral success the year before, Roosevelt felt obliged to bow to the storm of criticism evoked by this scheme and to withdraw it. But, in the absence of such a responsive attitude, demonstrations have little effect. Under these circumstances, the South African opposition to Nationalist expedients could have been effective only if it had been ready to resort to forcible measures, which might conceivably have led to a clash of arms. Natural reluctance to go that far, plus the fact that the opposition lacked a sense of personal commitment to the group that was being deprived of its rights, and even perhaps to the Constitution, which was a compromise between racial groups rather than a symbol of unity, led to an ultimate acquiescence in the situation by white South Africans (who hold the monopoly of political power). By so doing, however, the opposition left the way open for subsequent measures that imperil the rule of law. To lose the safeguard of established rules of procedure as limitations on the power of the parliamentary majority is to make possible the uncertainties of arbitrary rule.

DECONCENTRATION OF POWER

So far, we have been considering the limits that are placed on government through the protection of individual rights, the restraints of the constitution, and the functional division of powers among the executive, legislature, and judiciary. It is now time to look, in some detail, at the territorial division of power, or at least of responsibility, that is provided by local government and by federalism. Where local or regional subdivisions have their own jurisdictions, citizens have additional oportunities to participate in the process of government, and the exercise of authority is restrained by such diversification.

Historically, the limitations upon the authority of a central government that result from deconcentration developed long before constitutional and legal limitations. The "absolute" monarchies of prerevolutionary Europe, for instance, were much less absolute in practice than they claimed to be in theory. This was simply because the central government was not then technically equipped to deal with local matters in remote parts of the country. In developing countries, central authority still tends to be severely limited by difficulties of communication and also by clientele relationships of a local or regional nature. Increasingly, however, there, and generally in all developed countries, national government, and especially national administration, is so organized that it can and usually does operate side by side with the organs of local and of intermediate units of government, even in the most remote places. In fact, the distinctive feature of a federation, in contrast to a *con*federation, is that national law is operative throughout the country. This expansion of national functions and responsibilities, however, endangers the operation of those local and possibly regional levels of government that used to enjoy virtual autonomy, thereby removing whole areas from the influence of the central government.

Local Self-Government

Traditionally, one of the counterweights against too much centralized government was found in local self-government. It is often said, and with some justice, that the "grass roots" of democracy, and its essential training ground, are to be found at the local level, where people deal with problems of immediate and direct importance to themselves—problems, moreover, that are intelligible to them in terms of their personal experience. Significantly, local government in Germany, in the dual sense of local autonomy and of democratic participation by citizens, developed and was able to gain genuine importance at a time when German state institutions were still authoritarian. Again, after the German collapse at the end of World War II, self-government first reasserted itself at the local level. Not only have local self-governing institutions shown stubborn vitality in times of stress; they can also provide a healthy counterbalance to overcentralization, restraining the "apoplexy at the center and the anemia at the extremities" that are always threats in the highly organized, bureaucratic state of today.

It must be admitted, however, that, even in countries with long traditions of local self-government, there is a marked trend toward centralized supervision, financing, and even control that tends to turn local government into a device for mere decentralization rather than a counterbalance to the central administration. In Britain, for instance, many activities, such as education and public health, that used to be locally inspired are now organized on a national scale; genuine self-government on the local level thus threatens to become a casualty of the welfare state.

Yet, there still is a marked difference between the British and American systems of local government, on the one hand, and that of the French, on the other. In France, the authority of the prefect remains supreme within the department, the largest of the local divisions; but the prefect is the political agent of the central administration. In Britain and the United States, however, local officials are employed and paid by the local units, even though in many cases they must meet national or state-imposed standards.

The most serious evidence of decline in the vitality of local government in many countries is the lack of interest in local issues. In France, Britain, and Germany, for instance, local elections are increasingly looked on as trials of strength for the national parties, which interject national issues into local contests. Although this aspect somewhat increases public interest, it also entails the danger that political contests, like administrative programs, are merely being decentralized and have no firm roots in local needs. In this perspective, the localism of American politics may have more merit than is commonly recognized.

The issue of local autonomy arises even in totalitarian or authoritarian one-party states, where one might assume that central control on the part of the all-powerful and all-controlling party leadership would prevent any meaningful autonomies and self-government on lower levels of government and administration. We shall see below that this is nearly always true in regard to federalism; but, at the lowest level of urban and rural local affairs, there has been a trend, especially in the increasingly numerous "technical" areas of government, toward granting more leeway to local units and their officials (the latter, of course, carefully selected and checked by upper party levels). This kind of deconcentration is now noticeable in the Soviet Union, and even more so in China, where Maoist leadership uses decentralization and initiatives on the part of the people, both in agricultural communes and in industrial enterprises, as safeguards against the re-emergence of overstrong bureaucratic controls. Although such initiatives are supposed to be limited to technical matters, and are not supposed to interfere with politics or to question official ideology, they somewhat alleviate complete centralized conformity and control.

There is one problem the world over that may yet pose the gravest threat to meaningful local government in the traditional sense: the trend not only toward urbanization but toward the formation of huge metropolitan areas, the "megalopolises" of the future, sheltering tens of millions of people and covering vast, continuous territory that cuts through old local government areas or even the boundaries of "states" (in the United States or Germany) or similar political units. This development creates a twofold problem: how to make even local issues meaningful to individuals who are mere atoms in such huge communities; and how to coordinate the affairs of a megalopolis that, in terms of government and administration, is cut up among a large number of units. Coping effectively with the most urgent problems facing the urbanized mankind of the future—such as traffic and transportation, decent housing and education, public health and the pollution of the environment—requires new approaches to such newstyle problems of local government. Extending "participatory democracy" to provide subgroups with a share in running their own affairs, as has been tried in some large American school systems and welfare and poverty programs, may offer one constructive device.

Federalism

Federalism is a much more effective means of providing deconcentration of authority than is local government, since it establishes constitutional arrangements allocating power to the regional as well as to the national governments. In countries like the United States, Canada, Australia, West Germany, Switzerland, and India, where a federal division of power exists, the high court watches over the delimitation of the powers of both the central authority and the component units, as we have noted, and affords protection to their continued existence and spheres of action whenever a relevant case raises the issue. Yet, although this safeguard exists, the problems encountered in local government also appear to some extent where federalism provides an intermediary level of government between local and central affairs.

In the early days of nation-building, the role of federalism was often essential. The United States, Germany, Switzerland, Canada, and Australia, to mention some of the most important of federal states, could not have been immediately established as full-fledged unitary structures out of separate, independent units. Federalism in these countries is still comparatively strong, because some tradition of sectionalism has remained there to this very day. Similarly, in recent times, when large, little integrated units under colonial administration were established as independent countries, a federalist structure was often the only, or best, system to prevent their disintegration into separate ethnic or linguistic fragments. But what about federalism's continuing role once nations have been formed?

Even in the classical federal systems, whether in the largest or in one of the smallest democracies in the world—the United States and Switzerland—there is now a serious question whether units below the national government that are not mere administrative subdivisions of that government can effectively carry out more than strictly local functions at a time when so many activities are necessarily nationwide, if not still broader. National-planning and national-security activities tend to become ever more encompassing. Australia found that only the federal government could command the resources to finance its large-scale development and social-welfare programs. Switzerland even amended its Constitution in 1947 to enlarge the jurisdiction of the federation in economic matters. Moreover, in an age when ecological problems should compel even the largest nation-states to agree to international regulation, subnational units can hardly insist on separateness and "sovereignty." Where discharge of oil or waste into major rivers or at the coastline threatens to pollute the oceans of the world, discharge of such matter obviously concerns the nation and not just one or the other of its subdivisions; and only the nation commands the resources to finance large-scale tasks and programs of national concern. Thus, in the Federal Republic of Germany, the constitution has been changed to confer on the federal government increased powers to coordinate and legislate in ecological affairs. All of this has led to a marked trend toward centralization, at least in the older, established federal systems of the world.

In the face of this development, students of federalism have given much thought to classical questions regarding the distribution of functions and powers. Should the federal or the state sphere possess the unspecified residual powers? Should the administration of national laws be entrusted to national executive agencies, as in the United States, or should it be carried on, in the main, through state bureaucracies but under federal supervision, as in Germany and Switzerland? The same question arises, be it noted, in respect to the organization of the judiciary: Should there be, on the American pattern, two parallel columns of courts reaching from bottom to top in both the federal and the state spheres; or, as in Europe, Australia, Canada, and India, state judiciaries coordinated by one federal supreme court? Finally, there is the question of how best to organize that body which in federal structures customarily represents the member units on the federal level of government. Is it better to follow the American or Australian senatorial system, where delegates to the second chamber are representatives of the people, and elected by their votes; or, as might seem theoretically closer to the idea of federalism, to have the delegates represent the state units, i.e., their governments, on the German pattern?

All of these questions, in turn, are influenced by broader underlying forces and trends. While, for instance, the unit that enjoys unlisted (i.e., undefined) residual powers might seem to have the advantage, the real balance depends on how broadly the listed ("enumerated") powers are in practice defined and applied. In Canada, where residual powers are vested in the central government, judicial decisions by the Privy Council long acted to build up the separate jurisdictions of the provinces. In contrast, American constitutional history serves to show how terms like "interstate commerce" may be used to enhance central power at the expense of the member units, despite the vesting of residual powers in the latter. In the long run, what really counts is the viability of the member units, which today is determined by two major factors: financial and political.

Financial viability depends on the distribution of the richest financial resources, especially taxes. Even constitutional systems like the Australian and the German, which began by reserving most sources of income for the states, have ended by giving the federal government the major share of financial powers and resources. In countries like the United States, where, constitutionally, there is free competition between levels of government in tapping resources, the balance of income and expenditures has likewise shifted overwhelmingly to the national level.

Even more relevant than the financial factor to the survival and viability of federalism is the political factor. This resolves itself into the question of whether genuine and sufficiently strong social, economic, and cultural interests, possibly backed up by regionally concentrated ethnic, linguistic, or religious groups, seek protection from centralization through reinforcing states' rights. There is, in this respect, a striking contrast between old-established systems, such as the United States and the European federal states, and the new countries of the world. In the older federal countries, with the exception of Canada and Switzerland, strongly felt regionalism seems largely obsolete. As distances shrink in the air age, as metropolitan areas cut through state lines, and as people move like latter-day nomads from place to place, the traditionalist, regional sentiment that underlies genuine federalism tends to atrophy. It is even said that federalism has become largely irrelevant or inapplicable because of the jet plane, the superhighways, and the instant-communication

systems of our technological age. Yet, one could argue equally
well, that these and similar factors serve to render even
smaller countries out of date.

Nonetheless, certain interests in the older, federal countries
that by themselves have little to do with regionalism have
tried to underpin federal divisions. In Germany and Canada,
national political parties find their control of state governments a vantage point from which to influence national
policies. In Austria, the Social Democratic Party, whose doctrine is centralist rather than federalist, defends the Austrian
federal system because of its own entrenched position in the
member unit of Vienna; so does its chief opponent, the People's Party, which controls the rural and Alpine states. In the
United States, mining, oil, gas, and similar interests may become ardent supporters of federalism, by virtue of their dominant position in certain states and their consequent influence
on those states' senators in Washington. The American party
system and electoral provisions, of course, still operate through
local and state divisions. But strong, regional feelings are
rare, except for white sectionalism in the South.

Canada is different because of French-speaking Quebec,
with its resurgent spirit of nationalism and separatism,
sparked by linguistic and cultural distinctiveness, local pride,
and economic aspirations. Moreover, the Canadian provincial
units are far larger than American states and are divided by
natural features like the Rockies in the West and the St.
Lawrence River in the East. Canadian federalism has also
been reinforced not only by judicial interpretations, as we
have seen, but also by the not infrequent practice of the electorate of choosing different parties to control provincial administrations from those they support nationally—thus maintaining
some territorial checks and balances vis-à-vis powerful national
parties.

Nevertheless, regardless of local situations, the issues represented by political parties in the older, established states are
national, as inevitably are the interests and organizations of

the chief social and economic groups—labor, trade, and industry—in industrial countries. This is probably the chief reason why the federalism written into the postwar Constitution of Italy, traditionally a strictly centralized country, remained a dead letter for over two decades, with the exception of five geographically or ethnically distinct "border" units (among them, the two major islands of Sicily and Sardinia and the formerly Austrian, partly German-speaking Alto Adige), which were immediately given regional autonomy. Only in 1970 has regional government been introduced into the remainder of the country, with fifteen more units assuming regional controls. The major effect, however, has been that national parties have found additional strongholds in which to entrench themselves, as, for instance, the Communist Party in three regions of central Italy (including the regional capitals of Florence and Bologna).

Therefore, while, in general, federalism or regionalism rarely rests on strongly felt sectional foundations, units like Alto Adige frequently still have some genuine regional basis, at least in feeling that nationality, language, religion, or general historical background sets them apart from other groups or from the majority population. Often, this feeling of separateness is reinforced by economic grievances. Both factors apply even to regions such as Scotland and Wales in Great Britain, which, of course, do not possess federal autonomy; but some guarantees of autonomy would certainly have to be granted to the present Northern Irish counties if they should ever be united with the Irish Republic. Quebec in Canada, Bavaria in Germany, Catalonia and the Basque regions in Spain before the Franco dictatorship did away with their autonomy, all reflect the same distinctiveness. With industrialization, some of these differences are gradually being overlaid, but, as Quebec demonstrates, this process does not necessarily eliminate either an insistence on local autonomy or strains within a federation.

On the whole, however, the outlook for federalism in the

older systems is none too good. But this does not necessarily pose a threat to liberalism. It is far from certain that smaller units of government are more sensitive to the rights and liberties of individuals and groups than are larger ones. In the United States, it is quite the other way around as far as the protection of the rights of racial minorities is concerned. Moreover, central government at times provides more effective protection against the pressure of nongovernmental power, such as that of "big business" or other special-interest groups. Thus, as one student of federalism has pointed out, whether subnational autonomy and diversity are protected or not often depends more on the political culture than on structural arrangements like federalism. After studying paired countries, one unitary and one federal (such as New Zealand and Australia, Chile and Argentina, the United Kingdom and the United States), he found that in no pair of countries with similar political culture was the federal member of the pair significantly more sensitive to subnational interests than the unitary one.

Although federal divisions tend to become less significant in mature democratic countries, in dictatorships they are commonly irrelevant. Technically, the Soviet Union has a federal structure, but the division of power is far more apparent than real. In Germany under the Nazi system, it became entirely illusory. This is because the essential characteristics of totalitarian systems demand the concentration of power in one man or in a small group backed by a monolithic party that controls and permeates all operations throughout the system, functionally as well as geographically. In post-Stalin Russia, responsibilities between the national and regional spheres have been shared more than they were under Stalin, but the very fact that Soviet policy has repeatedly gone from centralism to greater decentralization and back again testifies to the inherent weakness of federalism under such a regime. Yugoslavia, with its quite pronounced federalism, seems to be the exception among dictatorially controlled countries; but the genuine federalism characterizing that country only serves to demonstrate that, where ethnic, linguistic, and historical diversities separate populations to the extent that they apparently do Serbians, Croats, and Slovenes, dictatorship, even of the one-party type, has a hard time to maintain its own control and the over-all unity of the nation.

In Latin America, federalism (largely copied from the United States), is often simply a façade, even where there is no dictatorship. Its general weakness is reflected in the ready resort to "federal intervention," which substitutes federal for regional control in the member units.

On the other hand, as we have already suggested, federalism seems to have particular importance today in nations that have only recently come into existence or that are about to. When large units gain their independence from colonial rule, federalism may be the only way to prevent their disintegration into weak and small fragments. India, whose federalism now reflects its wide range of linguistic groups, retained its unity only by yielding to their demands for separate divisions. The trend toward further subdivisions may, however, call forth a counteracting trend, with centralism enforced in the interests of maintaining unity. This happened in Indonesia, which was transformed from a federation into a centralized republic soon after gaining independence. In a similar move, Ethiopia absorbed its previously autonomous province, Eritrea. Even the former Cameroon Federal Republic, which unites a territory formerly held under trusteeship by France with one formerly under British supervision, has now adopted a unitary structure.

In the case of Pakistan, itself a splitaway from colonial "Greater India" because of the centrifugal force of religion, the bond of Islam proved too weak in the face not only of geographical separation but also of ethnic and linguistic differences that economic and social inequalities between the Western and Eastern portions of the country served only to exacerbate. Thus, after a bitter struggle and untold suffering,

East Pakistan became independent Bangladesh, while West Pakistan itself remains threatened by the separatism of subnational ethnic groups, such as the Pathans.

But, frequently, federalism has provided a means whereby diverse small units can group themselves into viable or even powerful entities. The United States provides the earliest illustration of this process. The Canadian and Australian colonies also took this route to national unity and statehood between 1867 and 1901. In Nigeria, the original form of federal association between three widely different, though economically complementary, regions, each with a dominant ethnic group—Yoruba in the West, Ibo in the East, and Hausa-Fulani in the numerically strongest North—facilitated the move to independence in 1960. Moreover, despite a bitterly fought civil war over the attempted secession of Biafra, a reunited Nigeria now functions as a federation of twelve states under overall military control. The Malaysian Federation, another recent addition to the independent members of the Commonwealth of Nations, is a further example of how the federal form has combined self-conscious, and in this instance separated, smaller entities. Despite its dispersed and varied units, Malaysia has exhibited considerable cohesion in the face of overt interference by Indonesia. Thus, federalism can provide a framework for experimentation and a flexibility in determining the allocation of power that help to make its form suitable to widely varying conditions.

If federalism can play this role in the making of new nations and thus provide the middle way between splinter units and excessive centralization, then it may yet come to play an even larger role in international relations. The increasing interdependence of countries in the field of security and the progressive economic integration of the world may, in the long run, suggest the value of a federal relation to countries with small resources and extensive needs of development. This would be particularly appropriate in West, Equatorial, and East Africa, where the race for independence has brought to a number of countries a political status that their immature economies can barely support. This reasoning perhaps applies even more to island groups and archipelagoes, such as those in the Caribbean and the Pacific, and to ministates striving for a meaningful autonomy.

It must be said, however, that, in many areas, national and territorial sensitivities and aspirations—either of the territorial unit, or of a particular group within it—have either complicated or prevented the progress toward, or consummation of, a formal federation. The Federation of Rhodesia and Nyasaland, founded in 1953, failed to secure the allegiance and support of its majority Africans and broke into the original component parts: now Zambia, Malawi, and Rhodesia. (Rhodesia unilaterally and unconstitutionally declared its independence to preserve white control, but has been pressured to change its racial policies through U.N. sanctions.) The West Indies Federation also broke up, though through local jealousies and even miscalculation rather than any problem of racial discrimination. Several attempts at federation in African-controlled Africa have also ended in failure: notably the Mali Federation of Senegal and Soudan, the latter now named Mali; and the projected East African Federation of Uganda, Kenya, and Tanganyika (now Tanzania). Thus, federalism can be an answer to diversity only when the units concerned make a common and sustained effort to achieve it.

It should be pointed out, however, that there are a number of looser associations in Africa, notably the Common Services Organization in East Africa and the Afro-Malagasy Common Organization (OCAM) spanning virtually all former French-controlled territories in sub-Saharan Africa, within which the Council of the Entente provides a closer relation between the Ivory Coast, Upper Volta, Niger, Togo, and Dahomey. All African-controlled countries confer regularly through the Organization of African Unity (OAU), which has endorsed certain common policies, like the acceptance of colonial-drawn boundaries, support for liberation forces, and asylum for refugees. They are also being drawn closer together through the establishment or expansion of existing links with the European Economic Community (which is itself undergoing a decisive enlargement through inclusion of the United Kingdom and some of its European trading partners). More will be said in Chapter VIII of this remarkable postwar development in Western Europe.

It is possible that out of such experiences not only the new countries of Africa but the older ones, too, may finally come to recognize the value of a federal relationship. Indeed, the more audacious among us might look forward to the use of federalism as a device to integrate the major powers, whose basis of genuine independence has disappeared along with their former "impenetrable" frontiers, and perhaps even ultimately to create a world federal structure.

IV

CHANNELS OF POLITICAL ACTION: ELECTIONS, POLITICAL PARTIES, AND LEGISLATURES

Although constitutions form the framework within which governments should operate, they cannot of themselves answer the most vital question for a democratic state: How is government to be kept responsive to the popular will? It is still possible in a New England town meeting to bring citizens together to make their own decisions on policy, as Athenians used to do in classical times. But national populations are far too large and too dispersed in modern times for that kind of direct action. On the other hand, the national plebiscite was a favorite device of de Gaulle for ratifying his Algerian policy and even for instituting the direct election of the President. It is also occasionally used in both the legislative process and that of constitutional amendment, as in Switzerland and in Australia in the case of the latter. These exceptions notwithstanding, modern government is essentially representative government. But this very fact raises a vast number of other questions: How are representatives to be chosen so that they will be responsible to their constituents? How can they make their influence effective on the executive? In other words, how can the vast variety of often opposing groups in a modern community be linked with the process of government in such a way that policy-making can be carried on speedily and decisively, and yet with due regard to the consent of the governed?

THE PROCESS AND PURPOSE OF ELECTIONS

The most obvious point at which citizens directly influence the conduct of government is at the moment of elections; the most obvious center of representation is the legislature. Through elections, democracies can achieve that peaceful change of administration that is the most difficult of problems for dictatorship. Through legislatures, the public is kept informed of proposals for policy and lawmaking and hears them thrashed out in the battle of conflicting points of view. Moreover, through investigations—either by legislative committees, as in the United States, or by the more flexible method of the parliamentary question—the executive may be kept under supervision even on points of administrative detail.

To say this, however, is not to answer a long series of questions, some of them substantive and some technical, but all revolving around these issues: How can representatives be kept responsible both to their own constituents and to the interests of the whole electorate? Whom should representatives represent, and how should they perform this function? And how should elections be conducted and on what electoral basis?

To be more specific: Should elections be held in single-member districts, where the decision is always clear, or in multimember constituencies, where the results, through proportional distribution of seats, more nearly reflect various shades of opinion? Part of the advantage of voting in single-member districts is that the contest is understandable and often dramatic, as in any race where only one person can win. Moreover, in this kind of voting there is no question but that the elected representative is directly responsible to a particular constituency as well as to the whole country in general. In addition, and very important, there is the fact that under this system powerful parties tend, at least in Anglo-Saxon countries, to win so high a proportion of the seats in the legislature that they easily fill the competitive roles of government and opposition. This makes for effective government, since the party in power has the votes to carry out its program; at the same time, the opposition becomes responsible for the clear presentation of alternative policies and for unremitting efforts to keep the government sensitive to its responsibilities.

The problem of single-member constituencies is that the minority stands in danger of being disfranchised. Beyond the apparent injustice that up to 49 per cent of those who exercise their franchise may not have their votes count in the final selection of the representatives, the presence of third-party candidates, not so rare these days in either Great Britain or Canada, may split the vote, so that the representative is chosen by as few as 34 per cent of the electors. Should there, therefore, be multimember districts and a system of proportional representation, so that minorities will be represented in proportion to their strength throughout the country? Proportional representation may mean voting for a list of party nominees from which the top names are selected in accordance with the number of votes the party secures; or using the single transferable vote, in which the elector ranges his candidates in order of preference and has his second choice counted if his first choice either has been elected already by other people's votes or stands no chance of being elected; or be carried on through a run-off contest, which may be followed either by a final vote restricted to those who received at least 10 per cent of the vote in the first round (as with legislative elections in the Fifth French Republic—a process leading to maneuvering and political deals to mobilize strength behind the right or left) or by a more clear-cut choice between the two candidates receiving the highest number of votes in the first contest (as in the French presidential election); or some other procedure. Regardless of details, the results of this system may seem to be fairer than those of contests in single-member constituencies. If Great Britain, for example, used proportional representation, the Liberal Party would have many more members in Parliament, for its proportion of the total vote is nearly always much higher than its proportion of MP's.

But this system also may give rise to several problems. The

elections under proportional representation are not so easy to follow as the other type. Nominations, especially under the "list" system of PR (as proportional representation is commonly called), may become the preserve of entrenched party elites or bosses, over which even the party members have very little influence. Moreover, under PR it is much more difficult to determine that highly important question in a democratic system: To whom is the representative responsible? Since proportional representation also tends to maximize the voting power of small, closely knit minorities, it tends to split the legislature into so many parties that effective government becomes difficult, if not impossible.

A considerable number of countries have long used, or are now using, one or another form of proportional representation, e.g., Italy, Israel, Ireland as well as several other small European countries, and Australia, which uses PR for electing the ten senators from each of its six states. West Germany's somewhat complicated election system comes close to being proportional. Most of the larger modern democracies, however, seem to feel that the liabilities of PR outweigh its advantages for choosing the members of the body that is usually the seat of political power—the lower house.

Some countries that do adhere to the system of proportionality have tried to eliminate some of its shortcomings through special devices. In West Germany, for instance, a "5-per-cent clause" denies any representation in the legislature to parties failing to poll a minimum of 5 per cent of the votes. This has successfully prevented the formation of a large number of splinter groups, although the evenness of the electoral strength of the two major parties has thrown disproportionate influence to the remaining smaller groups, notably the FDP, which manage to scale this barrier. But in general, as under the single-member district system, voters rally to the largest groups, perhaps in part to "climb on the bandwagon," but more particularly to have their votes count in the choice of the government. From the point of view of proportionality, this may be regrettable, but provides compensation through the greater stability inherent in a system of a few large parties.

Under the majoritarian principle, which underlies the idea and practice of democracy, every vote should have equal weight (with the one major exception that, in federal systems, the second chamber representing member states, if composed of popularly elected representatives, may reflect the equality of such member states through an equal number of delegates for each, regardless of population). Few electoral systems, however, make any attempt to satisfy this concept of equality in an exact, mathematical manner. But where discrepancy becomes too great, serious problems arise. Even so democratic a system as the British permitted double voting on the basis of special claims to representation—i.e., the university vote and the business-premises vote—until the end of World War II, when the Labour government abolished it.

The most frequent cause of inequality in the actual weight of votes, however, has been malapportionment of districts and failure to reapportion them over long periods of time and after great shifts in population (in recent times, generally from the countryside to metropolitan areas). Thus, in most countries with single-member districts, there are fewer voters in rural than in urban constituencies. This fact grossly exaggerated the political influence of American rural areas until forced "redistricting" under a Supreme Court mandate began to make representation of rural and urban areas more equitable. In South Africa, these inequities still provide a major advantage to the rural constituencies whose voting population is mainly Afrikaner.

Apart from nondemocratic arguments (such as that people "closer to the soil" are more valuable than the "urban rabble," or that educated persons should have stronger influence over political affairs), inequality, especially of rural and city areas, used to be justified by the argument that scattered communities covering large areas should have a measure of compensation. This argument is hardly valid any more in days of rapid communication, but it is still used by strongly entrenched political and economic interests that profit from the system. Thus, in the United States many districts became drastically unequal in size; electoral provisions for some state legislatures even guaranteed by statute that the rural population would receive greater representation than urban voters. Since redistricting was under the control of the selfsame bodies whose members were interested in the continuation of this situation, namely the legislatures, it was not possible to remedy it until the courts intervened. After having long refused to go into this "politically sensitive" matter, the Supreme Court in 1962, in *Baker* v. *Carr,* declared that denial of equal voting rights through malapportionment was irreconcilable with equality before the law as guaranteed by the Constitution. This case referred only to one chamber of state legislatures, but subsequent decisions have extended the principle to both state chambers as well as to the House of Representatives.

Important shifts in the power structure of the United States have resulted from this judgment by the court, illustrating once more the frequently decisive role played by constitutional jurisdiction. The reapportionment issue in America also raises the basic question of whether even a majority should have the right to deprive citizens of equal representation. Such an attempt was made by certain states, which tried to salvage the system of unequal districts through a plebiscitary vote on the question. The Supreme Court, however, taking its liberalism in this sphere seriously, decided that the minority disfavored by such a majority vote must be protected in its right to an equal vote and thus declared the results of such plebiscites to be inadmissible.

In Great Britain and many other countries, the responsibility for redistricting is "depoliticized" by vesting it in impartial bodies such as commissions of judges. While this has had salutary effects in Britain, the effort of South Africa to keep redistricting constantly abreast of changing population levels has created its own problems, since the boundaries of constituencies have been redrawn after every five-year census, and thus between each major election. Such frequent changes (as has also been true of British redistricting since World War II) tend to break down that sense of community within a constituency that contributes so much to the reality of representation. On the other hand, where redistricting lags behind changes in population, there is the opposite, and perhaps even greater, evil of districts becoming drastically unequal as the result of population shifts.

Even with their extraordinarily frequent redistricting, the South African election returns do not follow the popular vote with any degree of exactitude. The National Party did not poll over 50 per cent of the votes until the republic referendum of 1960 and the general election of 1961, though in 1958 it won 103 out of 156 seats in the House of Assembly. This discrepancy is partly the result of overweighting the rural vote, but it results more directly from a phenomenon also observable in British elections: the fact that a major party (in South Africa the United Party, and in Great Britain the Labour Party) can pile up such huge majorities in urban centers that it "wastes" many of its votes. In fact, redistricting in South Africa has seemed deliberately aimed at massing the opposition vote within constituency boundaries under the principle of similarity of interests, thereby reducing the number of close election contests and causing Parliament to look like a reflection of regional differences and of rural or semi-urban and urban divisions.

What seems evident from this brief survey is that there exists no electoral system that exactly reflects popular views and divisions. This in itself is not necessarily a cause for concern. What is important is to secure a rough approximation of popular sentiment through means that the public accepts as legitimate. Thus, democratic states do not need to worry about attempting to provide any exact, mathematical reflection of the electorate—an attempt doomed to failure before it is begun—nearly so much as about obvious subterfuges to secure the advantage of particular groups (such as gerrymandering the boundaries of constituencies), since this undercuts the sense of legitimacy that makes the public trust electoral results.

Even when, as in France under the Fourth Republic, it was the center parties upholding constitutional government that devised electoral rules to their own advantage, they were threatening the system they hoped to save. This danger also existed in postwar Germany and Italy, since the method of election, not being specified in their constitutions, could be devised anew by parliament for each election. Election systems have therefore tended to depend on the calculations of parties or majorities as to which rules would serve them best, and thus have tended to become the football of party politics. Since powerful groups are tempted to abuse their power to disfranchise small ones, such tactics inevitably help alienate parts of the electorate. For the moment, the result might be to the advantage of stable government. But, since the process of election is designed to provide representation with the aura of legitimacy, any drastic attempt to distort electoral provisions to the advantage of any group cannot but imperil the faith of the electorate in the democratic system as such.

In the new states of Africa, universal franchise is looked on, not surprisingly, as the key to political power. Where white minorities have long held control, as in South Africa and Rhodesia, the vote is the means of maintaining or securing power (as, indeed, it still is in diminishing parts of the American South). The old conflict between education and economic standing, on the one side, and numbers, on the other, which was waged in earlier days in Western industrializing countries, now permeates the multiracial states, and in a more virulent form. No one can doubt that, ultimately, numbers will secure in Africa the influence they have elsewhere—the political egalitarianism of the democratic creed is too widely accepted elsewhere to be denied indefinitely there—but this is only the first step. The franchise can put people into power. But it is far more difficult to ensure their continuing awareness of, and responsiveness to, the public will. This is particularly true in Asian and African countries, which as yet have had little democratic experience, though at least some of them e.g., India and Tanzania, have demonstrated that illiteracy is no bar to selecting their representatives, and particularly their leaders, shrewdly. Yet, not only in the new countries but also in the older democratic states, the issue remains: how to maintain a genuine link between representatives and those who put them into office.

There is, in fact, no real sense in which one man elected by universal suffrage can be said to represent the interests and wishes of all the voters in his constituency, or even the majority of them. The best that he can do, whether he is in the British House of Commons, the American Congress, or the Indian legislature, is to be aware of the most deeply felt preferences of his constituents, to be responsive to the views of important individuals, and to keep in mind the interests of the most important pressure groups operating in his constituency, if, indeed, they can be reconciled. But still more important are the demands of his party, the activities of its leaders, and his own sense of responsibility for viewing issues in the light of public interest rather than the more narrowly conceived advantages of particular groups or places.

In this framework, what distinguishes democratic government is not only that it is representative, but that it is also responsible. The highest voting records have been those in the Soviet Union, Fascist Italy, and Nazi Germany; but, since the election is for only one slate of candidates, the effect is merely, and inevitably, to endorse the existing regime and in no sense to check its use of power. Democratic states naturally encourage wide use of the franchise, and some, like Australia and Belgium, even make voting compulsory under penalty of a fine. Moreover, there is some significance in such drastic difference in voting participation as we witnessed in the U.S. and West German elections of November, 1972: a 55 per cent turnout versus over 90 per cent. Yet, the significance of an election lies less in the number of people voting than in the acceptance of this process as the legitimate means of putting a government into, or out of, office without violence, and thereby keeping it responsible to the electorate.

POLITICAL PARTIES

Political parties are the indispensable links between the people and the representative machinery of government. Their role is most obvious when an election is in prospect, but, in fact, they need to be continually operative if a democratic system is to work effectively. It is political parties that organize the vastly diversified public by nominating candidates for office and by popularizing the ideas around which governmental programs are built. They are the vehicles through which individuals and groups work to secure political power and, if successful, to exercise that power. They have a no less significant function when in opposition of scrutinizing the use of power and forcing the government constantly to justify its policies and actions.

What distinguishes political parties from interest or pressure groups is the breadth and variety of their followings and the orientation of their programs toward issues of concern to the whole country. Because awakening interest in these broader questions is a more difficult task than stimulating interest in matters that obviously affect the business or family of an individual, parties must make people politically conscious, i.e., aware of their role as citizens. This role cannot be fulfilled simply by voting but must be a continuous one if government is to be kept responsive to public interests. Thus, political parties are responsible for maintaining a continuous connection between the public and those who represent it either in the government or in the opposition.

Contrast Between Democratic and Dictatorial Parties

Dictatorships also find the political party an indispensable instrument, but they use it quite differently from the way democracies do. Whereas democratic political parties consciously emphasize diversity and mutual criticism, in the Communist or fascist dictatorship the political party is but the body of the faithful dedicated to maintaining the one truth that their leaders avow. Whereas, furthermore, democratic political parties are, apart from their elected members, informal, nongovernmental organizations (though their electoral activities may be regulated by government), the dictatorial political party permeates every government as well as nongovernmental activity and is virtually a part of the administration it dominates. Where democratic systems maximize opportunities for criticism and protect individual rights to free speech, dictatorial systems operate on the principle of "democratic centralism,"—i.e., comments may be offered in the early stages of a proposal, but, once the leaders have made their decision, everyone must accept it. Where democracies anticipate an alternation of leaders and provide the public with a choice of candidates for office, dictatorial leaders are self-selected through a power struggle within the party machinery itself. Where democracies use the fervor and slogans of an electoral campaign to publicize the differences between party programs, in a dictatorial state the party carries on continual propaganda campaigns in support of the government's objectives and is the chief means by which conformity is maintained throughout the society.

It is thus confusing and, in a sense, inappropriate to use the term "political party" both for the competing political associations in democratic states and for that group which has the full monopoly of political as well as all other power in a dictatorial totalitarian state. Such a group often owes the designation "party" merely to the fact that, in predictatorial times, it actually had been one of several competing political groups on the political scene, from which, subsequently, all but it disappeared, leaving the now official or "state" party in control of political life.

A prime characteristic of political parties as they have evolved in democratic countries is that they are voluntary groupings acquiring their cohesion from perceived and ac-

cepted purposes. They thus serve to integrate the people socially within their ranks by giving them a common objective
and a common organization. But the political party in democratic states is a vehicle to be used by its members, not a
master to be unquestionably obeyed. In totalitarian states, in
contrast, the political party is the chief means of control
throughout the state, and thus its membership is carefully
sifted to ensure conformity to the overriding purpose of the
small ruling group. Usually, therefore, its membership is
fairly small (in 1970, for example, Brezhnev reported that the
Communist Party in the Soviet Union was just under 11 per
cent of the population), unlike that of a democratic party,
whose purpose, indeed, is to attract as many members as possible. To a certain degree, the totalitarian political party
serves to express the sentiments of its members, but only to
the degree that is useful for the purposes of the regime. In no
case does it act to restrain the exercise of power. As the Nazis
used to put it: In democracies, authority comes from below
and responsibility from above; in dictatorships, authority
comes from above and responsibility from below.

The Totalitarian Party in a Democratic State

The fundamental differences between democratic and totalitarian-minded parties raise particular problems when one of
the latter is operating within a democratic state. At the beginning of the century, Lenin taught his Bolsheviks the secret of
successful subversion: to be a highly organized, highly disciplined group giving unquestioned obedience to its leaders in
tactics, in their interpretation of Marxist dogma, and in their
objective of radically reorganizing society. Hitler used much
the same techniques in building his Nazi Party into an instrument capable of taking over power from the Weimar Republic. Thus, fascist and Communist parties are understandably
suspected of seeking to overthrow the legitimate government
of the country within which they work, replacing it, if necessary by force, with their own control—either in their own interests or, in the case of a Communist Party, in their own and

probably also the interest of a leading Communist-controlled country: the Soviet Union or China.

Totalitarian-minded parties are most effective in seizing control within states whose machinery of government is weak and indecisive, and whose population has little sense of common unity. But, even without the hope of replacing the legitimate government with their own, totalitarian-minded parties can do much to disturb the smooth functioning of the state. In France, the Communists used to poll 25–30 (and still get 15–20) per cent of the vote and, until the Fifth Republic changed the electoral system, sent a large number of their representatives to Parliament. In Italy, the Communists have consistently polled the second highest number of votes and have elected substantial numbers of deputies. This process has two debilitating effects on democratic operations: It keeps a large number of voters from supporting democratically inclined parties, thereby forcing the latter to compete within a restricted milieu; and it places a strong group of deputies in a position where they can constantly impede the administration and thus divert it from its primary job of providing effective, responsible government.

The Communist vote in France and Italy reflects a high degree of mass support. The Communists have perhaps a third of a million Party members in France—more than the total enrolled in all other parties—and five times that number in Italy. In each case, a relatively small, but highly organized, group of militants dedicated to Marxism-Leninism direct the activities of the large number of people whose grievances these militants exploit by playing on the strains caused by every imaginable shortcoming of the respective society, economy, or political system, such as rising costs of living, unattractive labor conditions in industry, corruption or high-handedness of the civil service, or, particularly in Italy, the misery, backwardness, and exploitation of the farmers. Where Communist parties appear incapable of securing majority support, they may join "popular front" governments, as in France under Léon Blum in the mid-1930's and briefly after

World War II. In 1972, the French Communist Party again joined in an alliance with the Radicals and Socialists to challenge the dominant UNR in the 1973 election. Such partnerships, however, are commonly clouded by fear that the Communists seek only their own advantage, rather than that of the whole country.

Still more complicated has been the situation in regard to the Communist Party in India. As the only organized group endorsing the Indian war effort (which it did because the Soviet Union was involved), the Communist Party had special opportunities to develop during World War II. Shortly thereafter, and for the first two years of India's independence, the Communists were revolutionary in aims and action. Dealt with firmly by Pandit Nehru's government, the Communist Party then announced that it accepted the democratic framework and would secure its purposes through the peaceful winning of elections. Although the Congress Party has maintained its predominant position in India, as we have noted, the Communists formed the second largest party in Parliament until a general split in September, 1964, led to the creation of a new left-wing, pro-Chinese party known as the Marxist Communist Party. Since then, these two parties have been rivals in state elections and in the national legislature, with the result that their ability to undermine stable democratic government in India has been considerably weakened.

Because of the fear of Communist infiltration, some states, in particular South Africa and, until recently, West Germany have outlawed their Communist parties. But this tactic runs the danger either of forcing the organization underground, where it may be still more dangerous, or, as in South Africa, of using broadly phrased anti-Communist legislation to suppress legitimate efforts to change discriminatory practices. It is far more constructive to attack the conditions and grievances that the Communist Party can exploit, and to develop the national consensus and its reflection in mass popular parties that provide the best insurance against the rise of totalitarian-minded groups. At this point, therefore, it is important to consider the development of the mass party in democratic states.

The Rise of the Mass Party

Although political parties are now recognized as the dynamic of the democratic political process and the chief means whereby popular control can be exercised, this has not always been the case. When organized political parties first arose in Great Britain and on the Continent, they were aristocratic cliques or factions seeking to protect the interests of their particular group against monarchical demands, although, especially in Britain, some of their members had a strong sense of public responsibility. With the rise of the bourgeoisie came what Max Weber called "parties of notables," informal associations built around those persons who actually held parliamentary seats. This stage of party development was characteristic of British parties after the Parliamentary Reform of 1832, of the political groups in the German Parliament of 1848, of parties in pre-Fascist Italy, and among the center and rightist groups under the Third French Republic. There is also a parallel in the efforts of the Federalists in the early days of American independence to preserve the monopoly of political office by persons of property and position.

But this stage of party development has virtually ceased to exist. Its place has been taken by the mass party, as evident in the United States and Great Britain as it is in India or Mexico. The mass party is the natural outcome of universal suffrage and of the need to appeal broadly to different groups in the community. In contrast to the earlier party of notables, the mass party not only attempts to appeal to all groups in the community but also tends to be highly organized on a national level (at least at election time), with increasing power resting in the hands of party functionaries. At the same time, it is the mass party's representatives in parliament who are ultimately responsible for policies, and they rarely abdicate this responsibility to the professional party organization that did so much to put them in office.

Political parties in the older democracies, and especially the older, more conservative parties, reached the stage of mass appeal and professional country-wide organization only by degrees. In the United States, for instance, parties are still organized largely at the state and local (county) level and become national organizations only at four-year intervals. Recently, however, there have been two exceptional attempts on the part of ideologically minded sections in both major American parties—in 1964, the "conservative," or Goldwater wing of the Republican Party; and, in 1972, the populist wing of the Democratic Party under George McGovern—to establish continued central control over the entire party. But, having acquired control at the party's nominating convention, the Goldwaterites lost it again after the defeat of their presidential candidate, and decentralized controls were then instituted by various sectional party leaders, such as state governors and certain leading Republican senators and congressmen. In 1972, new and more equitable rules of selection for the national Democratic convention, based on the report of a committee chaired by McGovern himself, led to his nomination as the party's presidential candidate but more conservative forces took control after his defeat.

In Germany, a country of much higher centralization of party life and party organization, the "bourgeois" parties, such as the Christian Democratic Union (CDU), still have not attained the degree of cohesion that has long been characteristic of the Social Democrats (SPD), as attested by the much lower percentage of the CDU's formal membership, on the one hand, and the greater interest in party affairs taken by the average member of the SPD, on the other. Even in Great Britain, the Conservative Party only slowly adopted the high degree of organization it possesses today, and then largely to counter the impact of Labour, whose popular appeal and disciplined cohesion were its strongest weapons against the entrenched economic strength of the two older British parties. In both Australia and New Zealand, the more conservative parties—the Liberal Party in Australia and the National Party in New Zealand—were even slower to develop a high degree of organization or a popular mass appeal, doing so only as late as the elections of 1949, at which time both these parties ousted Labour administrations from office. In contrast, neither the Liberal nor the Conservative Party in Canada is as yet highly organized, except at election time. There, as in the United States, political parties tend to be great holding companies, incorporating conflicting interests and maintaining their cohesion through the imprint of characteristic attitudes —the Canadian Liberals and the American Democratic Party being innovators and social-minded; the Canadian Progressive Conservative Party and the American Republicans being concerned more with maintaining an existing status—as well as through the struggle for political power. Under these circumstances, there is less need to develop highly organized national structures such as are characteristic of present-day British parties or socialist parties on the Continent.

The party system that operates the British parliamentary structure is more akin to that of the United States, however, than is commonly believed. In both countries, there are customarily two large political parties, each vying with the other to win public office in order to promote its policies and purposes and to enjoy the material advantages that go with the possession of office. While it would ordinarily be argued that the British party system, with the Conservative and Labour parties alternating in office, has a far more defined class base than has the American, it must be remembered that to win an election both parties must appeal as broadly as possible to the electorate. Although Labour still receives a large share of the working-class vote, the Conservatives are increasingly attracting white-overall and white-collar workers, particularly in the newer industries. From its side, Labour is cutting into the Conservatives' traditional predominance in rural areas. Indeed, it may well be true that guessing a man's political allegiance on the basis of wealth and social status is easier these days in the United States than it is in Great Britain.

Nonetheless, a distinction can be made between what is

called a party of individual representation and a party of social integration. The former is concerned chiefly with political functions, as is still largely true in Canada and the United States, and even with these on a limited scale. Although the appeal is directed at the whole community, it is generally made only at election time. Moreover, the representative, once chosen, feels free to make his own judgments on issues, to the detriment of party solidarity—a particular characteristic of Southern Democrats in the United States, but by no means restricted to them. The party of social integration, on the other hand, demands much more of its members in terms of financial support, of continuous concern with issues, and of a coordinated view of life. Its representatives are under stricter party discipline. In this respect, the election system, as we have seen, has a bearing: The list system of PR makes the individual representative more dependent on the party leadership than do other systems. In addition, the constitutional system itself has an impact; for, where the threat of dissolution of parliament hangs over its members, as in Britain, at least those belonging to the majority party will think twice before kicking against policies of their leaders (i.e., the cabinet), whereas the absence of this possibility—as in the United States and Italy and formerly in France—contributes to the feeling of independence that the individual deputy enjoys.

Socialist parties, with their coherent world view and corresponding attitudes and policies, have been among the earliest to belong to the integrated type. But, as governments virtually everywhere assume more responsibilities for economic and social life, there is a natural trend toward turning any party of representation into one of social integration. As long as such a party neither aims at the total conquest of power nor operates in so exclusive a fashion as to imperil the basic consensus on which all stable democratic societies must rest, this process does not threaten but complements the mass democracy of the twentieth century.

The danger of imperiling basic consensus is illustrated, however, by one of the most distinctive of modern mass parties, the National Party in South Africa. Even in the nineteenth century, the Afrikaner people were organizing themselves into groups with suggestive names like Het Volk (The People). Within two years of the coming into being of the South African Parliament in 1910, the first Afrikaner Nationalist Party was formed. In 1948, when the contemporary National Party first came into power, it had become the political representative of the great mass of the Afrikaner people as completely as the Dutch Reformed Church was their religious vehicle. Moreover, the Nationalists have developed a highly organized party machinery that uses professionals to direct the constant activities of volunteer workers. Thus, the strength of the party rests on two powerful pillars: a high degree of organization, and a fervent sense of separate identity of the Afrikaner people, which is reinforced by appeals to their cultural distinctiveness as well as their genuine fear of being overwhelmed by the numerically dominant Africans.

The Nationalists represent an unusually close identification of a political party with a particular racial group. So close an identification with a particular racial or social group may well mean, as we shall see later, that the representative aspect of a political party outweighs the responsible aspect. In other words, a political party, like a political representative, has a twofold function: It must heed the wishes and interests of those who have put it into office as well as of the formal membership of its group; but it ought also to have regard for the interests of the whole country. For either political programs or political leadership to be limited to the interests of a single group tends to split or to distort the character of the community if that party acquires political power.

Two-Party Versus Multiparty Systems

The sharp and fundamental distinction between political-party systems, as we have seen, is between those in totalitarian and those in democratic countries. But there are also very considerable differences between characteristically two-party systems such as we find in Great Britain, the United States,

Canada, Australia, New Zealand, and South Africa, on the one hand, and the multiparty systems of Continental Europe, on the other. Most of the traditional two-party systems also include one or more smaller parties: Great Britain, for example, includes the Liberal Party; Canada, the New Democratic Party (NDP) and the Social Credit Party; South Africa, the Progressive Party. But the essential contest is between two parties only. The third, or the third and fourth parties, may secure a limited number of seats but not enough to become the official opposition. Thus, the election takes on the characteristic of a contest between two major opposing forces, and the voter may cast his vote for a political group that is certain either to form the government or to become its relentless critic.

In multiparty systems, however, the voter can never be sure whether the party for which he votes is going to form the central part of a governing coalition or not. The process of compromise that goes on within a given political party in the average two-party system (and particularly in one like the American or Canadian system, which finds business, labor, and farmers in both major parties) is transferred in a multiparty system either to the floor of the assembly or to the back rooms, where party leaders meet to hammer out the composition and program of a coalition government. The power to make and remake coalitions enhances the authority of the assembly as well as the independence of the ordinary member of that body. Unless his party is a strongly disciplined one, like the French or Italian Communist Party, the member has a chance to exercise his own discretion about policies, and particularly about who should be the premier, in a way that is completely foreign to two-party systems. The penalty (and it is a heavy one) is that governments tend to rise and fall with dismaying regularity, as they did under both the Third and Fourth Republics in France and still do in Italy. Moreover, it is difficult under such conditions to secure continuity of policies, except through the action of the administration, which then acquires a power otherwise denied it. Another great disadvantage is that the voter is usually not presented with a choice of leaders, one of whom, as chief of the party gaining the majority, will be sure to become the head of government; for, in a multiparty system, it is the postelection negotiations of the parties that determine who the prime minister will be. He may even turn out to be from one of the smaller parties forming the government coalition.

It is commonly said that what determines whether there is a two-party or multiparty system is the degree of unity within a particular state. Multiparty systems obviously reflect divisions within the community—in social structure, economic interest, racial composition, or ideological preference. But that naturally disparate groups can be held together by a strong personality and the overriding importance of a few major issues has been proved by the experience of West Germany. Much the same task as Konrad Adenauer performed in West Germany was carried out successfully by Pandit Nehru in India during its early years of independence. But, when cleavages go deep in a country and are felt intensely, only exceptional leadership—like that of General Charles de Gaulle in France—is capable of bridging them. Moreover, unless new allegiances develop that are stronger than the earlier divisions, old multiparty instability tends to reappear after the departure of the strong leader.

But two-party systems also have their problems, as in Great Britain, Australia, and New Zealand, where one party, Labour, claims to represent a class interest, or Canada and South Africa, where there are linguistic and cultural divisions to be bridged. Before 1924, some political observers even believed that Labour would never be able to achieve office in Great Britain without a violent reaction, since they felt that the propertied groups in the community would feel too threatened by its objectives to allow such a program to be imposed peacefully. That this did not happen reflects a major degree of agreement on fundamentals between the Labour Party and the other parties in Great Britain, and in New Zealand and Australia as well (where Labour achieved national office as early as 1908). It also reflects the fact that the programs introduced by Labour, when it came into office in those countries, corresponded to the social conscience or, in the latter two countries, to the equalitarian views of the community at that particular moment.

This fact explains two phenomena: why Labour was able when it first came to power to carry through its program so quickly and without difficulty in all three of these countries; and why, in each case, the Labour Party tended to lose its momentum and appeal so soon after instituting its reforms. What seems obvious is that, once a simple reformist program has been carried through by a labor party, it confronts the much more difficult issue of whether to introduce more than palliatives to curb the inequities and dislocations inherent in capitalism. It confronts the dilemma, in other words, of whether to be representative of its own particularism or whether to be responsible to the basic ways of action of the whole community. If it drastically attacks the prevailing economic modes, it risks alienating its own right wing and even more the middle-class groups on which it depends for electoral success. If not, it alienates its own more radical members and loses its drive. Thereafter, paradoxically, its greatest appeal to the electorate may well be that it can do better administratively than its conservative opponents—who, in the meantime, have adopted the more attractive parts of labor's program. The end result, in these cases, is that the consensus of the community is strengthened, while effective government is maintained.

This trend toward moderation has been characteristic of other labor parties, too, in particular the originally more radical and dogmatic socialist parties of the Continent. Many of these parties have played an effective role in coalition governments, and where, as in West Germany, they become the leading government party, there are few who are still afraid that their policies will deviate from the mildly reformist pattern set by their more recent party programs (such as the Godesberg program of the West German SPD). This entire development reflects the entrance of formerly proletarian and underprivileged classes (such as the industrial workers) into the "affluent society" of the industrially advanced nations. In the less advanced countries, class divisions are as yet less marked. But, in the developed nations, "pockets of poverty" are still found, and neglected groups may look for more radical representation of their interests if reformist parties overlook them.

The process of consensus-formation on the basis of moderation is more difficult where ethnic and linguistic, rather than social and economic, divisions are concerned. In Canada—with the exception of the sharp political and party division between English- and French-Canadians over conscription during World War I—the national-party system has commonly overbridged regional and ethnic divisions. The French-speaking minority is always represented within the governing party (in the long Liberal reign from 1935 to 1957, and again from 1963 to 1973, virtually all of Quebec's representatives were on the government side). But cooperation between the English- and French-speaking within the same party did not prevent the rise of such separationist movements as the *Front de Libération du Québec,* which, until outlawed after its 1970 kidnappings, capitalized on the considerable discontent in that province. Moreover, as the 1972 election returns demonstrated, the Canadian political system is still strongly influenced by sectionalism.

In South Africa, with its exclusively white party system, the United Party, which then combined practically all the English-speaking population with a small percentage of Afrikaans-speaking South Africans under an Afrikaner leader, was dispossessed of political power in 1948 by the National Party, with its exclusively Afrikaner membership and leadership. The result was at first a noticeable deepening of antagonism between the two groups. But, largely because most whites in the Republic feel a need to retain something of a common front against the blacks (Africans, Asians, and Colored, i.e., mixed blood), who outnumber them four to one, this divi-

sion between the Afrikaans- and English-speaking sections
tends to be bridged over by a common sense of increasing
danger felt by the largest resident minority exercising political (and, in practice, highly discriminatory) rule on the African
Continent. Thus, while, under normal circumstances, a political party composed of one racial (or any other exclusivist)
group tends to accentuate divisions in a country, and thus
lessen consensus, a strongly felt sense of danger may, on the
other hand, result in a new, either externally or self-imposed,
pattern of conformity. Thus, somewhat paradoxically, the
two-party system may also reflect a situation in which a reluctant minority increasingly conforms to the will of a parliamentary majority instead of performing the functions of
criticism and of presenting alternative programs that are the
essence of the constructive role of the parliamentary opposition.

Multiparty Systems with a "Dominant" Party

In the postwar world, as we have seen, party systems in
most democracies are either of the two-party type (which
should really be called the "two-major-party system," since
there are nearly always one or more minor groups in the legislature), characterized by the alternation in power of the two
major political groups, or of the multiparty type, with its
minimum of three, and often more, major political groupings
and its variety of possible party combinations for holding office. While the two-party system still has its strongholds in the
Anglo-Saxon world—the United States, Britain, and the older
Commonwealth countries—there is now a strong trend toward
it in West Germany and also in Austria. Among the multiparty countries, there are still a few, such as Belgium and the
Netherlands, in which the three or more major groups are
relatively equally balanced. Increasingly, however, we find a
further system emerging where one of these multiple parties
is "dominant," in the sense that it either is in control alone
or at least forms the central group of all coalitions.

Sometimes, this situation develops because a strong radical
party, such as the Communist Party in France or in Italy,

compels the other parties to rally around the only other strong group, such as the Gaullists (UNR) in France or the Christian Democrats (DC) in Italy. It may also be the rallying point for major conservative forces in a country: in Italy, the Church and business; in France, business and the "technocratic" administrative elite; in West Germany, where the CDU was the "dominant" party for twenty years, big business, agriculture, the churches, and officialdom—in short, the whole "establishment," with organized labor left on the outside. In Japan, the Liberal-Democratic party has dominated the political landscape throughout the postwar period, backed decisively by the business groups of an economically "exploding" nation. But it would be wrong to assume that this kind of system necessarily constitutes, or reflects, the dominance of "capitalist" or otherwise conservative groups and classes. For we also find it centering around socialist, or at least social-democratic, parties, representing labor, agricultural smallholders, or similar groups, in countries such as Sweden (formerly also Norway and Denmark) as well as in developing countries where, as with the Congress Party in India or the Institutional Revolutionary Party of Mexico, the dominant party is, or was, the major group leading that country toward political or economic independence. We shall see below that a dominant party, after independence, often remains the only legal party in the new nation. But where, as in India, parties are allowed to compete freely, the one symbolizing the independence struggle is likely to maintain its "controlling" position. Another "dominant" party is Israel's Mapai, which was the rallying political group even prior to the coming into existence of the state, representing as it did the major Zionist forces, namely labor (organized socially and economically in the Histadrut) and the socialist agricultural cooperatives (kibbutzim). No government can be formed in Israel without Mapai.

Since the dominant party is the king-pin of the political setup in such systems, a major political problem is the maintenance of its unity. Backed as it is by many different and often competing and antagonistic groups, the dominant party more often than not is an uneasy alliance of factions, and thus is threatened by factionalism and even disintegration. As long as they are disciplined by strong personal leadership (the CDU under Adenauer, the Italian DC under de Gasperi, the Indian Congress under both Nehru and Indira Gandhi, the Mapai under Ben Gurion and Golda Meir), these parties are the backbone of political systems that may function as well as do systems where two parties alternate in power. In the absence of such leadership, on the other hand, they are likely to become a cause of destabilization. They may become weakened by secession (Ben Gurion himself split away from "his" party, forming a splinter group), but even more so by constant internal strife between factions and leaders. Which wing prevails in a party such as, say, the Italian DC becomes, then, as important a general policy issue as that of the strength and policies of all the other parties.

Party Financing

With the rise of the mass party, the question of who pays for party work and party offices, party employees, and, in particular, campaign and other election expenditures has become an ever more urgent one. At the time of party "notables," persons of independent means could still finance their own campaigns. While this fact, of course, favored wealth, it was, so to speak, self-contained wealth, and the successful candidate, on the whole, was not beholden to persons or groups that backed him financially in expectation of reward. Today, the financing of a mass party and its election campaign requires vast amounts of money, which, in principle, can be secured in two ways: by numerous, generally small contributions of party members and voters, or by fewer, but larger, subsidies from special-interest groups, such as business enterprises, agricultural organizations, and trade unions. In our day, especially since the organization of nationwide campaigns (which include television and radio appearances of candidates), electioneering has become a fine and highly expensive art. Thus, the question of from whom, and how, a party secures its major support can be decisive not only for its subsequent attitudes and policies but for its very success at the polls.

It is here that the functioning of the democratic process meets a vital test. If equality of opportunity in the political field is to have more than a mere formal meaning, it must imply at least some degree of equality in the means essential for political success. But this ideal is far from being realized in most democratic systems. It is well known, for example, that in the United States the Republican Party is far better off financially than the Democratic Party (in the 1956 election, the proportion of their campaign funds was roughly 2:1 and in 1972 far higher). Although President Nixon vetoed a 1971 Democratic-sponsored bill permitting a one-dollar check-off for the taxpayer's chosen party, a more comprehensive measure became law in 1972. This legislation permits a $100 deduction by a taxpayer for a contribution to his party's electoral expenses, makes mandatory full disclosure of the source of campaign contributions over $100 made after a specified date (the time limit is removed for future electoral campaigns), and sets certain limits on political party use of TV during the campaign. Moreover, the law provides that, subsequent to the 1972 election, a taxpayer may indicate a one-dollar check-off on his income tax to the benefit of the party of his choice. While such provisions do not provide a full answer to the problem, they mark a significant advance on which further initiatives can build.

A striking example of "inequality in financial opportunity" was furnished, in the 1950's, by West Germany, where industry established so-called promoters' associations, which assessed individual enterprises according to their payrolls and distributed the tax-exempt levies among the government parties, chiefly, of course, the CDU. In 1958, however, the Constitutional Court outlawed the tax deductibility of campaign contributions as a violation of the "equality principle" of the Constitution. Thereupon, the parties, in order to lessen their dependence on private contributions, voted themselves subsidies from public funds on the basis of their proportional strength in the preceding election. This device, too, was subsequently declared unconstitutional, as far as financing the general activities of the parties was concerned, but reimbursement of their campaign expenses by this means was permitted as long as the funds were allocated equitably. This system of financing campaigns through state funds, while making the parties appear even more "official" organizations than they already are, has at least eliminated the worst effects of "big business" and other comparable influence over elections.

In Great Britain, a system more effective in limiting campaign expenditures than that in the United States has prevented the extremes of plutocratic abuses. The law specifies financial limits during the election period and restricts "treating" and other defined forms of influence. In Canada, big business commonly contributes to both major parties, though a higher percentage is given to the one in power. But the problem is a serious one, and, until it is solved, democracies will continue to be vulnerable to the charge that, behind their egalitarian façade, they are really controlled by rich men or powerful pressure groups.

The Mass Party in the Newer States

While mass parties evolved slowly in the older democratic states, they have been a characteristic of the newer states from the beginning. Where a nationalistic movement is struggling to bring a country to independence, its natural focus is in a mass party that unites virtually all elements in the country in a common demand for transfer of power. After independence is achieved, however, or often even when it is close at hand, strains may develop that split the mass party into communal or ethnic groups. In British India, for example, the Moslem League refused to work with the Congress Party because of the latter's predominantly Hindu support and secular philosophy, and this led ultimately to the partition of the subcontinent between Pakistan and India. Pakistan itself suffered further dismemberment in 1972, when, after a bitter civil war, its eastern half declared itself the independent state of Bangladesh. In Nigeria, the Ibos attempted, also by civil war, to establish the separate state of Biafra but failed against Federation forces under military rule. On the whole, therefore, states, in Africa as in Asia and, increasingly, in Latin America, either develop a single, dominant mass party or are threatened with anarchy or separatism, leading to army or dictatorial rule.

In emerging Asian and African states, the problem is still more social than political: It is the need to build a sense of unity in the country strong enough so that criticism and diversity do not seeem like treason. Wherever there was a serious split in the nationalist movement prior to independence, the group in opposition was almost inevitably labeled treasonable. If this split persists or reemerges after independence, either force, or a long period of stability are needed to heal it. The kinds of divisions that are welcomed in well-established democracies may shatter the fragile chances of national unity in ethnically diverse societies.

One-Party Democracy

Although few independent African states have a two-party or multiparty political system, the leaders of countries like Tanzania, the Ivory Coast, Senegal, and Kenya commonly assert that they are neither dictatorships nor totalitarian but "one-party democracies." The justification for this designation is twofold: that a formal opposition party would only accentuate existing differences and divisions, whereas these potential sources of strain can be given expression and can be reconciled within the single political group; and that there is no place for the traditional parliamentary battle when existing skill and experience are all too limited and all energies and talents are needed to advance national development.

Is this democracy? We have been accustomed to saying that one-party rule and dictatorship are virtually synonymous. But, even in the early days of the United States, there was only one party, the Federalists, until Jefferson stimulated the rise of what was little more than a personal political movement. When the Federalist Party collapsed, the country was left for some time without an organized alternative to Jefferson's Republican Party. Yet, in the long run, of course, the American two-party system emerged. While it is natural for the older Western democracies to look for two-party systems and ultimate alternation of office in the new countries, this process requires experience, a substantial pool of talent, and a fairly firm social structure. For most of the new countries, the touchstone of democracy will not be the number of parties engaged in debate in the parliamentary arena, but the right to express open criticism and the maintenance of the rule of law. If these two essentials exist, the future may well see the evolution of what we consider the more orthodox structure of democratic government.

What we have called "one-party democracy" differs basically, it must be emphasized, from the one-party totalitarianism of the Soviet Union itself or other Communist-controlled countries. In the first instance, the presence of only one party is not a dogma but an expedient. The objective is to mobilize the people voluntarily to work for the vastly important objective of national development. In this sense, "one-party democracy" has some similarities to the unity most Western democratic states established while they were fighting what President Franklin Roosevelt called "the war of survival"—World War II.

The possibilities of criticism within the one-party democracy provide in themselves a type of opposition that should not be underestimated. The mass parties in the newly developing countries are far from monolithic. It is far more difficult to identify and classify the kind of opposition that operates within these African countries than it would be if the opposition were organized as a separate party, but forthright, well-publicized criticism by backbenchers in both Kenya and Tanzania is not infrequent. In fact, it is possible for something very close to the interplay of government and opposition in mature democracies to take place within the single party of the new states, but only, of course, if opportunities for criticism are not stifled.

Army Rule

In a striking number of cases, new parliamentary democracies that failed to provide stability or to work efficiently, or that suffered coups for other reasons, have come under army rule. In Ghana, Pakistan, Burma, Iraq, Nigeria, Uganda, Zaïre, Argentina, Brazil, Bolivia—to mention widespread examples—military leaders control the civilian machinery of government. In part, these situations have been the result of either internal or external threats, but, more especially, they have come about because of parliamentary weaknesses and crises. Western democracies look with disquiet upon the establishment of military dictatorships—and justifiably so, in view of their own experience with the phenomenon known as "Bonapartism." But, in the new states, the military are sometimes more liberal-minded and better trained than are the politicians. Thus, their authoritarianism, if combined with self-restraint, may perform the function of an "educational dictatorship," which is progressive because it aims at modernization and reforms.

Much depends, of course, on the policies of the army leader who comes into power. Some army regimes are coercive, as in Sudan before 1964; some merely become bywords for self-seeking aggrandizement, as is threatening in Nigeria, despite the probity of General Gowan himself and his broadminded policies of reconciliation since the end of the civil war; some, like General Amin's in Uganda, are unpredictable; some, as in Peru and Brazil, are active modernizers. Although most military rules are intolerant of criticism, a few do, nevertheless, attempt to establish new and appropriate forms of representation as channels for promoting local self-reliance and social change.

Among the latter, Colonel Nasser in Egypt and General Ayub Khan in Pakistan both established new forms of representation; yet there is a great difference in the methods they used in attempting to shape their respective societies. As far as institutions are concerned, both established directly elected village and town councils as the lowest level of representation, arguing, with some justification, that illiterate peasants can choose better from among those they know personally than between rival parties. On this base, a pyramidal system of indirect election from one level to the next was erected.

This attempt to substitute consensus in a representative system for party government was said to avoid unnatural divisions and to reflect the traditional "village democracy" of which Asian and African leaders sometimes boast. But, while Ayub Khan concentrated on land reform and on tackling local problems, Nasser embarked on a radical reorganization of the economy, using nationalization as a major instrument. In the short run, the village-oriented social and economic program of Ayub Khan had a closer relationship to the local councils that form the basis of representation than did Nasser's plan; but, in the longer perspective, the view that decisions must be the result of a unanimous consensus overlooks its potential danger to independent thinking and free expression.

"Village democracy" arose out of circumstances providing limited alternatives, or even an absence of alternatives. It reflects narrow horizons, perhaps bounded by the physical limits of the village itself. Since, with modernization, the village is rapidly drawn into a much larger entity, with a wide range of alternatives, and is affected by swift-moving social and economic change, the strain on the traditional consensus becomes great. There is an arithmetic, if not a geometric, relationship between the number of possible alternatives of action and the speed of social and economic change. The opportunity to argue out these alternatives, at least in the interest of understandability and in order to check on possible arbitrariness, may thus produce a more solidly knit community than can be achieved by institutions directed toward glossing over such differences of view.

It is not only under army rule, however, that such issues

arise. The one-party democracies of which we have spoken are also eager to enjoy a consensus in regard to their policies. Since popular support is necessarily one of the criteria by which we judge the degree of democracy under such regimes, it is particularly important that we know how much of that support is secured by muffling opposition and how much of it is the result of a genuinely free discussion of alternatives.

Army rule is often established solely to serve as a transition stage leading to the establishment of a more stable democratic regime. Egypt is an outstanding example of how the army, under far-sighted leadership, can provide such a transition from a corrupt, privilege-ridden regime to a relatively democratic, though one-party, structure. It must be admitted, however, that, compared to the ease with which most army coups take place in developing countries, the process of establishing and then maintaining stable and popularly supported representative institutions is long and fraught with pitfalls. All too often, discontent or division leads again, as in Ghana in 1972, to army intervention.

Turkey, as we have seen, was initially transformed from a traditionalist, Islamic state into a secular republic, and acquired stability, economic growth, and a secure international position under the authoritarian rule of its great leader Kemal Pasha, better known as Atatürk. In 1945, President Inönü somewhat precipitously introduced a multiparty, Western-style parliamentary system with popular elections. In 1960, the Menderes regime was overthrown by an army group, but parliamentary government was re-established the next year. The army now officially keeps in the background but, in fact, determines which party is in power.

In the Sudan, a series of army coups in the first months of the 1963 military regime resulted in broadening the base of authority, but ultimately led to bloodshed, while repression of the Southern Sudan was, if anything, intensified. After a brief interlude of democratic government in 1965, the army again took over under new leadership dedicated to ending the long civil war, and ultimately succeeded in doing so in

1972 by granting a substantial measure of autonomy to the Southern Sudan. Thus, the character of the army leadership and, perhaps still more important, the way the leadership responds to the divisions existing in the country, determine the impact of army rule and the degree to which it provides a foundation for a more democratic system.

Postwar experience of types of rule in newly independent countries includes a wide variety of means to combine effective and, it is hoped, public-spirited administration with economic development and encouragement of national cohesion. Some leaders have maintained that authoritarianism is essential for the maintenance of stability and for demanding the sacrifices necessary for development; others contend that parliamentary institutions provide the framework within which leadership can be combined with public airing of issues and restraint on arbitrary action. Neither view is necessarily valid for a particular situation. It is important to recognize that the operation of parliamentary institutions in such a way as to provide effective and yet responsible government requires a considerable degree of experience and of restraint. The Belgians obviously gave such institutions little or no chance of success in the Congo by bestowing them only a few weeks before the territory achieved independence on June 30, 1960. Yet, among the former British- and French-controlled territories of Africa, some, like Senegal, Cameroon, Kenya, Botswana and Zambia, have not been unsuccessful in handling parliamentary institutions, which provide legitimacy and a known method of succession in a way that authoritarian regimes cannot duplicate. At their best, they also provide for the ventilation of issues, so that feelings are not bottled up until they reach the explosion point.

What the experience of responsible-minded army rule and one-party democracies may indicate is that the urge to express opposing views, and the corrective balance wheel to authoritarianism of such outlets, may be found in many more places than traditional political analysis has suggested. Within a democratic one-party system, the opposition may make itself felt through trade unions or youth or women's groups; it may be provided by the army acting in a nonpolitical but somewhat censorlike role, or by the civil service acting in the same nonpartisan fashion and allowed by the ruling politicians to do so. As long as this is the case, the stifling effects of authoritarianism are lessened, the opportunities for social growth are enhanced, and cohesion and stability are combined with criticism. In comparison with this somewhat sensitive balance, unresponsive dictatorship—whether veiled in parliamentary forms or exercised openly to the accompaniment of inflammatory nationalist propaganda—tends toward an enforced uniformity within which opposition can express itself only through violence.

LEGISLATURES

The chief objective of most political parties is to place their candidates in the elected, representative assembly (or assemblies) still usually referred to as a legislature. Under the presidential system, the chief executive is likewise the product of direct party contest and election; thus, in the United States, not only the two houses of the legislature but also the Presidency are based on direct popular support. In the parliamentary system, on the other hand, the executive issues technically from the legislature and, in this way, only indirectly from party contest and popular vote. But, especially where there is a two-party system, the electoral contest, though ostensibly concerned only with the election of members of the legislature, tends more and more to be tantamount to a plebiscite on the leadership of the government. This has been traditionally the situation in Great Britain, and more recently it has become so in West Germany.

Although, in a few countries—e.g., Norway and Israel—the legislature is organized as a unicameral body, it is commonly composed of two houses. The reasons for having a second chamber vary. Occasionally, it is a remnant of the predemocratic past, providing for the representation of the nobility and similar special groups. Thus, in Great Britain, the House of Lords

—by now shorn of most of its formerly vital functions—in part
still rests on hereditary succession, though in part on appointment also. In other instances, the objective is to provide a chamber that is more conservative (in the general, not necessarily the
party-political, sense of the word) than the popularly elected
house, a result usually achieved through an indirect method
of selection by persons themselves elected to other bodies.
This process, used in France and South Africa, for example,
tends to make the second chamber not only more conservative but also weaker than the popularly elected one. This is
true, of course, also for Great Britain (and Canada, where
senators are appointed), because, in a democratic period, people consider those popularly and directly elected to be their
most "legitimate" representatives. Thus, the second chamber
tends to recede into the background and to be useful (where
it is not hampering) as a place for considering issues that the
popularly elected chamber does not have time to explore ade-
quately or for providing another point of view.

The most frequent reason, however, for the existence of two
houses is a federal structure of government. In federally organized countries, as we have seen, the second chamber, representing the member units, can be organized in different ways.
In some countries, like West Germany, it is not elected but
consists of representatives of the governments of the member
states, thus only indirectly reflecting the party constellations
in these units. In others, like Australia, Switzerland, and the
United States, its members are popularly elected but from
differently demarcated constituencies. In either case, these second chambers may be of equal importance and on an equal
footing with the one selected through the over-all national
elections.

Where, as in the presidential-congressional system of the
United States, direct election underpins the power and prestige of both legislative chambers and of the chief executive as
well, there is a natural basis for the system of checks and balances, which can operate despite the links among all three
created by political parties. But, in a parliamentary system,

where the executive is not separate from the legislature, there is an almost irresistible tendency toward the dominance of either the cabinet or the lower chamber, even if both legislative bodies are elective. Few chambers were so butressed in power as the French National Assembly under the Fourth Republic; under the Fifth Republic, it has become a mere shadow of its former self as the President and Cabinet have become dominant. The British House of Commons occupies a position midway between the French National Assembly of the Fourth and Fifth Republics—a body of distinction but under the control of the Cabinet.

There was a time when democratic theory (originating in Rousseauian and Jacobin ideas) was inclined to look upon an assembly, which issued directly from popular elections and thus immediately reflected the "will of the people," as *the* supreme organ of government, in principle entitled to conduct all the affairs of state, and in particular to be in full and complete charge of lawmaking. But the idea that "representative" government requires a parliamentary body with the above-mentioned all-encompassing powers was based on a fallacy. Representative government, in this sense, could not exist even under the best of circumstances. To expect any large and varied group of average, inexpert representatives to frame the laws of a complex society and to coordinate a government's far-flung activities is to impose a burden that no representative assembly can be expected to bear.

What a well-organized assembly can do—and do well—is to analyze, criticize, and pass on the policies and proposals of the government; to voice the desires and anxieties of the mass of the citizens; to protect their liberties against any abuse of power by the government; to educate public opinion through its debates; and finally—as the term legislature implies—to participate in the process of lawmaking to the extent this is still possible in an area that relies increasingly on the expert and the administrator. In some ways, the legislature is particularly suited to these tasks. If its members lack the expert knowledge necessary to frame technical legislation, they possess a different kind of knowledge, which the experts themselves are not likely to have: the legislators, taken in the mass, represent a range of experience in terms of class and geographical origin and in intimate knowledge of their constituents that makes them exceptionally good judges of public opinion and of the acceptability and workability of laws.

In the Soviet Union, as one would expect, the aim is different; the Supreme Soviet is, in practice, expected to perform only a few of these functions. Great care is taken to make that body as representative as possible in a vocational and a national sense; but the purpose is not to permit these representatives to oversee and criticize the government, but rather to permit the government to educate them (and, through them, the people) in its purposes and policies. Thus, there is no criticism of the government's policies, and what criticism there is of administration stops short of the leaders of the Communist Party and, presumably, is permitted only with their approval.

The same applies to the parliaments of the Soviet-orbit countries, whatever the method by which they are elected and even if, as in the German Democratic Republic, other parties are represented together with "mass organizations." These organizations, as well as the non-Communist parties, are under over-all Communist leadership and serve to integrate specific groups that cannot be absorbed easily by the ruling party. One possible exception is the Polish Seym, where one parliamentary group (a Catholic one) has been allowed to voice occasional criticism, or even opposition.

When one turns to the Western democracies, it is evident that both the British Parliament and the French National Assembly under the Fourth Republic performed certain (though not the same) functions admirably. As protector of individual liberties against any abuse of governmental power, the House of Commons is unexcelled. As educator of the public on important issues, its well-organized and -publicized debates are remarkably effective. As critic of proposed legislation, the Opposition, at its best, is highly effective. The chief criticisms to which Parliament is subjected concern its lack of expertness (which detracts both from the cogency of its criticism of legislative proposals and from its ability to supervise the increasingly complex activities of the civil service), its rigor of party discipline (which allegedly destroys the independence and initiative of the private member), its failure to reflect with exactness the strength and varieties of political opinion in Great Britain, and its subserviency to the Cabinet.

In postwar France of the Fourth Republic, in contrast, the National Assembly reflected more accurately the diversity of opinion and the popular vote, and the system of specialized committees provided members with greater knowledge and rendered them more fit to cope with the technicalities of modern legislation and administration. Although there were complaints of excessive discipline among some of the parties of the left, the deputies in the center and on the right enjoyed a large degree of independence. And, unlike the British Parliament, in normal times the French National Assembly demonstrated its control over the Cabinet by rejecting or making serious modifications in its proposals. In spite of these merits, however, few people would consider the Fourth Republic's National Assembly a model democratic legislative body. The inability of the different party groups to agree upon an effective legislative program and to support a stable government; the violent and undisciplined debate, and the uncompromising hostility between different political interests; the eagerness of certain partisans on the extreme left and the extreme right to discredit parliamentary democracy by making effective action impossible—all helped to give currency to the popular picture of the legislature as a forum of bickering, irresponsible special interests. This tended to make men more amenable to follow a leader who promised political stability and the placing of the national interest above party interests, and thus paved the way for de Gaulle's Fifth Republic.

Nor did the German Parliament under the Weimar Republic offer a much more reassuring picture. Traditionally, the German executive was more independent of parliament and parties than was the French, with the result that, in Germany, parliamentary control of the executive was often ineffectual. But the ensuing conflicts between popular forces and an authoritarian-minded governing elite discredited democratic procedures and representative institutions time and again, thereby opening the way for the executive to assume uncontrolled power.

While it would be an exaggeration to suggest that the executive today in West Germany is unrestricted politically, it is nevertheless true that, in large measure, it controls the procedure of lawmaking. The expert ministerial bureaucracy drafts and initiates almost all important bills, adapts them to local and state needs through the second chamber (another bureaucratically composed body), steers them through Bundestag committees by its presence and powerful influence there, and subsequently, of course, oversees their administration. Moreover, in the course of this process, the legislature has made little use so far of the possibilities of surveillance and criticism that the Constitution and its own standing orders provide. Not irrelevant is the fact that, within the federal legislature, and even more in the state legislatures, public officials "on leave" constitute the largest bloc of deputies, there being no rule of incompatibility.

Even where they exist, parliamentary power and influence are at a low level in the new, or semidemocratic, countries. One of the characteristics of the mass party, as we have seen, is its dependence on its leader or leaders; the very effort of nation-making, and of attempting to assert a new importance in international affairs, encourages use of the legislative body as a sounding board rather than as a critic. Moreover, the lack of administrative training and experience, which handicaps legislators everywhere, is most obvious in capitals like Colombo, Jakarta, Nairobi, Dar es Salaam, Lusaka, and Mexico City. This is not to say that the legislators in these and similar countries do not work hard (they do, particularly in committees outside public view), but they have not yet ac-

quired either the responsiveness to public attitudes and needs
or the opportunity or skill for detailed supervision of executive action that is the mark of the better members of mature
legislatures. In countries only gradually emerging from caste-,
or ethnic-, or family-oriented social structures, it is also difficult to inculcate national loyalties and perspectives.

Some of the difficulties resulting from allegiance to local
rather than national interests are illustrated even in the
American Congress. A congressman's party affiliation may be
less important than the area from which he comes or the special interests in his constituency. This can lead not only to
"logrolling" in the passage of legislation but also to somewhat
erratic and even arbitrary supervision of executive action, as
has been true of the use of certain investigating committees.
Moreover, the power of congressional committees, especially
in finance, seriously limits the ability of the executive to present a coordinated program.

While, in contrast to the British Parliament, Congress has
effective power over the process of law- and budget-making
and thus, in principle, is one of the few remaining truly independent legislatures in the world, yet, in practice, it has developed a machinery of organization and procedure that acts
more often as a brake on action than as a spur to it (for instance, through the filibuster in the Senate or the role of the
Rules Committee in the House). Frequently, therefore, laws
reflect the power of entrenched groups rather than the majority will in the assembly. More than in any of the world's
other great legislative assemblies, bills may be stalled, pigeon-
holed, killed, or amended and compromised, at so many way
stations in their passage that Congress, rather than being a body
that makes laws sometimes becomes one that prevents legislation. This happens most frequently when legislation disliked
by some major interest group or powerful lobby is at stake;
while, on the other hand, bills favored by such groups sometimes pass like lightning, without even being debated. This
system, in general, favors the *status quo* and hampers reform.

Indeed, to enact significant and far-reaching reform legislation requires the rare combination of a reform-minded, activist President and a large, progressive majority in both houses willing to support him. This is a rare combination but it has occurred from time to time in the history of American legislation, notably in the post–Civil War "Reconstruction" period, under the two Roosevelts, and under Lyndon Johnson (before he became deflected by Vietnam). Thus, in the United States, reform through legislation takes place only spasmodically; there are better chances for it, in general, under the parliamentary system of the fusion of the legislature and executive.

What emerges from these comparisons is the fact that some of the frequently criticized defects of the British Parliament are, at least in part, assets: its freedom from the confusion, irresponsibility, and deadlock with which the legislatures of Italy or the French Fourth Republic are rightly charged, the potential deadlocks in the American system, and the lack of effectiveness of parliamentary action found in most of the newer countries. If the system of representation is far from perfect in Great Britain, both in failing to reflect shades of political opinion and in commonly exaggerating the majority of the larger party, these very distortions usually provide a stronger and more stable government that is capable of introducing a comprehensive program and of carrying it through. Party discipline not only reinforces this stability but contributes to the responsibility and the educational value of the British system. It is true that Sweden, with its multiparty system, also provides stable and clear-cut government; but this is largely because the party combinations that furnish the executive do not fluctuate sharply (as was the case in France's Fourth Republic), and also because its party groups provide fairly clear-cut alternatives at election time. But, if party members fail to vote as a unit, it is impossible for the voters either to understand or to judge the party's position; and there is no assurance that a party, once elected, will have either the desire or the power to carry out its promises to the voters. It is at this point, in particular, that the ultimate responsibility to the voters implicit in representative government links up with the legislature's role of supervision and restraint on the executive.

A word should, perhaps, be said about the problems of the technical organization of parliament in the twentieth century and the personal status of its members, for these questions are not without influence on politics and the functioning of government. While the more relaxed pace of life in previous centuries permitted a representative body to proceed leisurely and intermittently—with its members left to their own devices as far as income and information were concerned, and organized according to archaic rules that often reflected colorful customs but were hardly conducive to a smooth transaction of business—the conditions and demands of the technological age have required modernization here as elsewhere. The use of closure to speed the passage of legislation and the power vested in the Speaker of the House of Commons to allocate opportunities equitably help to meet, but do not wholly solve, the problem of chronically congested calendars. American legislatures, and especially Congress itself, suffer from stalling action when legislation threatens those with vested interests or their clients, status or interests. And, while Congress, at least now, has the technical assistance of ample staffs and an effective legislative reference service in preparing or coordinating legislative proposals and also provides adequate pay for its members, the state legislatures in the United States for the most part still meet only intermittently, pay their members too little, and provide meager assistance in their work. The West German Bundestag likewise does not provide its members with adequate reference services. In this regard, the British are also far behind, thereby penalizing those, particularly in the Labour Party, who can ill afford to pay personally for secretarial, research, and office services.

For a variety of reasons, the weight of government in this century has shifted from the legislature to the executive, and this development cannot fail to affect the image of parliament in the eyes of the public. Even as a forum for the executive leadership's pronouncements on important issues, parliament has declined. A chief executive, returning from an important meeting abroad, will be besieged for information by the representatives of the "media" as soon as his jet plane touches down at the airport. More likely than not, he will feel that he cannot withhold important facts until the next meeting of parliament, and thus its members will, in this situation, be relegated to the position of the general public, and their debate (if there is any) will take second place to that being carried on in the press and elsewhere.

Yet, it is clear that legislatures fulfill important, and indeed vital, functions, provided that their members are alert to public tasks and to the interests of the community as a whole, and avoid being mere mouthpieces either of their parties and "party lines" or of special interests concerned chiefly with how the big pie is cut. Above all, there must be perceptive and, if possible, well-publicized criticism of executive proposals and actions. If there is an official opposition, its members must know how to provide meaningful alternatives, even where there is agreement on fundamentals. Within a multiparty system, and even more in a one-party democracy, debate needs to be focused on essentials and to receive adequate publicity. For, in the end, what a legislature exists to do is not only to represent the public but also to ensure that the public is kept constantly aware of how the political machinery is performing, and what is planned for the future. Only thus can a legislature perform its essential function of maintaining continuous interaction between the people and its government.

V

POLITICAL LEADERSHIP
AND ADMINISTRATION

Throughout our discussions of how to keep government responsible, we have referred to the importance of political leadership. The spectacular growth in the functions of government that has taken place in every advanced country has caused the power of the executive to grow proportionately at the expense of the legislature. Since, as we have seen, the legislature is not well fitted to perform the tasks of framing and initiating, as distinct from discussing and passing, legislation, or to engage in comprehensive planning, these tasks inevitably fall to the relatively small group of political leaders and top-ranking administrators. Moreover, the leadership function presents in an acute form a basic problem of modern government: how to integrate the numerous and often dissenting groups and interests in our pluralistic societies and, at the same time, to check overintegrated or -concentrated power. Liberal democracy can all too easily develop toward the anarchy of diverse and uncooperating groups, while undemocratic systems tend to develop into authoritarianism and even, ultimately, dictatorship. In both situations, the balance wheel is responsible leadership. Thus, the effort to develop and maintain responsible leadership is the most crucial one for the future of the modern democratic state, with its mass electorate and vast multiplicity of tasks.

The Headship of the State: The Leader "Reigns"

Integration through leadership has a twofold aspect: symbolism and actual authority. Psychologists and sociologists

may argue about why it is that every human political organization needs a unifying symbol with or through which it
can identify itself as unique; but the fact is undeniable. The
unifying symbol may be impersonal (e.g., the American Constitution), but more frequently it is embodied in a person. The
extreme case of personalized symbolic (and actual) leadership
is the totalitarian dictatorship, with its Führer, its Duce, or its
"Great Father and Leader," as the Soviet press used to call
Stalin. But traditionalist leadership can be as strong as charismatic leadership. Not only "divine right" but also modern
constitutional monarchy is a case in point. It is perhaps no
coincidence that fascism as well as Communism, both of
which discard traditional symbols for new ones, have been
least successful where monarchy as an institution still has
strong roots. Thus, the British, Dutch, and Swedish crowns,
despite their lack of real political power, have proved an anti-
dote to totalitarianism. Moreover, in some developing countries, monarchs have promoted reform affecting vested feudal
interests, notably in Iran and even, to some degree, in Ethiopia.

This fact underlines the important function of a head of
state, as distinguished from the head of government. Where
constitutional monarchies exist, the chief function of the head
of state is to symbolize and represent the nation, especially in
its foreign relations. Without the monarchy, the Commonwealth might have disintegrated. Even the Asian and African
members which have adopted a republican structure acknowl-
edge the Queen as the symbolic "head" of the Commonwealth, in effect its most visible symbol of unity. Parliamen-
tary-type republican countries, lacking such a "given" head
and symbol, face the problem of providing for a dignified
headship that can serve as a unifying force. In West Germany,
for example, the restraint with which the first President of
the new regime, Theodor Heuss, exercised his function accounts in large measure for the high esteem this office now
enjoys. In France, too, the office of President, separated as it
was from actual executive power, used to depend for its respect and importance on the person of its holder. Under the

Fifth Republic, however, de Gaulle enjoyed not only great national prestige but also vast reserve powers, and, in practice, exercised a major degree of decision-making. Moreover, in an effort to provide his successor with comparable political influence and power, de Gaulle, using means of dubious constitutionality, pushed through a provision for direct election of the President. This constitutional change seems to have provided a unifying and directing executive, particularly while a strong party supporting presidential policies dominated the legislature. A regrouping of parties, however, leading to a strong party coalition *opposed* to his policies, might well lead to a presidential-legislative confrontation in the future.

In the United States, the head of state exercises so much real executive power that both dignity and prestige are never lacking. Although the Constitution is usually considered the primary unifying symbol in the United States, the degree to which the combined head of state–chief executive is the leader of the nation in the people's mind is sharply illustrated when a President dies in office or is struck by sudden illness.

But presidential systems face a serious practical problem: how to relieve the chief executive and political leader, whose tasks are already almost superhuman, from the additional time- and energy-consuming burden involved in his symbolic role. This is why even totalitarian regimes sometimes make use of a person other than the leader for the discharge of symbolic functions, e.g., the King under Italian Fascism, or the Chairman of the Presidium of the Supreme Soviet in the Soviet Union. In the United States, it has been suggested that the Vice-President might assume some of the ceremonial functions of headship. But symbolic leadership, once vested in one office or person, is not easily transferred, nor may its possessor wish it to be transferred. It involves more than legal or constitutional amendments; it involves the mind and the habits of a nation, and, where such a division of functions is an innovation, it might mean a change in the degree of influence exercised by the incumbent of the particular high office.

THE HEADSHIP OF THE GOVERNMENT: THE LEADER "RULES"

In Democracies

Even leaving aside the symbolic function of political leadership, there remains the bulk of the leader's tasks, enough to render the job trying under any standards of efficient one-man performance. Such a leader, in a democracy, must lay down the essential lines of policy in every field of domestic and foreign affairs; he must determine basic lines of military policy, even in peacetime; he must coordinate the innumerable agencies of what, in most modern countries, has become the biggest "business establishment"—the executive branch of the government; ordinarily, he must lead, and keep together, the majority party (or, in a multiparty system, one of the major parties, plus the coalition of parties that makes up his cabinet); he must manage a sometimes hostile, sometimes (in terms of majorities and minorities) unstable, or sometimes (in terms of political discipline) anarchic legislature; he must deal with a vast variety of interest groups and be able to resist their often powerful pressures; to be successful, he must be alert to, and yet manage, public opinion; he should be a spokesman capable of explaining the problems and policies of government in simple and effective terms; he must ordinarily be able to win an open, competitive election. In a parliamentary democracy, he should be able to participate successfully in the give-and-take of debate. He should be able to guide cabinet meetings, reconcile divergent opinions, and preside over the formulation of policy. He should, in addition, be a good administrator, not in the sense of detailed technical competence, but in the ability to oversee the range of administrative activity and to supervise the coordination of policy.

In Dictatorships

In contrast, the task of a totalitarian leader seems simpler. True, his job is still vast in terms of the top decisions to be made. The governmental machine to be organized and coordinated may be even vaster than in democracies, particu-

larly where, as in the Communist regimes, it involves planning and running the economy; as in democracies, it comprises
policy-making in the vital fields of foreign affairs and defense.
On the other hand, a totalitarian leader does not have to
manage a genuine legislature with an opposition or a party
with its own will and perhaps conflicting wings. Everything,
in this respect, is "coordinated." He does not have to deal
with free-ranging, independent pressure groups, though pressures, even dangerous ones, may work behind the scenes. If he
must interpret policy to the masses, he does so unimpeded by
the interference of a critical opposition or press. His popularity can be created artificially by the officially directed
instruments of a manipulated public opinion. Since no opposition is tolerated, he need never win an open election.

Still, it is easy to underestimate the job of a totalitarian
dictator. Since, in such a regime, there is no formal system
whereby he accedes to power, the leader must have attained
his position through what we term extralegal means. As we
know from a study of the rise of a Hitler or a Stalin, the
means may include brute force as well as devious scheming,
terroristic propaganda and purges, and manipulation of the
masses, of important power groups, and of close friends and
lieutenants. Under any circumstances, his rise, or that of a
small group of leaders, involves a selectivity in which only
the fittest—i.e., the toughest—survive. And, after having arrived at the top, the leader, or leaders, must stay on top
through whatever means necessary, since there is no constitutional legality or traditionalist legitimacy. Moreover, although
there is no need to respond to an independent public opinion,
the "purity" and at least seeming consistency of the official doctrine must be maintained through constant interpretation so as to leave no doubt about the basic standards—the
"line"—of the regime. This, in the case of Soviet leadership,
has involved the attempt to coordinate and even direct the
doctrinal lines and resulting basic policy approaches of *all*
Communist regimes. Failure to maintain this doctrinal leadership, at first in the case of Titoist "revisionism" and subse-

quently in the face of Maoist "doctrinairism," has accounted for the serious splits that have occurred in the Communist camp, most conspicuously the Soviet-Chinese rift.

The Two Compared

If quick and decisive action is what modern government requires above all else, then, some have argued, the authoritarian leaders—proven in cunning and ruthlessness and free from special pressures, constitutional inhibitions, and the need to conciliate genuine opinion—are far better suited to such conditions than are the democratic leaders. Especially in the vital fields of foreign, defense, and economic policies, concentration of power, unhampered by popular or parliamentary controls and free from the danger of periodic change of personnel, may appear the better guarantor of efficiency. But such arguments are based on doubtful assumptions. As a matter of fact, the pressures and special influences that openly harry democratic leadership also play on totalitarian leadership, though they are better hidden behind a (temporarily) streamlined façade. This became all too apparent in the examination of the Nazi regime after its downfall. Efficiency may suffer from overconcentration of power, overorganization, flight from responsibility due to fear of reprisals in case something goes wrong, absence of criticism, and, consequently, the possibility that vital information never reaches the top level. And finally—as was clearly revealed in the process of "de-Stalinization" in the Soviet Union—if unlimited power makes possible impressive feats, like Soviet industrialization under Stalin or German blitz-rearmament under Hitler, it also opens the way to possible blunders of equal dimensions, such as Hitler's later foreign policy or strategy decisions, or Stalin's wholesale purges and his policies toward the satellite nations.

Democracies are less likely to commit either feats or blunders on such a gigantic scale. It should nevertheless be noted that one-man rather than group leadership has characterized most of them in recent times. This is the case not only in democracies with a presidential system, like the United States, but also in many of those with a cabinet system (which, of course, implies collective leadership), like Britain. And it is true not only for older countries but also for new or revamped systems like those of India, Indonesia, Japan, and West Germany. In fact, it is chiefly in the backwaters of world politics, or in countries, like permanently neutralized Switzerland, that are artificially shielded from international pressures, that genuine group leadership survives. France used to be the exception that merely proved the rule, for the very fact that its premiers were rarely able to provide forceful leadership under the Fourth Republic was a prime factor in weakening that country and preparing the way for the strong executive of the Fifth Republic. Italy is the one major country where the trend toward personal leadership has not (yet) taken place.

PROBLEMS OF SELECTION, RESPONSIBILITY, AND SUCCESSION OF THE CHIEF EXECUTIVE

One-man rather than group leadership characterizes government in our century because of the increasing importance of speedy and decisive policy-making, especially in foreign and security affairs. This situation, however, throws into high relief the equally vital importance of the selection and responsibility of the supreme holder of power, the process of succession, the selection and responsibility of his chief lieutenants, and the access that they and others have to the leader, whether he be democratic or dictatorial.

Selection and Responsibility

Turning first to the problem of the selection of a responsible leader, we find that it is democracies, rather than dictatorships, that are faced with difficult problems. Dictators are self-selective and, in a constitutional sense, irresponsible. Fascist doctrine states this frankly and even boasts of it; the leader is answerable not to the "whims of the masses" but only to "history." Communist theory, it is true, proclaims the responsibility of the leader to the masses, whom, even in Leninist doctrine, he is not supposed to leave too far behind. But who decides? Who holds the "vanguard" to its proper task in the absence of institutionalized criticism and control? The revelations about Stalin disclosed a leadership that cared little what the masses, even the "class-conscious" proletarians, thought or desired. And, if Stalin's rule was attacked by his successors as a monstrous deviation, there was supreme irony in the fact that his main critic and successor was ousted in turn for arbitrary policies and even charged with fostering a "personality cult" along Stalinist lines.

In democracies, on the other hand, the decisive constitutional rules and procedures aim at providing responsible leadership. Whether selection is through direct popular election, as in presidential systems, or indirect, as in parliamentary systems—where the vote is cast for a parliamentary party, whose leader then becomes head of the government—it is the essence of democracy that the leader thus receives a mandate to which, because it is limited in time, he can be held responsible. Periodic elections, therefore, are still the indispensable foundation of democratic responsibility.

In a multiparty system like the Italian or the French under the Fourth Republic, the mandate is less clear than it is in the British type of two-party system, for the voter does not even know which one among the leading politicians of the various parties will eventually emerge as Premier. This problem was less serious in France than it might appear, however, because the Cabinet acted as a group, and thus under group policies rather than under one-man leadership, while Parliament exercised close control over executive leadership. Whatever disadvantages this had in other respects, it was a highly effective device for holding the Premier and his colleagues responsible to the popular will, which supposedly resided in the Assembly. This latter check is always a strong factor in the British system, for the Prime Minister, though in many respects in control of Parliament, is always subject to questions and criticism within that body.

In a situation like that in West Germany, where neither of the two strong parties has been able to form a government by itself, the popular mandate may be unclear. In 1969, as we have seen, the Social Democrats, with a lesser number of seats than the CDU, came into office through the support of a small, third party, the FDP. The CDU, thus thrown, to its great surprise, into opposition, has never since ceased to charge that this was a "betrayal of the electorate's will." The situation was clarified in 1972 when the SDP-FDP coalition got a clear mandate at the polls.

On the surface, there is less enforceable responsibility in the presidential system. The American President is free from direct legislative control (though he must work closely with Congress to have his program accepted), and also from the restraints that the collegiate (or Cabinet) system provides even in Britain. In this situation, the time limit of his term remains the only significant *formal* check. But certain *informal,* less institutionalized ways of rendering account to the public have developed, such as the occasional presidential press conference and direct TV reports to the nation on important policy decisions like the 1971 imposition of wage and price controls. These appearances attest to the significant role that the press and other channels of mass communication play in a modern democracy. Indeed, how would any legislature fulfill its role of public information without newspapers, radio, and TV, which report daily to a mass audience on its activities, often critically?

Yet, however effective the devices for checks and limitations and enforcing responsibility may be in democracies, the job, and therewith necessarily the power, of leadership remain uncomfortably great. This is the more so because of the necessity of granting an even less limited and less clearly defined power to government, and in particular to the chief executive, in time of crisis, when only such concentrated power seems able to cope with the emergency. Especially in our age of cataclysmic perils and fears, the temptation to resort to speedy and decisive action is great, and thus even long-established democracies have emergency or martial-law powers that, as happened in Canada in 1971, may be invoked in times of grave national crisis. A political theorist, Carl Schmitt, has gone so far as to declare that internal sovereignty belongs to whoever can exercise emergency powers. It is perhaps significant that he is German, for it has been in countries with weak democratic traditions that constitutions have most easily been abrogated or undermined through the use or abuse of emergency powers. But, no matter how strong its democratic tradition, no country can afford to disregard the dangers inherent in this problem. (More on this subject of the use and misuse of emergency powers will be found in a later chapter.)

Succession

If democracies have more problems than dictatorships in selecting leaders, the reverse is true when it comes to the matter of succession to leadership positions. In all systems where law determines what happens in government in fact, and not merely in form, succession will proceed in prescribed ways. In a monarchy, succession laws designate the heir to a throne; in a working democracy, the constitution or ordinary statutory law performs the same function in regard to presidents, prime ministers, or other leaders. Ordinarily, in such situations the transition from one leader to another thus proceeds without difficulty. In most democracies, of course, such a change happens in the normal course of regular constitutional procedures as a result of periodic elections.

As a rule, however, dictatorial succession creates a crisis for the very existence of the regime. Since such rule is commonly based upon the "unique" and therefore "irreplaceable person" of the leader, it is put to its greatest test with his demise. Actually, neither the Nazi nor the Fascist dictatorship survived to pass this test, since the death or overthrow of the leader was caused by the forcible action of external enemies. In case of an internal revolt, as in some Latin American countries, it may mean either the end of the dictatorship as such or the establishment of a new one on the basis of the successor's "charisma." Under such "praetorianism," it is often the top military who determine the successor.

But, after a dictator's death, as with Lenin in 1924 and Stalin in 1953, the transference of his "halo" to a successor is a difficult task. In Stalin's case, transference of power seemed relatively smooth on the surface, but, as we now know, it involved, in fact, a series of struggles for power before Khrushchev emerged as the undisputed leader. In contrast, Khrushchev's ouster, as well as the succession to his powers, was both quick and apparently without grave repercussions. It seems, therefore, that, as Communist regimes become older and more stable, the top level of party leadership becomes more institutionalized and the succession to leadership smoother. Here, the Central Committee, as we have noted before, plays an increasing role. Thus, in East Germany, Ulbricht's heir apparent, Erich Honecker, succeeded without difficulty to the leadership position through this mechanism in May, 1971.

Succession may be facilitated by a formal sanction already given to the future successor by the dictator during the latter's own lifetime; but this creates a "crown-prince" problem, and totalitarian leaders, from Mussolini and Hitler to Stalin, have been loath to take such action. In China, Lin Piao, formally announced as Mao's successor, subsequently disappeared. Chou En-lai now seems to be the heir-apparent. In Spain, Franco has long prepared to meet his problem, not by selecting a successor to the dictatorship but, rather, by preparing for a return of the monarchy. In Haiti, "Papa Doc" Duvalier sought to transform his dictatorship into a quasi-monarchy by stipulating that his son should inherit both his position and his power. But, though Jean-Claude Duvalier did, indeed, become "President for Life" on his father's death, with the paraphernalia of personality-cult dictatorship and titles like "Worthy Continuer," in practice power seems to be exercised more through, than by, him.

If, as is obvious, the sharpest contrasts over succession are between dictatorial and democratic regimes, it should also be noted that different types of constitutional systems produce their own characteristic ways of providing for the succession of their leaders. The presidential elections in the American system provide not only the chief executive but, simultaneously, the leader of the party whose nominee is installed in the White House; although most American Presidents have had experience either as members of Congress or as state governors, neither is mandatory, as General Eisenhower's election in 1952 proved. In the British type of parliamentary government, in contrast, the Prime Minister is the leader of the party that wins a majority of the seats; inevitably, he has had parliamentary experience and, almost inevitably (Winston Churchill proved an exception), he has headed the party organization for a considerable time.

A party leader may be chosen by the parliamentary members of the party, as is the practice in Great Britain, Australia, New Zealand, and South Africa, or by a party convention, as is done in Canada and in most Continental European countries. In either case, it takes a "palace revolution" to unseat him once he is selected. It is true that the Canadian Progressive Conservative Party picked three leaders in the space of sixteen years, hoping each time to find one who could lead it to victory, as did John Diefenbaker in 1957, to end temporarily a twenty-two-year period of office by the Liberals. The Australian Labour Party also twice renounced its leaders, once during World War I and once again during the Depression, when they were already serving as Prime Ministers; but, in both instances, it was the party, not the leaders, who lost office. But these are exceptions, as was Churchill's elevation to office in 1941, and normally the leaders of conservative, liberal, and labor parliamentary parties have long tenures of office. Thus, they bring to the highest executive office, when they achieve it, a breadth of experience in parliamentary and party affairs that few American Presidents can rival.

Moreover, the British-type parliamentary system grooms aspirants for office through the grueling responsibilities of leading the opposition. There is thus ample training and experience of leadership. In Continental countries, on the other hand, there is frequently a greater turnover of party leaders, especially in multiparty systems, so that leaders are less likely to acquire experience and thus forcefulness. We even find, occasionally, that the party leadership is separated from the leadership in government; thus, when Adenauer resigned his Chancellorship in favor of Ludwig Erhard, he retained the chairmanship of West Germany's Christian Democratic Union. Quite obviously, such a duality obfuscates the question of who directs policies, as well as of who is accountable to whom, and thus may result in conflict at the top level of political leadership. On the other hand, West Germans have developed the practice of having the opposition designate a "chancellor-candidate" well ahead of a new election—a leader who may or may not be identical with the formal party head; this has been done since the SPD in 1961, for the first time, chose a young, more charismatic standard-bearer, Willy Brandt, in place of an older and somewhat worn party leader. Since then, there have been more vigorous and dramatic political contests.

In countries such as Japan and India, which have one major party—or where one major party is practically always in government, while another one is in the "opposition of principle," as in Italy—political leadership is to all intents and purposes decided within the party. This obviously makes for factionalism. In Japan, it has also meant that what is decided elsewhere by general elections, i.e., who shall become Prime Minister, is determined by the intraparty processes within the leading Liberal-Democratic Party. Thus, it is factions rallying around different leaders that, in practice, take the place of parties, feuding and stalling for position, when the issue arises, as it did in Japan in mid-1972, of who should succeed as party leader, which, in effect, meant as head of the government. What goes on within the party may be politically more important, therefore, than what happens in the larger, outside arena of Japan's political life.

In the United States, the absence of an organized and cen-
trally led parliamentary opposition has meant that a defeated
presidential candidate generally has only a nominal and politically meaningless leadership function, especially in cases
where defeat has discredited him as a leader. The defeated
party then usually turns to someone new for leadership in
the next election. Thus, somewhat paradoxically, the system
that, potentially, vests the greatest authority of any democratic country in a single figure does least to provide training
and experience for the tremendous responsibilities of the
Presidency.

Among the new countries, the problem of succession is
made more difficult by the relatively small number of people
capable of assuming such responsibilities. Any country may
have a charismatic leader—and, in any system, the demands on,
and the response to, leadership will depend greatly on whether
the leader is charismatic or not—but the importance of personality is particularly great where there is little sense of
national unity and the party structure is fairly rudimentary.
Instead of being organizational, as in more developed democracies, leadership in the new states tends to be personal and
even self-selected (often rather through ability to hold conflicting groups together than through a struggle for power).
The steady disintegration of the Moslem League and its inability to provide coherent direction in Pakistan after the
death of one leader and the assassination of another illustrates
the great dependence of party organization on leadership in
developing states. There is not only a disturbing reliance on
one or a few leaders to hold together political organization
and to direct development, but, almost as a corollary reflecting the uncertainty about the succession, a degree of haste in
achieving results that may threaten constitutional procedures.
The large number of military takeovers in Africa, Asia, and
Latin America is a reflection of the lack of stable social unity
and settled patterns of action able to survive existing strains
and divisions.

The Selection and Responsibility of Lieutenants

The differences between the ways democratic and totalitarian states select political lieutenants are even more striking than are those concerning the selection of chief executives. Where political lieutenants obviously share power, as do the members of the cabinet in parliamentary systems, they are either formally appointed by the chief executive or (as is the case in Australia when the Labour Party is in office) selected by the caucus, i.e., the parliamentary members of the party. Under the doctrine of collective responsibility, everyone in the cabinet not only considers but also must publicly support government policy. If a minister wishes to oppose a policy outside the walls of the cabinet chamber, he must resign to do so. So long as he is in office, however, he both runs his department and assumes full responsibility for its policies before parliament and the public. The American Cabinet is also composed of political heads of departments, but it is a pale reflection of the British or Australian Cabinet as far as sharing power is concerned, for the extent of its members' responsibilities and policy-making depends on the will of the particular President. Under President Eisenhower, for example, Secretary of State John Foster Dulles had virtually unlimited discretion in the field of foreign affairs, while his successor, Christian Herter, had little and William Rogers under President Nixon much less. Cabinets in multiparty systems like that of the Fourth French Republic reflect impermanent coalitions, but for this very reason a minister may possess more independent authority than a British Cabinet minister, since, in the multiparty system, he is usually an individual of competence as well as the representative of a party whose support is essential to the life of the coalition. Moreover, in the realm of foreign affairs, for example, the tenure of a minister in the Fourth French Republic was often far longer than that of the Premier. Under the Fifth Republic, the concentration of power in the executive, the fact that a minister may not hold a seat in the legislature, and the tendency to use civil servants as ministers, have produced a situation in which the French Cabinet is more like the American than the British, while the chambers are far less vigorous than those of either Congress or the British Parliament. The same holds for West Germany, where the Chancellor, once he has been appointed by majority vote of Parliament, has the power (used vigorously by Adenauer throughout his tenure, though less so by his successors) to appoint, shift, and dismiss ministers without concern for Parliament or even for his party's approval in cases where the minister is of his own party.

In totalitarian states, lieutenants to the dictator occupy a far more equivocal position than do cabinet members in democratic states. Their selection is a reflection of the internal power struggle at a given moment. Even when the dictator seems to occupy an unquestioned position of authority, shifts may go on—as was seen throughout Stalin's regime—that exalt one person temporarily and then cause his disappearance or demotion. China has been notable for the constancy with which its top figures, Mao Tse-tung and Chou En-lai, have worked together, but, on the other hand, many, if not most, of their former associates disappeared during the "Cultural Revolution." Most Communist states, in practice, have felt the impact of the permanent purge or of the struggle for ultimate succession all the way to the highest levels.

INFORMAL CHANNELS OF ACCESS TO THE LEADER

In a period when government seems to consist largely of impersonal regulations applied to vast numbers of similar cases and situations, it may appear strange to put great weight on questions like: Who has the ear of a president? Who is most influential in the cabinet surrounding a prime minister? We expect *camarillas* to play their role in uncontrolled dictatorships, but in other systems stories of personal influence and intrigue in high places, of "gray eminences" and ruling mistresses, seem to belong to a past of dynastic and similar personal rule. Yet, personal friendship, kitchen cabinets, and similar influences have never ceased to play a role in democratic as well as in dictatorial systems. The problem has indeed gained new significance with the heightened tasks of political leadership and the increased urgency and secrecy surrounding it in the age of nuclear insecurity.

The area of governmental secrecy has grown increasingly for security and related reasons. The top level of policy-making has, of course, always been conducted in secrecy, even in the most advanced democracies, as witness the meetings and discussions of the British Cabinet or those of the American Cabinet and National Security Council. This is inevitable if there is to be free and frank discussion before policy decisions are taken. But the question remains of when, and to what extent, a democratic leadership should take the public into its confidence with regard to matters of grave and lasting concern, e.g., committing the nation to a new alliance, or honoring military obligations under old alliances, or, as in the case of American involvement in Vietnam, escalating or winding down a war. This, indeed, was the very issue around which centered the vehement, and sometimes violent, debates over the publication of the "Pentagon Papers."

While participation in such bodies is highly important, we discover from time to time that their members are not necessarily those whose words will be most influential on ultimate decisions. Department or agency heads in the United States, or even Cabinet Ministers in Great Britain, may be less influential, in practice, than unofficial aides, personal friends, or lieutenants, especially where, despite the enormous growth of his functions and powers, the leader is not provided with an appropriate official staff of his own. More important than top-ranking official advisers may be secretaries, appointment officers, or special, personal assistants, like Sherman Adams under Eisenhower, or Henry Kissinger under Nixon, or Hans Globke under Adenauer.

The mere fact of a chief executive's limited time points up the problem of access. Policy decision may depend on the appointment calendar—i.e., on who gains access to the holder of power and who does not, or on what the leader hears and reads and what he does not. Connected with this is another problem that looms so large these days—how best to coordinate "intelligence." The leader can absorb only so much; what is selected, and in what form it is presented, may determine his action or inaction, with far-reaching results. Instead of emphasizing the vast powers of the leader in a modern industrial state, some observers stress that the chief executive, perhaps particularly in the United States, is the prisoner of his staff.

The recent trend in the United States has been to give the President a large number of "assistants," formally based in the White House and with bureaucratic staffs inevitably duplicating the traditional departments and, in some instances, notably Henry Kissinger as Special Assistant for National Security Affairs, far outstripping these departments in influence. This situation creates a special problem for maintaining responsibility to the legislature and the public, because the President may refuse to allow his aides to testify before Congressional committees or to be publicly questioned. Thus, while it is vital to give executives the maximum aid of highly responsible assistants, it is no less important to ensure the kind of inquisitiveness into the wide range of governmental affairs that keeps ultimate decision-making in the hands of those to whom the public has entrusted that responsibility.

The Role and Selection of the Bureaucracy

The higher bureaucracy is as important in providing advice, aid, and also policy proposals as is the second line of executive leadership, the ministers. No man can hope to keep abreast of the multitudinous factors of modern administration. One of the most important talents a leader must have is the ability to delegate powers, although, if he is to fulfill his mandate from the people, he must also retain ultimate responsibility. The chief executive is also and necessarily the head of the administration. But, in democratic states, the administration carries the responsibility not only of executing the laws but also of seeing that they fulfill the purposes for which they were designed. Thus, the administration, and particularly the higher bureaucracy, must be constantly alert both to the purposes of the political leaders of the country and to the needs, as well as desires, of the public.

One major problem here is the relationship of the higher bureaucracy, which is supposed to be nonpolitical (in a party sense), and the political minister. It has often been feared that, with the democratization of the top-level executive, the impact of a permanent bureaucracy advising elected or transitory ministers might be injurious to the public interest. Nonexpert ministers might come under the influence of expert civil servants, who would take advantage of their position and their expertise to sabotage policies (in particular, reformist ones) or in other ways deflect them or shape them according to their own political preferences. Experience, for instance under Labour governments in Britain, tended to show that there was no danger of sabotage or outright resistance to political policies. It is always possible, however, especially in our times, where issues are growing increasingly complex, that bureaucrats may manage, by indirection, to stall or inhibit action simply by not making all possibilities or alternatives available to the political top. Here, again, we meet the problem of "access" to the decision-maker, only now it is access of information rather than of persons.

Another issue is that of a "representative" bureaucracy. The representative role of the bureaucracy, according to which the civil service should represent not only the political leadership but also the needs and desires of the public, is now generally accepted in democratic states. Yet, this concept was disputed in earlier times, with after-effects to the present day. The Prussian and subsequently Imperial German view was that the primary duty of public administration was to serve the purposes of the state rather than to provide services for the people. This concept had the advantage of establishing clear-cut and single-minded responsibility to the monarch, and it was saved from promoting arbitrariness by the insistence on the *Rechtsstaat,* the rule of law. This has been one of the reasons why, to this day, the ministerial bureaucracy in West Germany predominates in many political processes, especially vis-à-vis the legislature. But this view fitted ill with the notions of popular sovereignty characteristic of the French Revolution. Under their impact, law came to be regarded not merely as the will of the state, enunciated by its supreme figure, but as a collection of rules devised for the better organization of the affairs of the community. In this perspective, public power became transmuted into public service.

In France, syndicalism went a step further, maintaining that public employees were no different from private employees and should have the right, therefore, to organize in trade unions, engage in political activity, and publicly express their opinions even if these were contrary to those of the political leaders. But activities along these lines were among the factors that weakened Italy and Spain in their pre-Fascist period and facilitated the accession of authoritarianism; they were not without effect in undermining the postwar Fourth French Republic. What may be termed the public-service state, at least in countries following the Anglo-Saxon tradition, now, therefore, endorses these views: that the interests of the public are superior to those of any group of public servants; that employment by the state differs from private employment in the techniques and tactics that may legitimately be used in attempting to change conditions of service (in particular, strikes are not an acceptable means of pressure); and that, while government employees should have the right to exercise the franchise in their private capacities, there is a basic incompatibility between government employment and open political activity, at least at the level of government (i.e., local or national) at which service is being rendered.

These distinctions, it must be admitted, make less sense in jobs comparable to those in private service than in jobs that are unique to public service. In cases where some sectors of the economy are nationalized, there would seem little reason for treating employees differently from what would be the case if the services were privately supported—except that nationalization either creates or grows out of monopolies and often in spheres that provide essential public services, like transportation. Thus, a strike in a nationalized industry or service, like coal mining or air transportation, has far more impact on the country as a whole than would a strike against an individual enterprise. Nonetheless, as government spreads into new areas of activity, there is increasing reason to separate what might be called genuine public-law and basically private-law employment and to treat them differently. Few people can doubt, however, that special provisions and traditions are essential for the type of government employment for which there is no parallel in business.

But, if there is agreement on this fact, there are wide differences in the ways democratic states have handled problems of selection, training, and promotion, particularly for that all-important group, the higher bureaucracy, which is involved in policy-making almost as much as in administration. The British have recently eliminated their former rigid categories for particular types of responsibilities and broadened their recruitment processes. They use written and oral tests to evaluate intellectual capacities and character rather than demanding specialized courses of study and particular types of experience. The French, in contrast, have a special School of Administration, with three years of training in particular subject matters interspersed with firsthand experience in an administrative unit.

The British, and the older as well as a few of the newer members of the overseas Commonwealth, choose the highest departmental officials from the permanent service, thus making it a career service of great distinction, although they run the possible danger of substituting ability and experience for genuine sympathy with the programs being introduced. In France, a minister brings with him his own "cabinet" of administrators, who work with the regular departmental officials to see that the minister's policies are carried out in accordance with his wishes. Americans, on the other hand, have never wholly discarded their belief that practical experience in business or commerce may be more useful in government service than academically tested ability and long experience in government. Although it is more common these days to find top officials retaining their posts (particularly posts requiring technical skills) despite a change in administration, there is far more infiltration from outside into all ranks of government service in the United States than is the case in Great Britain or in European countries. This can be particularly valuable when a "new deal" is instituted and knowledge is combined with enthusiasm in those most concerned with introducing new measures, but it also limits the attractiveness of public service as a career. Moreover, short-term "political" appointments make decisiveness and continuity of policy difficult. In systems like the American, furthermore, there are the dangers ever inherent in "patronage"—that is, the practice antedating the establishment of a genuine "merit" system of civil service, in which public office is used to reward unqualified persons to whom party leaders are obligated politically or possibly financially (e.g., for contributions to campaign funds), or of appointing those who, in turn, will be beholden for their jobs to the person making the appointment or to the party. In such circumstances, by no means uncommon in other countries also, the danger of corruption—whether in the moral or even the criminal sense—is always present. On corruption, more will be said later, but, even without this danger, there is the other not inconsiderable one, particularly in the field of foreign service, of jeopardizing the national interest through inexperienced or incompetent representatives.

In these days of ever increasing and ever more demanding governmental planning and activity, the problem of "permanence" in the bureaucracy is intimately related to that of policy stability and consistency. No policy can be stable and consistent without some stability of roles. And these roles are played, of course, by those charged with putting a policy into effect; i.e., the executive bureaucracy. If there is a constant changing of cast within the administration, with personnel coming and leaving, or a too frequent exchange between governmental personnel and that of business, or interest or other groups, there cannot be reliance on consistent policies, or even attitudes. Some measure of experience outside government service is important for broadening points of view, but bureaucratic permanence and stability seem particularly important now when ecological catastrophes threaten, countermeasures become urgent, and the long-range concern for survival stands in contradiction to the short-range objective of particular interests. In a literal sense, then, the "common weal" must be taken care of by trained servants of the public and not by private individuals or by some extraneous group. These advantages of a stable and permanent service must be weighed against its potential disadvantages: red tape, clannishness, and caste spirit, the last of which seems almost inevitable wherever huge bureaucracies are built up (particularly in nondemocratic societies). But still more serious are the by-products of impermanence: inadequate policy implementation and the danger that special interests might permeate the service.

Subtle differences may result, however, from the class structure and the prestige of the higher civil service. If, as was long true in Great Britain, ministers and the higher bureaucracy are drawn from a certain group of families, schools, and universities, they tend to have similar implicit assumptions about how policy should be executed; yet, as we have said, the British Labor Party, upon assuming office, found that it could work well with the higher civil servants. But such a degree of national consensus on essentials did not exist in Weimar Germany, where the permanent service hampered, and even impeded, the implementation of democratically inclined or socially advanced policies, and thus contributed to that regime's weakness and ultimate collapse in 1933. The less class-conscious and more equalitarian American educational system leads to a more differentiated, if less intellectually inclined, higher public service than what exists in either Great

Britain, France, or Germany; though this has the advantage of representativeness, it does not balance the limitations of less marked ability.

The prestige a bureaucracy enjoys also has a bearing on the type of person it is able to attract. In Germany, at least until recently, the public official has had greater status than in any other European country, or possibly any place else, which reflects both a belief in the expert and an identification of bureaucracy with the state. In Sweden, Denmark, and Holland, he is trusted, but he is not regarded with anything like the same deference. The Swiss, French, Italians, and Spanish are openly critical of their public servants, though the last two with more reason than the first. Americans, with their traditional idealization of the businessman, are only gradually acquiring the degree of respect for public service that the British have long held, and they are also learning that such respect and the standards of the service tend to reinforce each other.

If such factors are so influential, can it be said that the higher civil service is ever neutral in its attitudes toward public questions? Perhaps not; but should it be? The kinds of issues dealt with by the top level of bureaucrats for the most part are not those that can be handled by reference to rules. They are policy-raising issues for which no legislature and no executive can provide all the directives. Higher civil servants are confronted constantly by the need to use their own discretion in determining how best to carry out a policy so that its results will be in the public interest. This necessitates a sensitivity to tensions within the community and to genuine needs, as opposed to spurious claims, that taxes every faculty. The best members of the higher bureaucracy are likely to be those who are not hidebound either by ideology or by special class interests, public servants who can retain an open mind and a sympathetic understanding of public needs and purposes. If, as is true in democratic states, the public servant is immediately responsible to the elected executive, the ultimate responsibility of both is to the people.

Bureaucracy in the New States

Nowhere are administrative skill, experience, and public responsibility more needed than in the new states. Their very poverty of material resources and accumulated capital thrusts upon them a multitude of tasks in their efforts to become "modern." Almost all these tasks must be directed or supervised by the public service. Yet, it is generally in this field that their needs are greatest. The five hundred top Indian administrators who, up to the time India attained independence, shared the subcontinent's major governmental responsibilities with an equal number from Great Britain itself, constituted perhaps the most valuable heritage of British rule in India. That Pakistan could claim only about seventy of those trained for high posts under British rule caused major difficulties in Pakistan's task of administrative construction and contributed to the laxities that paved the way for army rule. India's more than four hundred trained administrators were of vast help in its early years of independence and ambitious development projects.

In comparison, the independent African countries have been handicapped, indeed. In the former British and French territories in Africa, arrangements were commonly made for former colonial officials to remain in office until Africans were trained to take their places. Moreover, many of the new African states found it necessary to increase the number of expatriate employees in their public service in order to keep up with the expansion of responsibilities resulting from development projects; they have also drawn on the resources of international agencies. The Africanization of their administrative services started later and, in all too many cases, was accelerated at the expense of training and quality.

The new states face special handicaps in building their administrative services. Their educational structures taper quickly to the point of the pyramid; primary education is now widespread, but secondary-level facilities remain inadequate. Moreover, those who succeed in completing secondary schools frequently go on through the university, thereby increasing the numbers available for professional administrative posts, but leaving almost no one to fill the highly important secondary rung of executive and even secretarial posts. A further problem arises from the need to replace traditional family-oriented loyalties by loyalty to the state. Traditional norms in many non-Western societies demand what we condemn as nepotism, i.e., providing jobs for family members; there is also a less sharp differentiation between public money and private money. A further problem is that, if one member of a family has a well-paid post, his relatives often assume that he will support them, or that, if training takes place abroad, there is the temptation to remain there. Thus, even where administrative skills exist, the new states have their own particular problems in developing the kind of relationship between the elected executive and the public administration that befits a democratically organized state. In the light of all these difficulties and of the great pressures for development, therefore, the achievements of the new states rather than their shortcomings should be highlighted.

The Phenomenon of Corruption

Bureaucracy is often accused of either arrogance or corruption (or, sometimes, both). It has been perceptively observed that, "A bureaucracy may be corrupt, but if it is accessible to the ordinary citizen, corruption by itself will not be seen as very important. Conversely, an efficient, incorruptible civil service will be seen as acceptable even if it is aloof. But the combination of corruption with arrogance is impossible to ignore."*

However this may be (and one may doubt whether the two are really unbearable only in conjunction), corruption may become as serious a problem for the moral and actual survival of a democratic community as does unlawful use of force by its officials. Corruption is primarily a phenomenon of

* See editor's introduction to A. H. Syed, "Bureaucratic Ethic and Ethos in Pakistan," *Polity*, IV, no. 2 (Winter, 1971), 159.

discrepancy between the fundamental moral and legal norms of a group and their actual observance (or, rather, nonobservance). Even in developing African countries, or other "modernizing" regions, where patronage in favor of the extended family is an integral part of their way of life, development and modernization also mean the introduction of standards of probity, of nondiscriminatory and nonpreferential recruitment, and so forth. Inevitably, therefore, the old community standards will begin to clash with the new rules; and the "modernizers," who accept the new standards as morally binding, will begin to regard the observance of the old ones as corruption.

In the modernized countries, corruption implies the clash between what one pays lip-service to (the "Sunday creed" of good and honest behavior patterns) and what the political or moral "culture" tolerates, or even prescribes as acceptable standards and patterns. This type of corruption must be distinguished from that existing in generally uncorrupt societies, where, as is bound to happen, corrupt deeds are occasionally committed, though they are few and far between, performed surreptitiously and condemned by most. In the latter situations, fighting corruption becomes a matter of effective criminal law and prosecution. The problem is much more serious where corruption has become the way of life for entire groups, such as, for example, the public service, or some section of it. Here, not only is it not condemned, but it becomes so much the standard of behavior that uncorrupted members of the group are considered "disloyal," indeed, traitors to the group; they are ostracized and threatened with revenge, and are often unable to find redress even at the highest level of government or, indeed, the courts.

This is illustrated by one statement by a public servant:

I remember in Denver, I think 1961, the Police Department was relatively free of corruption. It developed a burglary ring among some of the patrolmen there, and another patrolman became aware of it, reported his findings to the chief, and the chief sent him to the psychiatrist for examination. When the psychiatrist

sent him back to the chief, saying he was perfectly sane and tell-
ing the truth, the chief reluctantly acted on the accusation. There
were indictments. . . but the chief had to leave, had to resign,
and the officer who uncovered it had to resign and leave the city.

So this is the problem—that policemen know that if they ex-
pose corruption, they are taking a substantial risk of alienating
themselves from their fellow officers.*

Because groups are able to engage in such behavior patterns only with the connivance or collaboration of outside individuals or groups, corruption becomes contagious. It draws
in entire segments of society, and thus the value-pattern and
way of life of the community is undermined. Particularly
glaring "scandals" make the headlines for a while, but, since
too many people and activities are involved, it becomes un-
likely that much will be achieved either through trials and
prosecution or by way of reform, and public attention will
soon be diverted to some other scandal. Thorough investigation of police corruption in the city of New York revealed
what has been pointed out above. "Informers" (the term itself reflects the negative image, in the eyes of the corrupt
group, of the uncorrupt who lend their services to the investigating authorities) may subsequently become victims of frame-
ups or of outside groups, such as the Mafia, with a vested
interest in continued corruption.

This kind of corruption, with "unwritten codes of honor"
(see the self-assumed name of the Mafia: the "Honorable Society") and its own "esprit de corps" as group-integrating factors, does not appear only in bureaucracies. It can be found
as well in groups like the military, which, as in the case of
war crimes committed by members of the U.S. armed forces
in Vietnam or in the case of disregard of orders coming from
the top civilian level (as revealed in the Lavelle case—likewise
in Vietnam), may engage in exculpation and covering-up to the

---

* From testimony heard by the Knapp Commission on Police Corruption in New York City, *New York Times,* October 30, 1971. The Report
of the Knapp Commission, released in August, 1972, refers to the "code
of silence" that brands anyone who exposes corruption as a "traitor."

highest level. What, under totalitarian structures, is a result of "legal" orders (as the Nazi atrocities), may become, under authoritarian structures in democracies, a matter of "illegal," but tolerated and even expected, behavior. For the victims, however, the effect is the same. For democratic society at large, such corruption becomes one of its gravest threats, for it puts into doubt the underlying norms of that society.

Bureaucracy in Totalitarian States

Totalitarian states face an inherent dilemma in regard to their administrative services. They depend on them far more than would any democratic state, particularly one in whose economy private enterprise assumes a major role. Their very dependence on administrators to manage the economy as well as all other services, however, threatens to run contrary to the concentration of power in the hands of the party. Efficient administration dictates its own rules of organization, i.e., fixed jurisdictions, hierarchical chain of command, reliance on written orders, dependence on specialists, and stable routines. Yet, this regularity contrasts sharply with pressures of what we have called the permanent purge. In other words, the two major means whereby totalitarian states, and in particular the Soviet Union have controlled all aspects of life—the bureaucracy and the Party—require opposing conditions for their maximum effectiveness: the former, stability; the latter, constant ferment.

These counterpulls have evidenced themselves throughout the history of the Soviet Union. Marxist dogma, of course, condemned bureaucracy as an instrument of bourgeois oppression. Lenin originally thought the workers themselves would be able to administer the state and industry. Since the importance of administrative skills and responsibility quickly became apparent in the Soviet state, however, Party members were assigned to watch over managerial operations. Under the Five-Year Plans—the channels for the great industrial expansion of the Soviet Union—professional administrators began to achieve a privileged status, and they became important

Party members. Even then, however, they were exposed periodically to impossible demands and to the fear of punishment for failure to meet them. In order to fulfill their quotas, ministries would try to corral supplies, transport, and labor. Khrushchev himself was our authority on some of the resulting absurdities that led to duplication of effort in some instances and lack of use of resources in others (one ministry, for instance, moved goods in its own ships in one direction only, allowing the ships to return empty, while another ministry was doing exactly the same in the opposite direction). Khrushchev's own administrative reorganization in 1957 sought to avoid such waste by breaking up the top-heavy ministries centralized in Moscow under the Stalinist regime. Still more important from his point of view, however, the reorganization undercut the power of the managerial class, broke up the bureaucratic concentration in the capital, and brought industry under the control of well-entrenched regional Party agents. As with so many other policies that Khrushchev promoted, this one was designed to enhance the power of the Party by simplifying its task of maintaining supervision over the economic bureaucracy, i.e., that part of the administration that directs industry. Yet, inevitably, the new administrative patterns that developed soon solidified.

The dominant characteristic of the Brezhnev-Kosygin regime is the relatively harmonious cooperation between Party and administration from the lowest level of industry throughout the entire structure. The Party in each segment, and hierarchically from the top down, applies the whip to achieve stated goals, but the goals are worked out rationally with administrative specialists whose technical know-how is respected. Thus, ultimate political power is vested firmly in Party hands; but the Party itself works with, and through, the heavily bureaucratized state, whose expertness also exerts constant pressures toward technical advance.

Other Communist countries have confronted similar problems affecting what they call their "cadres" (staffs). In China, the chief cause of the "Cultural Revolution" appears to have been Mao's fear that the revolutionary enthusiasm of the first-generation revolutionary cadres was yielding to routinized bureaucratism, in the Party itself as well as in the general administration. Thus, he ·called upon the young, in particular the Red Guards, to rise against these cadres and to invest their offices with the spirit of "permanent revolution." In a system like the Maoist, with its emphasis on decentralization and workers' initiative, such an increasingly elitist and ossified administration becomes a threat that must be expunged. Yet, as with all such movements, the "Cultural Revolution" went too far, threatening to throw the entire system into chaos; it even found itself setting up bureaucrats of its own, this time drawn from the military. The Maoist faction lost no time in warning these, too, not to presume to seek dominance, as witness the subsequent disappearance of Lin Piao, who had been named in 1969 as Mao's heir-apparent.* Whether, however, a final balance has been struck among the various factions in China is still an open question.

THE ROLE OF PRESSURE GROUPS

Modern "pluralistic" society, which is dynamic and consists of large numbers of economic, occupational, religious, possibly ethnic, and other groups, inevitably confronts the problem of the relation between these "interests" and those of government and politics. In an open society, interest groups will be permitted to organize themselves freely; they will, therefore, not only engage in an interplay of forces vis-à-vis each other (such as employers and employees in worker-manager relations) but also tend to bring their influence to bear on the machinery and the processes of government, which affect them through laws, rulings, licenses, taxation, and innumerable other legislative and administrative acts. "Interests" thus turn into "pressure groups," and their activities into

---

* According to the official Chinese version, given by Chou En-lai in 1972 to visiting American journalists, Lin Piao and several other members of his clique attempted and failed to bring off a military coup, and died when the plane in which they fled China crashed in neighboring Mongolia.

pressures upon government. Indeed, "group theory" in political science has tended to interpret almost everything that goes on in government and politics as the outgrowth of the interplay between interest groups, on the one hand, and government, on the other. While the effect of this interplay may be exaggerated, it is advisable not to commit the opposite mistake and, as political scientists did for a long time, either underestimate or neglect the role of pressure groups.

In speaking earlier of the way in which influence is brought to bear on key men, particularly the top figures in the executive and the administration, we mentioned the influence of aides and advisers, and the importance of their recruitment, their access to the leader, and so forth. But the general problem of influence in government is far more complex and has many more dimensions than we have so far indicated. Every administration, whether democratic or dictatorial, has its own internal rivalries, strains, and divisions of opinion. Some of these strains derive from self-seeking, some from genuine differences of view among leaders or the parties they represent, some from overspecialization, and others from lack of knowledge and experience. Finally, there are some strains—and these may be particularly important—that are the result of outside influences and pressures.

Many people feel that pressure groups are necessarily harmful, because they seek to exalt the interests of small, though possibly wealthy or highly organized, segments of the population, thereby disregarding the interests of all, or of a substantial segment of, the people. But this view is not necessarily correct. Much depends, in this respect, on whether *all* interest groups, and not only the more powerful and better organized ones, get a hearing, and, second, on whether these groups, in their own internal organizations, function in such a way that their entire membership rather than entrenched oligarchies determine their policies. In other words, it is a question of how much democracy, in the sense of responsibleness, there is in the internal structure of these groups, as well as in their relation to government and society at large.

It must thus be one of the objectives of political democracies to bring into the open the pressures of, and response to, influence groups, so that their source and impact can be evaluated by the general public. Public responsibility requires sufficient openness about how political and administrative decisions are reached, so that undue influence can be corrected. In this process, the alertness of the press, and the investigations and exposés by political commentators like Jack Anderson in the United States, may be of great value in turning a spotlight on the self-seeking interactions of interest groups and public figures. It is a major shortcoming of undemocratic systems that the pressures which do exist, in fact, even under the most centralized dictatorial controls, are kept secret, so that the people have no way of knowing who is in charge and responsible for what.

Where they work in the open, however, pressure groups fulfill a necessary and potentially wholesome function. They may form a link between the people and the government, of which administrators or legislators can make use to secure information on facts and attitudes. For example, any democratic government would expect to consult farmers' organizations before instituting new farm programs and also in evaluating existing ones. As a matter of fact, lobbying can claim to follow two essentially democratic procedures: the right to participate in the formulation of policy and the right to redress of grievances. So long as pressure groups are not permitted to usurp the political function, their specialized knowledge of attitudes and facts can provide that connection between the ruled and the rulers without which the latter cannot be responsible to its public. Thus, the problem created by pressure groups is not that they are consulted, but that they sometimes use corrupt methods, like bribery or more subtle favors, to influence legislators or administrators. Under these latter circumstances, they not only lower standards of public morality but also distort to their own advantage policy that is or should be designed for the public interest.

This danger of distortion can become great in countries

with highly organized interest groups, some of which have developed the techniques of influence into a fine art. Where, in addition to this situation, the public has become used to such practices, expects them as a matter of course, and accepts their effects without much questioning, politics threatens to degenerate into a mere "Who gets what, when, and how." More, perhaps, than in other countries, pressure groups have, in fact, become something of a fifth estate in the American system of government, and it is not without reason that the most detailed studies of pressure groups and pressure politics have been of those operating on the American scene—which in itself provides some safeguards through the resulting publicity of pressure-group activities.

The American party system, with its lack of centralization (except at election time), of discipline, and of firm leadership, lends itself to the pressures of special-interest groups. So, too, does the separation of powers, which opens the way to exploiting not only rivalries, but what is often a disturbing lack of communication and integration between, and even within, the different branches. Moreover, the public passively acquiesces, for the most part, in the open tug of war between rival interest groups and, in what may be still more costly, alliances between them through which potentially conflicting claims are resolved in a manner detrimental to the public interest. Management and labor, for example, may agree on large wage increases, but such an agreement often runs counter to the interests of consumers in preventing higher prices and consequent inflation. Such connivance, combined with other factors, had resulted in such severe economic strains in the United States by 1971 that the government felt forced to intervene with virtually unprecedented peacetime wage and price controls. Also, lobbies may combine in order to raise tariffs, with some of the same inflationary pressures.

Because economic concentration has gone so far in the United States, there is constant and all too often well-founded suspicion among liberals that political power is subject to economic power, whether exercised through open lobbying or through the influence of businessmen who hold high office in the administration for a period of time, or through dubious practices. According to the Communists, of course, government in a capitalist economy inevitably becomes an instrument in the hands of dominant economic interests, and the political leaders become the "running dogs" of the bourgeoisie. While this view grossly exaggerates the impact of economic power, there can be little question that corporate wealth does influence the power of government. In Great Britain, France, and Germany, as well as in the United States, administrators find it more convenient to consult with big business and its representatives than with the multitude of small ones. In an effort to consider both large and small interests, the British have institutionalized a whole system of advisory councils; similarly, each ministry in Bonn also has its *Beiräte,* or advisory councils of interest representatives. But organizations of big corporations are more streamlined, their information is more clearly defined, their actions are more predictable, and thus their influence is greater. Beyond this, the resources of big corporations make it possible for them to exert pressure on the many levels of the American administrative and legislative processes. So, too, do the resources of the big labor unions, some of which have as marked a concentration of authority as do corporations. All the more important, therefore, to have a permanent civil service capable of withstanding undue and improper pressures.

Interest groups may also exert pressure for change through the judicial system. The most striking examples of this approach have been the successful effort of the National Association for the Advancement of Colored People to secure the U.S. Supreme Court judgment that the segregation of the races is unconstitutional, and the continuing series of cases brought to secure the implementation of that judgment in schools, public accommodations, and other particular situations. On the whole, however, pressure groups concentrate on administrative bureaus or ministries and on committee chairmen and party leaders. Many of the proposals for new public policy come, it must be noted, from such pressure groups, but, on balance, it seems as if pressure politics have had less effect through causing innovations than through preventing change. The long campaign against national health insurance in the United States was a classic example of the latter process.

If the party and governmental systems in the United States facilitate the impact of private pressures on policy-making, the strength of the national consensus to some extent limits their divisive effect. But in France, under the Fourth Republic, the situation was more serious. The growing lack of discipline in the political parties, other than the Communists, opened the way for an ever increasing influence by pressure groups, particularly those of the business lobby, until at times it surpassed that of the parties themselves, while the lack of public agreement on political and social values provided a milieu in which conflict became exaggerated rather than resolved. Contemporary Italy suffers much the same problems. In Great Britain, in contrast, a highly structured bureaucracy and highly disciplined political parties keep the decision-making process firmly in control, and pressure groups become a major means of keeping them constantly in touch with a wide variety of attitudes toward public policy—a situation paralleled by that in West Germany.

It is apparent, therefore, that the strength or weakness of the political decision-making process is of great significance for the role that pressure groups play in particular political systems. In addition, the type of the political system has a good deal to do with the way in which pressures operate. In that type of parliamentary system in which basic decisions are made at the top level of the executive rather than in parliament, as in Great Britain or West Germany—i.e., where most bills originate with the respective executive departments and their ministerial bureaucracy—pressure-group lobbyists are more likely to besiege the executive than they are members of parliament. Where, as traditionally in France before the Fifth Republic and now in Italy, the legislature predominates, at least in the lawmaking process, the deputies bear the brunt.

Under a system of separate powers, as in the United States, pressures are likely to affect both branches equally. Likewise, the way in which parties represent or reflect particular interests has a bearing on the chances and methods of pressures. Where, as in the United States, both Republicans and Democrats appeal to all the major strata of society, pressures operate on and within both. What becomes particularly important, then, is: Whom does an individual congressman or member of a state legislature represent? How susceptible is he to influence? And so forth. Where, as in Britain, the two major parties represent (among others) two distinct classes and their interests, these two parties themselves, in a way, function as interest groups. This fact becomes clear when one counts the number of trade unionists among Labor MP's or of businessmen among Conservative MP's. In West Germany and Japan, a substantial number of officials from the staffs of professional and occupational organizations serve as elected deputies in Parliament. Thus, the lobby, so to speak, invades and infiltrates the representative machinery itself.

The "takeover" phenomenon, however, is not limited to the legislature. To the extent that executive departments are set up to deal with specific areas of the economy (e.g., labor, commerce, and agriculture), they may come to be considered, and themselves act as if they were, servants of the corresponding interests (e.g., outposts of the trade unions, the business community, or the big farmers' organizations). To some extent, this is legitimate; but, if the top incumbents forget that, in addition to safeguarding the interests of their particular clientele, they must also protect those of the public as a whole and implement the over-all policies of the government as such, the danger arises that the government may become merely the arena of a fight in which opposing forces and interests pull hither and thither and the common weal is submerged.

This tug of war is what is so often implied in the term—and phenomenon—of "conflict of interest" (and the scandals provoked by it in government and administration). Big business, big labor, and big agriculture, as well as their subdivisions, in many respects tend to resemble a new "feudalism," under which public power and interest become vassals of the dominating interests. A system like the American, with its many political appointees and the constant interchange of persons between public service and business or similar outside professions, inevitably creates conflicts of interest among those temporarily occupying an official position. The Pentagon official (or general) in charge of defense contracts, already visualizing himself in the corporation post of his opposite number after he resigns (or retires) from his present job, may not seek to represent the public interest wholeheartedly in negotiating a contract. The lawyer in the antitrust division of the Justice Department may already think of becoming an attorney for big corporations, where he can then apply what he has learned in government service against the government. Can he, then, be trusted to act forcefully as an official of the government? A wildlife official in the Interior Department, at the insistence of ranchers, lends his services to destroy rather than to protect a species; mine inspectors of the Department of Labor, beholden to, or under pressure from, coal interests, apply regulations laxly; and so forth. Preventive action and its enforcement are here of the essence in protecting the public interest. Thus, the Bonn Defense Ministry has issued regulations under which no former official is allowed to reappear as a negotiator of defense contracts for the opposite side for a number of years after leaving office. No such restrictions, however, exist in the United States.

Yet, the top level of government usually has a better chance of combating undue pressure than the local level. A local community, anxious to keep an industrial enterprise and the employment it provides, may be pressured into not taxing it enough to help provide for decent schooling or urban renewal, or into closing its eyes when that factory pollutes its river. A ministry is not under such direct pressure. This is another reason why, if the great community tasks of our age are to be taken care of efficiently, they must be at least supervised by the central government.

In this connection, too, the type and attitude of leadership will be decisive. Especially in a country like the United States, where the parties are the chief representatives of competing interests, the national mandate of the Presidency is of utmost importance. If there is no integration of the plurality of groups and interests at this point, there will be none at all. Still, the American system, where interests, though working in and through parties, are not organized *as* parties, is at an advantage compared with systems where coalition governments made up from interest parties have difficulty in rising above a mere dividing up of the commonwealth to their own advantage.

Much also depends, in this connection, upon the social origin of the political elite. In countries where, as until recently in Britain and still largely in Germany, political leadership is restricted to an educated class drawn from a relatively small upper stratum, leadership may identify national interest with that of narrower groups and classes. But this is not necessarily the case. Not infrequently, a feeling of *noblesse oblige* leads persons of aristocratic or similar upper-class backgrounds to act in a more broadminded, liberal, and even democratic way than those from a lower stratum would do. This has been true in America, too. More democracy in the selection of the political elite has not always resulted in less personal, social, or similar bias. At the same time, while European countries may display class restrictions in selection, the "classless" society of the United States still manifests actual, though not legal, restrictions based on ethnic origin, or religious affiliation, or sex, or color.

A free world engaged in competition with a system in which a jungle type of struggle for political survival tends to bring the most ruthless to the fore can ill afford to place restrictions on the selection of the ablest among its citizens. It is, therefore, confronted with a twofold educational problem: first, how to educate the citizenry so that, free from bias and unaffected by the hullabaloo of the hucksters, it will make intelligent choices; and, second, in what amounts to a modern version of the age-old problem of the "education of the prince," how to develop in its potential leaders that combination of knowledge, ability and integrity, out of which they will act both with authority and with responsibility, the hallmarks of democratic leadership.

The importance of such leadership is heightened by two relatively new developments. One of these situations is found primarily in the domestic sphere of developed countries, where the increasing affluence of a considerable proportion of the population is shifting the urgency of governmental functions to the much neglected public sector. Since, by now, it is a collection of minorities rather than, as in the past, a majority that is seriously underprivileged economically or racially, it is more difficult, though no less necessary, to marshal support for them through a framework of majority procedures. Internationally, the developed nations are confronted with a somewhat comparable situation. Here, *they* constitute the affluent few who must help the vast masses of the developing world. Democratic leadership, in both situations, has the difficult task of convincing a majority of their people to act on behalf of the interests of others, even though this may involve severe sacrifices. But, if they fail to do so, the democracies will not only be defeated morally and politically by their chief opponents, but will deny their own basic values.

VI

BELIEF SYSTEMS AND POLITICS

The Role of Ideology

At the beginning of this book, we pointed out that the deepest challenge of totalitarianism lies in its claim that it alone can fill the spiritual void left by the decline of established religion in the modern age. Beyond their material wants, men need a belief in the meaningfulness of their lives, a faith in some higher cause to which they as individuals as well as the groups to which they belong can be devoted. Many believe that in this period of change and crisis, liberal democracy is failing to answer this need.

Behind these issues lies another problem. It can be summed up in these questions: What ties political communities together? What is it that forms those feelings and attitudes of attachment to the group—that minimum of allegiance without which a political community can neither be established nor endure? We live in an era of numerous and strongly devisive views, interests, and centers of allegiance, and even those of us who live in relatively normal conditions cannot overlook how large is the incidence of strain and emergency in this century: What percentages of populations have had to flee from persecution or have become victims of domestic strife or foreign wars? How many have tried to escape rural starvation only to vegetate in overcrowded shanty towns? How many have become victims of military or police brutality, or, out of dire need, criminals, drifters, drug addicts, in short, "dregs of society?" How many have been condemned to a lifetime sentence served in slums or ghettos? What, under such conditions, gives cohesion to a political community?

We in the West have long ignored these problems, largely

because we have been under the influence of individualism—that mainstream of modern social and political thought. Whether it bases itself upon the concept of an original social or political contract or upon the concept of utility, individualism has assumed that political units, like nation-states, are founded upon, or could and should be founded upon, the free and voluntary association of self-determining, rational, enlightened human beings. We have tended to overlook the impact of sheer coercion; the impact of irrational, emotional attitude patterns, born of frustration and despair, that may lead to the rule of the few and the subjection of the many; and the impact of tradition and custom, especially in the "socialization" of the young—i.e., the way in which younger generations are adjusted to the "establishment" into which they are born, whether it be through formal education or through the influence of the family.

Edmund Burke, two centuries ago, pointed out that a country is more than a utilitarian or contractual association; that its cohesion rests less on interests and is less braced by reason than it is founded on custom and tradition; and that even prejudice may serve to preserve the "ancient order into which we are born." To many moderns, this may sound like tribalism; but even Rousseau, who differed from Burke in so many respects, called for a "civil religion" so that the "general will" of a free community would be sure to prevail.

To talk of maintaining or even instilling the right prejudices, or of enforcing a civil religion, points up a basic dilemma in the relations between the individual and the community. We have been apt to forget that the attempt to render the individual autonomous and to make him the foundation of free communities and limited government has been relatively rare and recent in history. For, during most of the history even of Western Europe, and of most of the world until the present or the recent past, political communities, however they were first established (i.e., by war, by conquest, or, occasionally, by free compact), have been kept together by an unquestioning, traditionalist allegiance of the ruled to the rulers. Generally, there was no conscious effort to indoctrinate the people, nor even to mold their attitudes and opinions through formal education; this was not necessary. It was the prevailing atmosphere, the transmitted value and belief systems, that provided these standards. And it was in large part the churches that provided whatever institutional and organizational apparatus was required to ensure their hold. Only rarely, with the complete disintegration of a belief system, was there a chance for basic change or even revolution.

But with the era of the Enlightenment came a great change in attitude. To many people, it seemed desirable to conduct human affairs on the basis of conscious, deliberate, and free acceptance of value standards, whether they eventually turned out to be religious or not. Loyalty freely given, so one believed, provides a stronger and more democratic foundation of nations than does an enforced allegiance—or even a less consciously and more traditionally established allegiance. Thus, such loyalty has become the truly democratic ideal.

The Appeal of Fascism

Frequently, however, it is only the few who know how to develop their own personal beliefs and how to make these beliefs the basis of living together with others in political communities. This explains why, after traditional authoritarian rulership has lost its grip, it is often a new, irrational emotion, nationalism, that ensures the cohesion of existing units or makes for the formation of new ones. When nationalism is simply a moderate and relatively calm feeling of belonging to that group which constitutes the nation, it could still be reconciled with a liberal-democratic individualism. But, to the extent that nationalism becomes the substitute religion of those who need one or are possessed of more extreme and fervent feelings of attachment, it becomes a focal point for emphatic identification with one group, and antagonism, even hatred, toward all others. Thus, nationalism, in many parts of the world, became converted into an ideology of exclusivism and, in a variety of forms (racialism, bellicism, imperialism, Social Darwinism, political romanticism), emerged as the doctrinal foundation of various fascist movements, of which Italian Fascism and Nazism have been the most conspicuous examples.

Nationalism is one basis of modern totalitarian ideology. Another has been the need for a coherent philosophy of government and politics, a political *Weltanschauung*, that arises once the masses of the people have been called upon to participate in politics. It is well known how this need contributed to the appeal of Nazism: The individual who is frustrated by a society that has lost its grip begins looking for a new allegiance and identification through common hatreds and enmities, and finds an outlet in nationalism; nationalism becomes the feeling that separates him and "his" group from all outside "foes." But the friend-foe relationship in fascism becomes the basis underlying *all* political attitudes and action. The foe may be within, or without, or both: it may be Jews, considered as a racial group, in the Nazi version of anti-Semitism; it may be Africans, as in the racism of potential poor whites in South Africa, or blacks, as in American Southern (and now also other) states. Such protofascist attitudes may take the form of xenophobia—the antiforeignism of the Enoch Powell variety in Britain or of the James Schwarzenbach variety in Switzerland directed against immigrants and foreign workers—or of anti-Catholicism, as of the Ulster Protestants; it may assume the shape of syndicalism, which characterized the earlier stages of Mussolini's as well as Franco's fascism, directed against both foreigners and domestic "exploiters"; or, finally, it may reveal itself simply as anti-Communism of the McCarthy or Birchite type, which finds internal as well as external foes in the global conspiracy of world Communism. The masses supporting such movements are frequently people lost in the maze of modern society, who, alienated from traditional ways of life, look for safe and absorbing new ones in belief systems of this nature. The leadership usually emerges from those who fear that their economic interests may be harmed by new trends in the economy (e.g., small businessmen afraid of being wiped out by corporate concentration) or from those frightened by the threats—imagined or real—of revolutionary unrest and upheaval. Where socialism, Communism, or the demands of hitherto discriminated racial groups seem to threaten vested interests, these quickly despair of democratic processes to counter the threat and turn to the person or group promising stern reaction and strong leadership.

We have so far been talking of fascist ideology and fascist movements, not of the fascist type of government and its politics (with which we have dealt in preceding chapters). But it is important to realize that a kind of "protofascist" atmosphere of the type just outlined may well exist in nontotalitarian systems, even liberal-democratic ones. Such an atmosphere, or trend, then indicates a weakness, or even sickness, in the existing system. Protofascism may all too often cloak its program by adopting the slogans of a seemingly progressive and reform-minded "populism." When groups like blue-collar workers and others become alienated from established parties, they may fall for the partly antiestablishment and antirich but partly, also, racist, anti-Semitic, anti-intellectual, xenophobic, in short, illiberal slogans of a Duplessis in Quebec, a Poujade in France's Fourth Republic, or a George Wallace in the United States. A similar pseudopopulism was a basis of European fascism.

Thus, the rise of a fascist atmosphere has been classically based on the failure of party regimes to live up to democratic ideals and objectives. Especially when accompanied by widespread corruption and a pervasive feeling of "anything goes" and *"enrichissez-vous,"* deep distrust of existing political processes ("it's all politics") and of those who operate and control them ("dirty politicians") may lead to a loss of authority that may presage the downfall of a regime. It is under such circumstances that disintegration of a nontotalitarian system sets in. Events may then lead to revolution, either of the fascist-authoritarian or else of the Communist variety. Even though, as we shall see in our next chapter, chances of such a development, at least in the industrialized countries, are not great, the danger that, under the impact of such movements, a liberal-democratic system will turn in the direction of authoritarianism is considerable.

The Appeal of Communism

If fascism has provided one kind of modern totalitarian ideology (especially in the form of Nazism), Communism, in the form of Marxism-Leninism, provides another that, at this point, is even more virulent than fascism. While the fascist *Weltanschauung,* in its various shapes, is fuzzy and emotional, Communist philosophy has some rational appeal because of its allegedly scientific explanation of historical evolution and current conditions. This characteristic has attracted many, especially intellectuals, who would reject the irrational mysticism and the racial or ultranationalist fanaticism of fascism.

Just as there is a moderate form of nationalism out of which grows the extreme type underlying fascism, the original Marxist ideology was by no means the extreme, doctrinaire "Communist" creed that it became in the hands of Lenin and his followers. Into Marxism went many eighteenth- and nineteenth-century trends and ideas of a liberal and democratic character, ideas and ideals of equality of classes and races, the right of individuals freely to develop their personality, opposition to war, and an internationalism that believed in the common brotherhood of all men and nations. Its development toward the emphasis on power, on organized violence in the service of a revolutionary movement, on the "dictatorship of the proletariat," and on intolerance toward all competing movements, while to some extent inherent in original Marxism, came mostly because Lenin believed that all of these were necessary for ultimate victory; once socialism had been attained, there could be a reversion to the original ideals of liberation and nonviolence.

Another, quite different outgrowth of Marxist doctrine appeared in progressive labor movements. These movements shared its criticism of the exploitative conditions of developing capitalism and industrialization. Nineteenth-century socialism tended toward more extreme forms in Russia, where Tsarist autocracy maintained social and cultural backwardness despite the small but advanced industrial structure. In countries like Britain and the United States, on the other hand, where there was a more flexible response to industrialism, the impact of socialism on the labor movement was more pragmatic and less doctrinaire.

The rapidly forming proletariat in Germany lay between these two extremes. There, Marxism had a special appeal to people suffering from the *anomie*—lack of basic communal attachments and values—that characterizes the transition stage from the traditionalism of a rural population to the "modernity" of urbanized crowds (the same *anomie* can be observed in developing nations undergoing the same transition). On the basis of this new *Weltanschauung*, German Social Democracy established an entire "subculture" of a class not admitted to the "higher" culture of the German elite. Subsequently, amelioration of working conditions and increasing integration of the proletariat into a common society attenuated the hold of the doctrine or led to its replacement by a social reformism characteristic of, for instance, the Fabian "gradualism" of the nonideological British labor movement. Thus, in the developed countries of the West, the appeal of Communism has lessened. In a somewhat cynical vein, one might, perhaps, say that the British and American worker never was a Marxist; that the German was, but no longer is; that the French and Italian was not, seems to be now, but is getting more reformist every day; and that the Russian had better be.

In studying belief systems, we should not forget that democratic socialism, when it had a *Weltanschauung*, gave rise to many reforms that helped the exploited to attain better material living standards as well as human dignity. But, having attained these levels, as we shall see in the next chapter, many among the formerly exploited become so pragmatic that they are no longer concerned with the fate of those for whose betterment they used to fight. There is something to be said for ideology if it manages to avoid the fanaticism and exclusivism pervading its more totalitarian variations.

Communism, in the meantime, still attracts many outside its area of control, especially in the Third World. By interrelating the station and fate of exploited individuals and nations with the future destiny of mankind, Marxism-Leninism answers their yearning for a coherent philosophy of government and politics. What often impresses the half-starved, miserable human being affected, first, by the "revolution of rising expectations" and, subsequently, by "rising frustration," is the example of societies that have been able to pull themselves up by their own efforts from similarly miserable beginnings to their current levels of economic development and political power. In this struggle for the minds of men, the Maoist version of Communism seems to have an advantage over that of Moscow. This is partly because the Chinese can pose as the advocates of the cause of nonwhites all over the world, but also because their doctrine of the battle of all the poor rural people of the world against the rich, in their industrialized fortresses (who include the Russians), partakes of more revolutionary fervor than does the Soviet ideology.

Within their establishments, however, Communist regimes are liable to run into ideological troubles of their own. Not only can such regimes never entirely keep out Western thought and ideas, as *samizdat,* the underground press, and the recent, astonishing growth of a nondoctrinaire literature in the Soviet Union have shown; they face also the danger of apathy and *anomie.* For there seems to be a law of diminishing returns with regard to indoctrination. Although, to be sure, individuals in a mass society long for safe beliefs, they are nevertheless easily satiated when doctrines are too emphatically instilled, or when, in the present conflict of systems and ideologies, one has replaced another in bewildering sequence. The case of a young Pole seems still to be valid. He told an American journalist in 1956 (*New York Times,* May 11, 1956):

> When I was ten, I ceased to believe in my fatherland. I had God. When I was fifteen, I ceased to believe in God. . . . A friend gave me help. He was a Communist. He restored my faith in mankind. These were my happiest years. . . . Now it has turned out that what my family said about the dictatorship of Stalin was true. . . . I do not know how to change my soul for the fourth time. . . . I have no basis for believing anything.

Such an experience can hardly fail to make an individual cynical or apathetic. He avoids taking sides or positions of responsibility; he will not be caught napping again. Such attitudes are especially common in countries that have gone through the experience of totalitarianism and its aftermath of nazification and denazification, of purges and counterpurges. But the problem is an even more general one, connected with the phenomenon of "depoliticization." The less the chance of the individual in a mass society to control events, the lower his political *and* his ideological concern, and—in an endless and vicious circle—the more frantic the ideological appeals of those actual or would-be rulers who feel the need for ever more fervent adherence. For totalitarian regimes, this means increasing difficulty in binding the ruled indefinitely to their control. In its turn, democracy has to steer the difficult path between political apathy, creating what the French call *incivisme,* and the ever-present temptation of doctrinaire ideologies.

The Future of Ideology: De-ideologization or New Belief Systems?

What role are ideologies likely to play in the future? From the vantage point of the 1970's, one is tempted to say that the heyday of opposing ideologies and clashing systems based on them is over; that it was reached in the 1930's, 1940's, and early 1950's of this century and has since yielded to less doctrinal antagonism, to what some have called "depoliticization" or (an even uglier term) "de-ideologization." Fascism, at least in its extreme, Nazi variety, lost its appeal after the defeat of the Axis powers and the postwar revelations of their atrocities. Communism of the Stalinist variety also lost some of its attraction with revelations of the abuse of personal power that came with de-Stalinization. Moreover, as we have seen, for those living under totalitarian regimes there is a law of diminishing returns with regard to indoctrination. Apart from this, even regimes once founded on the doctrinal-revolutionary fervor of their leaders are liable to turn into "establishments," in which an elite motivated more by technology than by doctrine rules bureaucratically rather than by ideology. Doctrine, then, may still be used to induce conformity, but as a tool rather than a master. It tends to be replaced by the ideology of technological progress and economic growth, an ideology that Communist regimes share with Western elites and, above all, with those of the Third World. In this sense, there does exist some degree of "convergence," in particular between the Soviet-bloc countries and the advanced countries of the West. Being dominated by technology, on the other hand, implies for many if not for most, mechanization— spending one's life within the machinelike structure and atmosphere of the big society; at work, for instance, on the mind-deadening assembly line. In many instances, the individual escapes into his private sphere, and his inward-looking life frequently means depoliticization again.

But there have been reactions against this trend. There is the new phenomenon of the "revolt of the young," often involving political extremism and strong ideological commitment, affecting particularly the elite of the younger generations, the students, all over the world. These movements, almost all of which tend toward the left, constitute a revival of political ideology. But it is not generally a revival of traditional Communist doctrine. While Mao and Castro (or, rather, Ché Guevara) figure among the heroes of the New Left, they do so not as representatives of particular regimes (which, as "establishments," inevitably exhibit establishment features of bureaucratism and even of repression and manipulation), but as symbols (justly or not) of the struggle against *any* kind of established regime or government. In other words, it is in most instances a doctrine imbued by ideas and ideals of anarchism rather than of Communism. Anarchists, as anti-authoritarians, may agree on what to attack and destroy, but they usually fall out into warring factions over the question of what to put in place of the "old." The sorry history of anarchist movements—from the religious sectarians of the six-teenth century through the adherents of the workers'-council (or soviet) movements of 1905 and 1917, and thereafter—leaves little hope that the new anti-authoritarians will fare better in their attempt to create strong and effective movements. It seems that their future will be marked by nebulous standards, values, doctrines, and objectives.

But not only theirs. Contemporary elites, both in the East and in the West, likewise seem to have become victims of uncertainty and bewilderment. This characteristic stands in contrast even to recent periods. When Communism, as a clear-cut doctrine, opposed democracy as an equally unambiguous set of principles, one at least knew who opposed whom. Now everything seems to have become uncertain. The Communist elite, at least in the older regimes, is no longer wedded to the original doctrine and is thus unsure of the future. In the West, the elites' old belief in democracy's unfailing ability to bring about progress, economic growth, and increasing afflu-ence for all yields to doubt when confronted with the new problems posed by a deteriorating environment as well as by the apparently intractable nature of many of the social prob-lems, such as poverty and racial inequality. These are the same questions that make many of the young—who are sup-posed to occupy elite positions in the future—despair of solv-ing the world's troubles, "cop out" of society, and vent their frustration by resorting to violence.

This disintegration of traditional as well as newer belief systems seems matched by uncertain leadership and despair on the part of both leaders and masses. It has led many to return to the "womb," as it were, of traditional belief, especially established religions. We shall discuss the role of religion below. But, at this point, we would like to stress that this sort of "reactionism," rationally, is not the only way out of the dilemma. In principle, there is no illogic in the idea of merging different and dissatisfied groups in a common and bold approach which would confront the great new tasks of mankind. The "cop-outs," for instance, could become actively interested in the problems of social justice, and the critics from the New Left, as well as "older" liberals, could become involved in ways to solve ever more urgent ecological problems. A response to some demands *can* go hand in hand with the solution of others: for instance, decent housing, with ample air, space, playgrounds, and parks, would save or restore the environment and, at the same time, provide jobs for the "underclass." If such priorities were made the basis for social and political action, a new ideology of "conservative" (in the sense of value-conserving) progress might evolve. In a subsequent chapter, we shall try to demonstrate that a similar confluence of concerns and attitudes is needed on the international level to tackle the great global problems requiring universal concerns and policies. A partly idealistic, partly pragmatic ideology of "housekeeping on a small planet" might be evolved. We might then enter an age characterized by a more positive approach and a more unified, cooperative policy than are now visible.

CHURCH AND STATE

Consideration of the role of ideologies in the modern political world inevitably brings us to the problem of the relation between church and state. While political science cannot presume to pass on the ultimate validity of religious truth, it can, and indeed must, recognize the existence of individual religious beliefs as objective facts and of organized religion as a socially and politically relevant institution. Needless to say, it is the political consequences of both individual belief and organized religion that are our proper concern here.

We may usefully return to the phenomenon of *anomie*, the lack of values of the individual in mass society, to understand the role religion plays in a modern nation and, in particular, the problems created by the sometimes conflicting demands of churches and the modern state. Industrialization, urbanization, and the resulting mechanization of life have confronted religion with new tasks, which it can shun only at the risk of becoming a mere "Sunday creed," without vital commitment to, and connection with, modern life. If, in the past, religion served the social function of transmitting from generation to generation generally accepted values, it can today assume the function of providing individuals who are lost in a directionless maze with new or new-old standards, and thereby give direction and meaning to the lives of many who have failed to develop their own.

In assuming this responsibility, however, different religions may follow different paths, and it is important, in relating them to the state and to politics, to understand these differences. Protestantism, for instance, turns primarily to the individual and asks him to turn to the word of God and to interpret and live up to it on his own responsibility. Catholicism, with its belief in the Church as the divine organization for guiding its members, confronts both the individual and the polity with fixed standards and established demands. It is, therefore, not surprising that conflicts, wherever they arise between the secular and the spiritual, the law and policy of the state and the creed and dogma of religion, tend to become more conspicuous and sometimes more violent when the more tightly organized churches are involved. In the modern world, it is Roman Catholicism and, possibly, Islam, rather than Protestantism or Buddhism or the Orthodox Church in Russia, that stand up to secularism with the coherent and unified power of a "living faith." And, since the Catholic Church and the Moslem religion still have a powerful hold over the people of many countries and regions of the world, the issues in which state and religion are opposed are often most clearcut where these two religions are involved. For example, the states where the relation between public and religiously controlled education has been most difficult—France, Germany, and Italy—are precisely those states where Christian Democratic, i.e., strongly Catholic, parties feel deeply on this issue.

We must keep in mind, however, that the issue of religion and education concerns all countries and all religions, whether the state is friendly or hostile to religion or, in a system of greater or less separation between church and state, tries to be uninvolved. Apart from the family, the school is the most important "youth-socializing" institution. The degree and kind of religious influence through schools and other sources determines whether religion becomes the underpinning of the value standards and the belief systems of the adult population or, if it fails or the people are deprived of its influence, whether non- or antireligious ideologies, or *anomie,* will prevail. The hold over educational systems by religion or the churches, therefore, has had and still has its particular impact on the development of political systems. This may be through the influence of missionary schools in the colonies and dependencies of Christian countries where many future leaders of independent countries were raised. It may also be seen in countries where one of the chief local political issues is the influence of church or religion on secular affairs from Bavaria to Ireland, or from Tel Aviv to Cairo.

In considering different types of relationships between church and state, we must note, further, a more general phenomenon, namely, that of the involvement of *all* religion and *all* churches in the general historical developments of their times and, thus, in the changing patterns of, and approaches to, social and political life. This involvement is illustrated most impressively by the most strongly organized, worldwide church, the Roman Catholic, in its recent travail, which amounted almost to a revolution. This has been true in regard to internal organization, as the Church has been transformed from an absolutist system to a kind of aristocratic constitutionalism (with democratic forces still battling for greater influence on the part of the lower clergy and for lay participation). It has been true, above all, in regard to doctrine and policies concerning the great problems of our times, national and international, economic, social, and political. Vatican II, the Ecumenical Council (1962–65), called to codify Pope John's policies of *aggiornamento* (updating) of the Church, considered, and in part revolutionized, all these matters. True, Pope John's successor, faced with what he and many Church leaders came to fear as a "runaway" development, have tried more recently to stem this tide and return the Church to more traditional attitudes and policies (a reactionism that had perhaps its most significant and fateful effect in the issue of family planning and birth control). But the changes can hardly be undone. Thus, the Encyclical "Populorum Progressio" (1967) sided with the developing nations against neocolonialist insistence on the rights of investors. "Pacem in Terris" (1963) spoke out forcefully for far-reaching policies of peace organization and disarmament, while another pronouncement, the Pastoral Constitution on "The Church in the Modern World" (1965) not only condemned the use of nuclear weapons, area bombing, and so forth, but even advocated a world authority for the enforcement of peace.

In many places, Church figures encourage trends toward conscientious objection, and some clergy have engaged in nonviolent demonstration against war policies, such as American involvement in Vietnam. It is true that, officially, for the most part, the hierarchy has continued, as heretofore, to bless those participating in war, but the rift cannot be denied. It has also been apparent in areas of social conflict and social reform, from the movement of the French "worker priests" (subsequently suppressed) to the siding of priests and even bishops in Latin American countries (specifically, Brazil) with the impoverished and exploited peasants and their sometimes radical political movements. These developments again do not imply the complete transformation of a still often overwhelming conservatism of the Church in such matters. But they must be kept in mind when studying the present impact of churches and religions on political affairs.

To return to the issues that may divide churches and states, we must note that the aforementioned issue of education is only one among many over which church and state have been divided in modern times. There may be conflicts over the claim of secular power to participate in appointments to clerical office, in particular where the clergy, in turn, participates in civil matters like education or administering marriage contracts; over the Church's claim to have the sole right to administer such contracts, or to have its view prevail in matters of family law (divorce) or criminal law (abortion, euthanasia), or such matters of more general and increasingly serious concern as family planning and birth control; or to pass on, if not exercise censorship over, publications and other channels and media of communication. And it is by no means only in relation to the Catholic Church that such conflicts may arise. Any similarly comprehensive belief system is likely to get involved in conflicts. Orthodox Judaism, for example, is represented in Israel through its own political parties, which, if they were able to do so, would force their own Sabbath and dietary laws on orthodox and nonorthodox alike; as it is, they have been able to prevent the adoption of a modern family law. So it is also with Islam in Pakistan and the Middle East, where it has or seeks predominant influence. And so it is to a considerable degree with the Dutch Reformed Church in South Africa—with its rigid Calvinism and strong "elitist" and authoritarian overtones.

In understanding the issues and conflicts that may arise, we may distinguish three types of situations: (1) where there is an established or an actually dominant church; (2) where there is either complete separation between church and state or where there is separation in principle and the churches have certain defined privileges; and (3) where religion faces its most powerful modern opponent, totalitarianism.

State Relations with a Dominant Church

There are still a good many states where the dominance of one religion and one church is accepted, and where the

church, the government, and the general life and society of
the country are closely connected. This situation, of course,
reflects the premodern historical relationship between church
and state, in which the church, particularly through its control of education and its influence on the prevailing moral
and spiritual atmosphere in the country, in effect provided
the ideological foundation of the political regime. Frequently,
too, the church was related socially and economically with the
regime either through ownership of land or because important state positions were held by members of the clergy. The
church could then be identified with the *status quo* by both
adherents and opponents of the clergy. To opponents, it
might become, as did the French Church, Voltaire's *"l'infâme,"*
an institution to be crushed by a violently anticlerical and,
quite possibly, antireligious revolution. But such a revolution, on the other hand, could appear to many people as
destructive of the moral foundations of a country and thus
would rally against it not only the defenders of the old regime but all those fearful of atheism, laicism, and similar tendencies. Both in Spain and in Mexico in the first half of this
century, such a conflict enmeshed the power and influence of
the Church with all the other great issues of ideology and
politics that divide a nation.

There are many modern states in which such close ties
exist. The Ethiopian Constitution of 1955, for instance, declared the Orthodox Church the established church of the
state. Pakistan calls itself an "Islamic Republic." In India, the
Hindu Mahasabha made a strong, though unsuccessful, bid to
establish Hinduism as the official religious basis of the new
polity. Even in Israel, Jewish law is still part of the secular
code. It is Catholicism, however, that provides perhaps the
most significant case in point, in view of the large number of
countries, especially in Latin America, that maintain a close
connection between the state and the Catholic Church. In
Colombia, for example, the Roman Catholic religion is established as the "official religion of the nation under the protection of the public powers." Similarly, the constitution of the

Irish Republic contained a clause recognizing the "special position of the Holy Catholic Apostolic Roman Church as the guardian of the faith professed by the great majority of the citizens," recently abrogated to lessen strains related to the conflict in Protestant-dominated Northern Ireland.

Spain illustrates the problems and difficulties that can arise under such a system. The Franco regime, actively allied with Catholicism in the Civil War, recognized the Catholic religion as the "religion of the Spanish state [which] will be given official protection" (Article 6 of Franco's "Spaniards' Charter" of 1945), while Article I of the Succession Law of 1947 establishes Spain as a "Catholic, social, and representative State which . . . constitutes a Kingdom." While, thus far, Spain is a kingdom without a king, whose genuinely social and representative character may be in doubt, there can be no question about the role that the Church (together with the army and the Falange) has played as one of the three pillars of the regime. What has united Franco and the Church is, above all, a common fear of an anti-Franco revolution, which, whether liberal, socialist, or Communist, would threaten the Church with a loss of the prerogatives it considers vital.

It is perhaps the more significant that, despite this common interest and the predominant Catholicism of the Spanish people, conflicts between the state and the Church have arisen more recently. Franco was unwilling to grant the full measure of the Church's claim to internal organizational autonomy; and, in his Concordat with the Vatican (1953), he reserved to the state quite far-reaching rights over appointments to high clerical office. Moreover, in the contested issue of secondary education, with its system of parallel public and religious schools, the Church has had to grant the state supervision over its educational system. On the other hand, the Spanish clergy has frequently criticized (and some of the lower clergy have openly and actively opposed) some of the more repressive policies of the political regime, in particular its suppression of labor demands and its lack of concern for the living conditions of the poor, since both these trends directly chal-

lenge the social tenets of the Church. It is worth noting that
failure to take note of such conditions has in the past alienated large classes from organized religion. Still more recently,
the Spanish Church, through Opus Dei, a lay Catholic organization, has undertaken to become active within the state
organization itself, with its members staffing important governmental positions, and trying to combine Franco authoritarianism with modernization, especially of the economy.

Separation of Church and State

If issues between public power and organized religion arise
even where there is an official church, it is hardly surprising
that they may become even more acute where such a connection does not exist. Usually, the least ground for conflict is
found where, as in Anglo-Saxon societies, separation prevails
on the basis of mutual toleration and mutual freedom in the
vital field of education. This presupposes a meeting of minds
or of basic value standards—as in Britain between the general
public spirit and the Anglican as well as the nonconformist
creeds, and in the United States between the spirit of the
public schools and that of the private, including the Catholic,
parochial establishments. In the case of America, the potential gap between Christian tenets and the objectives of a competitive society has been bridged by a common acceptance
of a set of values and ideals that are indicated in the necessarily somewhat vague term the "American way of life."

But where, as in most Continental European countries,
either disestablishment has taken place against the opposition
of the churches, or the churches, though not recognized as
official, enjoy certain privileges, we frequently encounter a
conflict situation. The issue then tends to oppose the religious
side to "laicism," which rejects such privileges and opposes
any attempt on the part of the disestablished churches to re-
gain their former privileges. Such a conflict may result in
antireligious discrimination, and churches may be deprived
not only of their former privileges but also of the rights they
would customarily enjoy even under a system of complete

separation. On the other hand, a grant of privileges, such as the right to control education either through a system of church-run schools or through public schools in which instruction proceeds in the spirit of the respective denomination, might tie the church so closely to secular authority that religion assumes an almost official character; this is especially the case where churches are subsidized by the state. Thus, in the Protestant regions of Germany, religion in the past was so closely tied to the state that the pastor functioned, and tended to be considered, as part of the state bureaucracy. In France, on the other hand, where "laicization" was enforced upon the religious part of the population, the antagonism of church and state perpetuates itself even to this day on the local and personal level in the relations between priest and (laicist) school teacher; the same is true in parts of Italy. In either case, the issue can become one of the most profound ones dividing a nation, especially where it leads to the formation of Christian or Catholic parties or other parties whose platforms are characterized by their stand on the religious issue. Matters are made worse when the schism is accompanied by division in nationality or language groups. Thus, in Belgium, where the Flemish are more religious than the Walloon part of the population, a conflict over the education of teachers and state subsidies for the denominational school system not only involved the Social Christian Party in a struggle with the Liberal and Socialist parties but revived old and bitter antagonisms between the two population groups. All three parties split thereafter into Walloon and Flemish segments; the constitutional system had to be changed into a federal one; and there are even doubts about the continued viability of the Belgian state as a unit. Some of the same religious-ethnic divisions affect contemporary Canada.

Wherever the law of the state decides issues in a way irreconcilable with religious tenets, individuals may find themselves in agonizing conflicts of conscience. The most obvious example is the conscientious objector who will go to prison rather than bear arms. But large-scale passive or even active resistance to state authority may occur if national policies clash with the standards of a group that holds a nonconforming supranational creed or ideology. Democratic states are usually too tolerant and too responsive to the pressures of particular groups to permit public policy to violate drastically individual or group consciences. But such conflicts can easily arise between religion and a totalitarian regime.

Churches and Totalitarian Regimes

In the past, churches, as one of the famous two pillars of feudal-monarchical rule—"throne and altar"—have often endorsed established social groups and conservative political forces. This made them suspect to reformers, and especially to socialists, as dispensers of "quietism," who, in Marx's phrase, purvey a spiritual opium to the ruled to keep them in an obedient frame of mind. Those who became alienated from religion for this reason often subsequently turned against churches and religion as such, especially if they themselves attained political power. The churches, in turn, tended to consider "atheistic Communism" their chief political enemy. When totalitarian movements rose to power under anti-Communist slogans, religious groups were therefore tempted to align themselves with these movements as allies in a common cause. This was clearest in the case of Spanish Falangism; but, even in the case of Nazism, major portions of German Protestantism at first welcomed Hitler, and the Vatican concluded a Concordat with him in 1933 (as it had done earlier with Mussolini) in the hope of mutual accommodation.

Usually, however, it has not taken long to persuade churches and religions that, short of sacrificing their own fundamental interests and beliefs, they cannot hope to come to terms, and even less to make common cause, with any kind of totalitarianism that takes its own ideology seriously. Both Protestantism and Catholicism ended up in conflict with Nazism in Germany; conflict with the Church arose irrepressibly even in a Catholic country like Argentina under Peron, and exists today in Brazil; and, as we have seen, Church and state are not free from tension in Franco Spain. Religion and fascist totalitarianism (in the broader sense of the term) are incompatible, because they represent rival and total ideological claims. Even where fascism does not profess hostility to religion, it is so fundamentally wedded to ideals and principles that Christianity abhors that any real conciliation is impossible. Mussolini's ideal of bellicism and the warlike virtues, his glorification of integral nationalism as an end, and of force, violence, terror, cunning—in short, all the Machiavellian devices—as proper means, were no less pagan than Hitler's racialism and all that it involved. In South Africa, with the increasingly oppressive racialism of the regime, the churches have divided, with the Dutch Reformed Church officially supporting the government and most other denominations becoming openly critical. Increasingly, moreover, the regime reacts to liberal views and actions aiding black South Africans by expelling expatriate churchmen from the country, placing South African clerics under house arrest, or laying charges against one or the other under vaguely worded statutes that carry severe penalties.

Communism is no less fundamentally opposed to religious tenets than fascism, since it, too, demands the complete allegiance of its members. Thus, the church-state conflict in Catholic countries under Communist rule has been inevitable. Moreover, Christian parties have been in the vanguard of anti-Communist coalitions and policies in the postwar period, and, in Italy, they constitute *the* one big non-Communist party. A 1949 decree by the Congregation of the Holy Office in Rome declared that any association of a Catholic with the Communist Party, either as a member or in other ways, or through any activity in support of Communist doctrine and practice, was forbidden and would incur automatic excommunication.

Can there ever be a *rapprochement* or even a *modus*

vivendi between organized religion and Communism? Until recently, and particularly during the cold-war period, prospects seemed rather dim that an accommodation could amount to more than an uneasy truce, in which churches would avoid overharsh criticism of the regime and the regime, in turn, would avoid persecution of the churches. But, at that time already, the argument was made that, while fascism is pagan, Communism is a "Christian heresy"; i.e., that the ultimate ideal of Marxian socialism, which Communism professes, is not entirely incompatible with religious ethics: It is humanitarian and even personalistic, concerned with the better life of the individual rather than with the glory and power of nations or races or with the power of an elite or a *Führer*. Communism, especially during the Stalin era, perverted these ideals. Since then, however, the conflict has softened to some extent, due to changed attitudes on both sides, though not profound changes in doctrine. The Catholic Church, in particular, especially vis-à-vis countries with Catholic populations, like Poland and Hungary, has given up its extreme anti-Communist "crusade"-type of policy in an attempt to "normalize" its relations with the Communist regimes. On the part of the regimes, too, there has been some readiness to arrive at accommodation, in practice, in matters like keeping churches open for services, training clergy, etc. Where, as in Poland and East Germany, "Christian" parties are permitted (though, of course, under "reliable" leadership), concessions are occasionally made in more general matters, such as religious instruction (but outside the public school system). In the Soviet Union, while there has been no profound reversal of doctrine and practice even in post–Stalin days, militant atheism and similar extremism have vanished in a climate that is now less ideological than in the early days of the regime. The churches, on the other hand, have throughout history proved themselves adaptable to a wide variety of situations without sacrificing their ultimate goals; they have been able to cross the divide between continents, races, and civilizations; and they have been wont to take the long-range view, especially when the fate of many of their members was at stake. Thus, although the basic issue remains, and occasionally flares up into conflict, it seems generally attenuated at present through some measure of détente.

THE LIBERAL AND THE TOTALITARIAN POLITY

For the time being, Communism remains a challenge to religion as well as to the democracies. In view of this fact, the latter will naturally ally themselves with forces and movements opposed to any form of totalitarianism: with churches and religions as long as they do not support fascist regimes or trends, and also with those governments that, while not completely democratic, according to the standards of the older Western democracies, yet recognize some necessary restraints and limitations upon power in order to protect individual and group rights and liberties. Some of these latter governments, because of their authoritarian heritage, have failed thus far to live up fully to all the criteria established by British or American democracy. This is still true of Germany and likewise of Japan, whose modern political developments resemble those of Germany in so many respects, and whose late industrialization and strong authoritarian traditions have so far hampered genuine democratization. Not all modernized countries have been fortunate enough to enjoy the steady growth over several centuries of that incubator of liberal and democratic institutions, a rising middle class. And the newly independent countries of Asia, Africa, and the Middle East have had an even more sudden break with the past.

Recognizing the existence of such handicaps to democratic development, nations committed to democracy can profitably draw the distinction between political democracy and liberalism that we have previously suggested, and welcome as allies in the nontotalitarian camp nations and regimes that, while less democratic in their political institutions or in their approach to decision-making, are yet liberal in the sense of respecting and protecting the dignity of the individual and the free expression of personal and group interests.* As the Central European *Rechtsstaat* shows, this combination is a practicable one. In other words, where traditionalism does not exclude individual freedom and the development of personality, it may constitute a bulwark against totalitarian inroads.

This distinction between authoritarianism and totalitarianism may possibly also become a reality should some Communist regime develop a system in which individuals and private groups will be granted substantial and reliable protection of basic liberties, even though the ruling group and Party do not give up their decision-making controls. It is too early, at this point, to venture predictions about when and where this might happen, but, if one or the other of the former East European satellites of the Soviet Union, or even the U.S.S.R. itself, should enter upon this path, Western democracy would no longer have to consider such a regime its "natural enemy." An ideology of anti-Communism that, for doctrinal reasons, should fail or refuse to take notice of such developments and transformations in the opposite camp would be as dangerous as a dogmatic totalitarianism of the Communist variety. As Czechoslovakia so tragically demonstrated in 1968, one should not expect too much too soon in the way of "liberalization." But the contrasting example of Hungary, defeated in revolution but since then successful in quiet and gradual reform, indicates that it is not impossible.

Thus, in distinguishing between dictatorship and democracy, or totalitarianism and liberalism, what counts even more than the rule, or absence of the rule, of the majority is the right, or at least the reasonable chance, for individuals and associations of individuals freely to develop themselves. Particularly in our mass societies, where the people can exercise at best only a limited control over crucial matters of

---

* Thus we exclude, of course, regimes that are, or have become, illiberal in addition to being undemocratic—such as Greece under the colonels —and whose spurious claim to be allies of the Western democracies is based merely on their anti-Communism.

domestic and foreign policy, the difference between free and totalitarian countries seems to reduce itself ultimately to one question: whether there exists an inviolable sphere of privacy in which the otherwise organized, mechanized, ordered, and oftentimes bullied and manipulated individual may yet proceed according to his will, whim, or fantasy, his beliefs or disbeliefs, in a socially useful and adjusted or even an entirely "useless" and unadjusted fashion. Any genuine freedom in the personal and group spheres presupposes, as we have seen, the placing of limits upon political power. It is only when there are limits on what government may do and on the way in which it may do it that citizens are free. Thus, if religion may be an ally of democracy in its conflict with nondemocratic systems, liberal democracy, in turn, provides the setting within which human beings can most freely maintain those beliefs, religious or secular, that enhance their individuality.

VII

THE ROLE OF FORCE IN THE DYNAMICS OF CHANGE

In the preceding chapter, we asked the question: What ties political communities together? We found at least a partial answer in those feelings and sentiments of their members that can be summed up in the term "allegiance," and which confer "legitimacy" on political units and their governments. This legitimacy is closely related to the degree to which the established channels for peaceful change function satisfactorily in response to the needs and aspirations of the society.

But there is another aspect to the question. If legitimacy fails or is lacking from the outset, then the political unit depends for its coherence on the threat or application of force by those in control. According to Max Weber, the modern state is characterized by the capacity to maintain the "monopoly of the legitimate use of force" (or violence, or coercion, as the German term *Gewalt* may also be translated) in a given area. And, indeed, it would be unrealistic to disregard or de-emphasize the role that force and the control over its instrumentalities have played in the history of countries, and this not only in their foreign relations but also in regard to the maintenance, or else the change, of internal governments and regimes. But we are not directly concerned here with the role of violence in the foreign, i.e., international, relations of nations (although something on that will be said in the following chapter). It is rather with its impact on domestic affairs that we shall deal in this section.

Political violence or coercion is ordinarily not a political end (i.e., except for marginal persons or groups) but a means to other ends. Even as a means, however, its use is all too common. We have had occasion before to indict an overoptimistic trend in Western thought that suggested that systems based on concentrated power, such as authoritarianism and dictatorship, are on their way out, and that systems based on consensus and limited power constitute the "wave of the future." There was a similar and equally fallacious belief that the incidence of violence and coercion would diminish with the progress of civilization. The ballot has not been universally substituted for the bullet in these regards. Government and politics in the twentieth century have taught us a bitter lesson. As one of the outstanding students of political violence has said:

> The belief that some kinds of social arrangements or political institutions are intrinsically immune from violence or capable of satisfying all human desires is only a partial truth. Disruptive violence can [occur] and has occurred in every twentieth-century political community.*

Our century, unfortunately, has not been less marked than preceding ones by the number and intensity of violent domestic conflicts, whether in the form of civil war and revolution, racial or ethnic turmoil, large-scale rioting, or their violent suppression.

Before discussing in more detail the ways in which anti-state and antigovernment violence occurs and functions in today's world, we should say a word about the use that governments themselves make of that force whose exercise they claim as a monopoly, i.e., the state's enforcement power and apparatus of coercion. The organization of public force, through police, prison systems, and, last but not least, the military insofar as it is used domestically, tends to be concealed in "democratic" discussion as something "shameful" and hidden behind the fig leaf of popular institutions and constitutions. But, for all that, its existence is no less real and tends to come

---

* Ted R. Gurr, *Why Men Rebel* (Princeton, N.J.: Princeton University Press, 1970), p. 350.

to the fore whenever the "fatherland," i.e., the system or regime, is or seems to be in danger. Thus the universal availability and not infrequent use of that exceptional power that, depending on country and system, can proclaim a "state of emergency" or "necessity" or "martial law." When dealing with the executive, we briefly referred to the virtually universal possibility, under crisis conditions, of concentrating in one hand the powers and jurisdictions that ordinarily are dispersed, limited, and checked (at least in constitutional regimes). This hand, usually, is that of the top executive, which, in turn, controls, or sometimes is controlled by, the top echelon of the military. Totalitarian dictatorship, as we have seen, is almost identical with a "permanent state of martial law" (e.g., in the case of the Nazi dictatorship, which was even formally based on power from a presidential emergency decree of February, 1933). But even the more democratic polities provide for such powers, either explicitly, as in the case of Article 48 of the Weimar Constitution of Germany or Article 16 of the Fifth Republic Constitution of France, or implicitly by accepted constitutional usage, as in the martial-law powers of the President of the United States.

In Britain, emergency powers are based on the Emergency Powers Act of 1964 (based, in turn, on a law of 1920), which permits the government to declare a state of emergency in major crises. In Canada, as we have seen, a War Measures Act (as amended in 1960) permits use of the military to meet domestic or foreign crises. Two countries usually referred to as among the most democratic also have special provisions. In Switzerland, a constitutional amendment (1949) conferred on the executive powers to issue emergency decrees to counter threats to the democratic order (with a one-year limit for such measures). Sweden also amended its constitution in 1965 to grant emergency powers to a 50-member group of parliamentary deputies. This body resembles the "mini-parliament" of 22 that may assume such powers in the Federal Republic of Germany. In the latter, even the sorry experience with abuse of emergency powers under the Weimar regime did not prevent renewed experimentation twenty years after the adoption of a constitution (the Bonn Constitution), which, for once, had been simon-pure of such unpleasantness. Carl Schmitt, as we have seen, was not entirely unrealistic (though somewhat exaggerating) when he defined the "sovereign" as the one who holds control over the state of emergency. This statement reflects the role of concentrated power that is at the back of any and all political organization.

Force and Counterforce

But there is a dialectic in this situation. If it is true that, ultimately, governmental authority rests on power, which, in turn, must be able to avail itself of the instruments of coercion, it is also true that, the more government makes use of force, the less authority it is bound to have in the sense of legitimacy, and the more it is liable to provoke counterforce on the part of those who are "out-groups" or, for other reasons, oppose or challenge governmental authority. This applies particularly to democracies whose concept of the legitimate and therefore restrained exercise of public power is in sharp contrast to concentrated and unlimited control. But, in our century, even nondemocratic systems must rely on at least the appearance of democratic institutions for their legitimacy in the eyes of those subjected to them: thus, even their continued reliance on force may provoke unrest, if not counterforce, as events in some East European countries have documented.

There is a dialectic also in the relation of force and counterforce, i.e., in the interaction of "legal" (governmental) force and "illegal" (revolutionary) counterforce. Contrary to what used to be the "conventional wisdom," revolutions do not usually occur when classes or masses are at the nadir of poverty, exploitation, dependency, and despair; they are more often revolutions of "rising expectations." They originate in feelings of "relative deprivation," i.e., a perceived discrepancy between expectations and actual conditions that creates frustration and aggressiveness. As de Tocqueville, in his analysis of the *ancien régime,* discovered more than a hundred years ago:

> The evil, which was suffered patiently as inevitable, seems unendurable as soon as the idea of escaping from it is conceived. All the abuses then removed seem to throw into greater relief those which remain, so that their feeling is more painful. The evil, it is true, has become less, but sensibility to it has become more acute. Feudalism at the height of its power had not inspired Frenchmen with so much hatred as it did on the event of its disappearance.

This realization, of course, is particularly applicable to our century, when not only "developed" countries find their "proletarians" and, even more so, subproletarian groups, revolting in the face of affluence and perceived "relative deprivation," but the vast "Third World" of the underdeveloped cannot help experiencing anger and frustration as their rising expectations turn into disappointment over developmental failures.

In contrast to relative deprivation, abject poverty or absolute oppression usually leads to resignation and passivity. Thus, in the absence of perception of any possibility of improvement, deprived minorities, such as American blacks, Chicanos, and Indians and those under colonial oppression, tended, with rare and explosive exceptions, to be resigned to, if not more or less satisfied with, their condition as long as there seemed to be no chance of change. This, then, constitutes one kind of what political scientists and politicians are apt to term "stability," but it is stability based on oppressive hierarchy and autocracy, not on group harmony and satisfaction. Such stability should not be mistaken for democracy. Herbert Marcuse has pointed out the totalitarian potentialities inherent even in an outwardly tolerant and seemingly liberal society. Class rule, or ethnic or racial discrimination, or similar oppression and inequality reflect authoritarianism, and no excuse of ensuring "law and order" can hide this fact. State power and force that are too overwhelmingly strong to allow for counterforce, or more subtle means of maintaining a discriminatory *status quo,* may well whittle away the tacit underpinning of allegiance that is the strongest cement of a democratic society.

DYNAMICS OF CHANGE

Change, of course, is not always the result of force and violence. Here again, democratic-constitutional political systems contrast sharply with authoritarian-dictatorial ones. It is the *raison d'être* of the former to allow for peaceful change throughout societal life and to put at the disposal of organized society the governmental institutions and processes that structure such change. In dictatorial regimes, change is dependent upon the arbitrary will of the ruler or rulers, who usually are much more interested in preventing change so as to perpetuate their control. Even dictators, however, may be exposed to pressures for change originating in various classes, groups, and even "pressure groups." Occasionally, as apparently in the case of Mao and his "cultural revolution," an ideology of "permanent revolution" may even induce them to become the inaugurators of change in order to oppose rigidifying trends of party and other bureaucracies. Military or similar autocracies in developing countries may also inaugurate change in order to modernize their nations.

More frequently, however, change in autocratically run societies is the result of what may be called avoidance policy. Fear of rising discontent, of riots, violence, or revolution, renders those in control amenable to concessions and reform. Bismarck is said to have remarked: If you do not want social revolution, you must give the people social reform. And, to some extent, he did so, enough to turn a revolutionary workers' movement reformist. Avoidance policies may also be prodded by outside competition. Thus, reforms are inaugurated to counter a threatening (domestic or foreign-instigated) Communist movement.* It may, indeed, be questioned whether, in the domestic affairs of nations, any peaceful advance or reform—such as extension of suffrage or labor and welfare legislation—would have occurred or succeeded without the prodding of forces threatening revolution or similar kinds of violence. In this sense, the threat of force has usually been the midwife of progress.

But avoidance policies, especially in the relations between developed and developing countries, for example in regard to foreign-aid policies, have often not taken into consideration what we discussed before: namely, that alleviation or even advances may well create only frustration and thus stimulate revolutionary attitudes. Rational choice, therefore, is between more or less complete satisfaction of wants, or else so complete an oppression that resignation ensues. Since the latter alternative is incompatible with liberal-democratic ideals, only a policy of radical improvement and far-reaching reform seems practicable. In the relations between the United States and Latin American countries, for instance, such policies would involve backing the "next most radical reform movement"— i.e., the one next to Communism. But the blindness of vested interests and opposition to expropriation have ordinarily inhibited such rational choice and thus contributed, on occasion, to the perpetuation of indigenous oppression rather than to reform. In all too many instances, the United States, rather than backing the forces of "freedom and progress" as it once did, supports the *status quo*.

But there is another, more elusive, but no less serious, problem in the relation between democracy and change. Inasmuch as in most developed, industrialized nations democracy has come to mean that the majority of the population shares not only in political power but also in "affluence," its interest lies in the general maintenance, more or less, of the existing eco-

---

* According to a news report from South Vietnam, "A peasant from a village outside the delta city of Cantho who received an acre of land several months ago, summed up his feelings: 'I wonder if they would have given me this land if there weren't any Vietcong.'" (*New York Times*, January 4, 1972.)

nomic, social, and political system. As long as major groups, such as labor, were economically disadvantaged, political democracy still implied policies of change; it meant that these groups had to find majorities to enact the reforms that fulfilled their wants. To the degree that they did so, the disadvantaged and discontented classes were transformed into participants in the "affluent" society through the workings of the democratic process. In the United States, it is true, a governmental-political framework, characterized by mutual checks and balances, has rendered more difficult an equitable allocation of the benefits of industrial capitalism. Thus, compared with other industrialized societies, great changes by means of the democratic process have been irregular and belated. As pointed out in Chapter IV, the system required (and requires) an active *and* reform-minded President backed by a strong reform movement controlling a majority in Congress; this constellation did occur, notably under the New Deal.

The American middle classes and labor by now constitute that broad, compact majority on which the major parties—Labourites and Conservatives in Great Britain, Christian Democrats and Social Democrats in West Germany, Democrats and Republicans in the United States—concentrate their interest. This situation, however, means that minorities that are still economically or otherwise disadvantaged or simply have different ideas may find themselves without political advocates. Democracy then tends merely to stabilize the *status quo* and to prevent what further progress the remaining minorities need. Society then faces the danger of petrification, conjuring up the emergence of what Gunnar Myrdal has aptly named the "underclass" of the poor and racially or otherwise discriminated against who, in contrast to the exploited but working proletarians of rising industrialism, remain excluded from integration into the active economy and mobile society.

The challenge is then to traditionally progressive classes and parties, such as liberal-democratic and democratic-socialist ones, to resume their earlier concern for social justice and the needs and welfare of all and not only for those of the majority of which they now form a part. Democracy can degenerate into a system in which a satisfied and therefore conservative majority, operating through its major parties, protects itself against change. This danger could be accelerated as "affluence" diminishes with the sacrifices that *all* will have to make for the protection of the environment. Where the pie no longer grows larger, the chances of an increasing share for the poor and otherwise neglected grow dimmer. Where peaceful change is no longer attainable through majority vote, *status quo* majorities may be pressured into making concessions through campaigns of civil disobedience; sometimes they succeed, but sometimes they provoke a "backlash." This backlash can even take the form of martial law or similar measures countering riots or uprisings (actual, threatened, or merely alleged) on the part of minorities. One policy of force tends always to provoke the other.

REVOLUTION IN MODERN TIMES

Even a very cursory overview of twentieth-century history shows that the incidence of revolutionary and quasi-revolutionary violence has been at least as high as in preceding centuries. Types of such violence have been (with many shadings and overlapping between one or another):

(1) what one may call "old-style" revolutions, the uprisings of middle classes, allied with peasants and workers, against authoritarian-feudal regimes or bourgeois regimes still permeated with feudal-authoritarian remnants; in short, the type of the various "French revolutions" of the late eighteenth and nineteenth centuries. These revolutions partake of the character of nineteenth-century events, i.e., they reflect the claim of masses in industrializing countries to participate in political power. What the French achieved through their earlier revolutions (and the British and Americans through peaceful extension of the suffrage), Germany and other European countries tried to attain early in the twentieth century. The Chinese Revolution of 1911, the Mexican Revolution of 1910,

and two of the Russian revolutions, that of 1905 and the first of the two in 1917, were also of this nature. By and large, this kind of revolution has been disappearing: Peasants in the industrialized systems disappear as a class, while workers and lower middle classes fulfill their principal demands, and become part of the "compact majority" described before. In the preindustrial or industrializing parts of the world, on the other hand, revolutionary movements, as we shall see, tend to assume a character different from that of the "classical" European revolution.

(2) Occasionally, especially where a more or less liberal-democratic regime established by the type of revolution listed under (1) proved weak and unstable, Communism gained control through a second revolution. Here, the Russian October Revolution of 1917, which followed upon that earlier one that year, is the prime example. In China it took longer. In Cuba, Castro transformed the earlier type of revolution "peacefully" into the latter. By and large, however, Communist revolution seems to have little chance where democracy has given labor and other major groups their share in affluence and political power. In those situations, Communist parties either become insignificant or, where they remain strong, as in France or Italy, tend to become reformist. These parties have a chance where they ally themselves with anticolonialism (see below), or where the "revolution" is imported with the help of foreign bayonets, as in Eastern Europe after World War II. Thus, this type of revolution, too, seems to be a matter of the past, at least in its classical, "Leninist" version.

(3) Fascist revolutions or coups are usually reactions against a perceived danger from the "left," Communist or allegedly Communist. They occur especially where democracy seems either feeble, and thus vulnerable to overthrow by Communism, or where leftist movements seem to threaten vested interests through the use of the ballot. Under these circumstances, big business, the military, the upper bureaucracy, and sometimes the Church hierarchy may ally themselves with conservative, lower-middle-class, or peasant groups to estab-

lish authoritarian or dictatorial rule. This happened in Italy, Germany, and Spain, in all of which democracy had been established recently and was still shaky. In all three cases, as well, the Communist threat was blown up far beyond reality by the right. As an Italian anti-Fascist put it, Fascism was "a counterrevolution against a revolution that never took place." But where democracy is stabilized under the "compact majority" system described above, the chances of fascist revolution are as minimal as are those of a Communist one.

(4) The second half of this century, in particular, has witnessed a type of "revolution," or uprising, that often accompanies decolonization. It occurs where the "winds of change" that came to topple the colonial empires were disregarded by colonial rulers, or were met too reluctantly or too belatedly. From the first (anti-French) Indochina war to the Algerian war, violence was needed to achieve "self-determination" and independence. This type of violence now occurs only where colonialism still persists, as in Portuguese-controlled Africa —Guinea-Bissau, Angola, and Mozambique—and perhaps ultimately in minority white-controlled southern Africa—Rhodesia and South Africa—with their domestic colonialism; or where anticolonialist movements come under Communist control and then encounter foreign anti-Communist intervention, as in Vietnam. The latter situation is a borderline case of civil and international war.

(5) "Revolutions of rising expectations" occur not only in dependent countries but also in those formally independent, developing countries that are economically dependent on, or even controlled by, developed countries. Prime examples are found in Latin America. The endless coups and countercoups of the past were more of the "praetorian" type, which will be dealt with below (see 10). More recently, however, with the "awakening" of previously "dormant" masses (whether urban or *Indios* in the backwoods), movements tend to reflect genuine revolutionary ferment directed against feudal-military elites or foreign (now particularly American) interests and controls. Military elites, traditionally the chief guardians of foreign in-

terests, now sometimes espouse the cause of social reform. A military takeover, therefore, can no longer, as in the past, be termed "counterrevolutionary" *per se.*

(6) Antitotalitarian upheavals may take place where totalitarian or dictatorial regimes prove too weak, too divided, or too clumsy to prevent violence by satisfying economic wants or making political concessions. Such economic and political discontent led to the workers' uprising in East Germany in 1953, the Hungarian revolution of 1956, and two upheavals in Poland. "Counterrevolutionary" violence by the regime may ensue, or, as in Poland, a certain yielding to the original demands. Sometimes, as in Czechoslovakia in 1968, counterviolence (in that case, from abroad) follows the mere *fear* of popular upheaval.

(7) A curious and exceptional case of upheaval in a totalitarian regime is provoked, not by the "masses" subject to the regime but by leading groups within its own elite. Such seems to have been the case of the elite-inaugurated Chinese "Cultural Revolution," during which Mao, allied with other leading figures, called upon the "people" to rise against entrenched Party and other bureaucrats.* Somewhat similar was Hitler's violent destruction of one of his own chief party organizations, the SA. This kind of action shades over into a purge, a kind of "violence from above" characteristic of most totalitarian regimes. The purge may range all the way from "show trials" of a few selected victims to the killing of millions (as under Stalin). In its milder form, the purge is used to maintain party discipline and objectives by the constant threat of exclusion from the ruling party.

(8) Unrest based on ethnic conflict, racial discrimination, and similar "minority" (or, sometimes, majority) issues had seemed to be "out-of-date" what with progress and enlightenment, tolerance, and the benefits of constitutional guarantees

---

* A Chinese intellectual said to an American reporter: "The purpose of the Cultural Revolution was to recreate the atmosphere of the nineteen-thirties for our young people. Now they know what a struggle is." (Joseph Kraft, *New Yorker*, May 6, 1972, p. 114.)

of basic rights and "equal treatment under law." But, in the latter part of the century, it has come to the fore again; *vide* not only the continued discrimination against blacks, Chicanos, Indians and other nonwhites in the United States and ensuing protest activities and rioting, but also the conflict in Northern Ireland, the antiforeigner demonstrations in Britain, the violence in Quebec and Brittany, France, and even among a French-speaking minority in Switzerland (canton Bern). Frequently, as in the United States, Canada, and Ulster, the racial, ethnic, or religious conflict has social and economic aspects, with the haves and have-nots lined up on opposite sides of the barricades. These situations demonstrate all too clearly the persistence throughout our century of irrational sentiments that set human groups against each other.

(9) Much of the turmoil in newly independent countries, especially where the attempt is made to leap from the traditionalist, premodern stage into modernity, is based on the disintegration of belief systems and the ensuing *anomie* or the clash of old and new ideologies. Modernized or modernizing urban elites clash with traditional authorities. Similar disintegration of traditional beliefs, accompanied by confusion about what should take their place, seems to underlie much of the turmoil of the young, especially students, in developed countries, as well as the ferment within the strongly traditionalist and hierarchical organization of the Catholic Church. Such radicalism, while often resulting in mere nonviolent "dropping out" of society, also results in individual or smallgroup terrorism or alliance with groups that are otherwise revolutionary. Inasmuch as the political elites and other "establishments" of modern society are most fundamentally questioned through denials of, and attacks on, their underlying creeds and ideals (such as economic progress and "growth"), the reaction may well be more or less violent.

(10) When mentioning "praetorianism" and military coups in connection with Latin American violence, we referred already to what may be the "rock-bottom" basis of political force: namely, the almost "natural" resort to physical force on the

part of those who are in possession of the tools of force and are trained as "technicians of violence"—the military. Sometimes, as we have seen in regard to many of the developing African countries, the recourse to the military is seen as a stop gap to permit the re-establishment of order and the functioning of government. But, in more seriously divided situations, when everything else fails, power reverts to those who are in control of the instrumentalities of coercion. If, as Mao, for instance, contends, political power issues from the mouth of the gun, then it is particularly so where nonmilitary organs of government have lost "legitimacy" (or never acquired it), where they turn against each other without one being able to gain the upper hand, or where the very territorial basis of new political units is shaky, as it was in Pakistan. In the face of chaos, or the collapse of legitimacy, only military organization and power seem capable of governing.* But, if such government is based on nothing *but* military power, then it, in its turn, is shaky, for it is ever subject to the disunity that a falling out among its leaders, or factions can bring, so that one coup follows upon another. Thus, the seemingly strongest type of rule is also among the weakest.

If we look at the great variety of revolutionary and otherwise violent resorts to force in the twentieth century, we discover certain variables whose impact on such events, while not unknown in preceding centuries, seems to be particularly characteristic of our own. One factor is the interaction of domestic and international affairs: Wars, for example, create conditions favorable to revolution, especially in defeated countries, as happened at the end of World War I. Such war-born revolutions may, then, lead to further conflicts between ideologies

---

* What this means to the little man caught in the middle was graphically described by a Vietnamese peasant (quoted in the *New York Times,* August 10, 1972) who told a reporter: "When the nationalists come they claim they are the government and when the liberation forces come they claim they are also the government. So both sides are also our government. Both sides have guns."

and regimes, as with the clash between the fascist systems of the post–World War I period and Communism, both of which were products of that war.

Another factor affecting violent change is also connected with international affairs. In former times, even smaller and weak nations could, to a large extent, determine their own affairs themselves. Revolutions, too, could be "revolutions in one country," even though the doctrines and ideologies of the revolutionaries were internationalist. But there is a difference today, when almost every country is closely tied to international economics, trade, and finances. Isolated revolutions, especially when they aim at a radical (socialist, Communist, or similar) economic transformation, may, as in the case of Chile, depend for their success on arrangements with, or at least toleration by, the "capitalist" or similar interests with which the country was traditionally involved; or else, as in the case of Cuba, on lining up with the "camp" of the big power, either the Soviet Union or China, that has undergone a similar revolution before. "National self-determination," in this respect, has become a dependent variable.

Still another factor that is particularly noticeable in our century is the impact of the growth in world communications. The universe of information that by now integrates the globe and renders events instantly known everywhere has its obvious impact on the spread of violence. Violence often proceeds in waves, as with student demonstrations spreading from Berkeley, California, to Berlin and Paris, as well as to most other major universities outside the Communist orbit. Similarly, race riots may sweep major centers, as in the United States in the late 1960's. Instantaneous visibility on the television screen helps the acceleration.

TECHNOLOGY AND VIOLENCE

These observations lead to the more general question of the impact of technology upon violent action. Again, the relationship seems to be a dialectic one. On the one hand, the technological superiority of organized society over antistate groups has grown immeasurably since the times of primitive barricades. Government can organize its enforcement machinery speedily, equip it with the most modern means of repression, and throw it rapidly wherever needed. Thus, the "underclass" in modernized societies can protest and create turmoil, it can riot and wreak large-scale destruction, but its chances of gaining the upper hand through revolution are dim. This is true whether the "underclass" is a disadvantaged minority in a developed country or a suppressed majority as in South Africa. In some developing areas of the world, however, where majorities are on the rise against indigenous or foreign rulers, guerrilla warfare has shown up the helplessness of even vastly superior technology. Partisans may enjoy, and make use of, the support of people at large, as in significant parts of Vietnam and Portuguese Africa. Also, in World War II resistance forces in friendly territory inflicted heavy losses on technically and strategically superior forces whose visibility made them "flies on the flypaper."

Technology may give entirely novel opportunities, on the other hand, to individuals and small groups in a technologically advanced society. The functioning of modern, highly developed society is at the mercy of innumerable incidents or "malfunctions," which can throw it out of gear. A power-station failure may mean the blackout of large areas, and a virtual standstill of all activities. Acts of sabotage from innumerable vantage points can create vast danger or turmoil. As we are all too aware, one person armed with a gun (or merely a popgun) may highjack a jumbo jet with hundreds of passengers aboard, or kidnap an important indigenous or foreign political figure. "Urban guerrillas" can utilize the combined features of the urban "jungle" and urban integration for their purposes, and go undetected for long periods of time.

USE OF VIOLENCE TO PROMOTE CHANGE

If the gap in living standards between the wealthy developed "North" and the heavily populated and much more slowly developing "South" grows ever wider, it is safe to predict that the deterioration of life and ensuing increase of despair in the latter will lead to more acts of violence, some out of sheer hatred and frustration, others for pressure on local regimes or foreign interests. This progression will accelerate if the wealthy "North" encapsulates itself away from the poor, who cannot "rise in revolt" against the distant rich. The radicalized will then go on kidnapping foreign ambassadors, highjacking planes, assassinating political leaders, whether for mere protest or vengeance, or because, this way, they can extort at least a small amount of what they consider due to them. Increasingly, such acts can be expected even within the confines of the rich countries. It is also possible that, within the latter, the representatives of the "exterior proletariat" might join forces with members of the radicalized "underclass." Even outside this class, aggressiveness arising from alienation and frustration in the face of an increasingly depersonalized world, may hit blindly at anybody and anything, thereby making for more and more violence and use of counterforce. Such possibilities underscore the urgency for developed countries to face the needs of the developing world as well as those that face them domestically. Withdrawal into "fortress America," or "fortress Japan," or "fortress Soviet Union" will be self-defeating.

Government is faced with a particularly difficult problem whenever force is exerted against it to extract some concession or change of policy. In that event, the general reaction not only of governments but also of the public is usually that "one cannot yield to force or the threat of force without undermining the foundations of government." Inasmuch as organized society must claim the "monopoly of force," this reaction is understandable. But the social scientist cannot leave it at that but must dig deeper, especially when such acts are not those of "ordinary criminals" but have a political motivation. The action itself may be meant primarily to draw the attention of the domestic or international public to a situation claimed to be basically wrong, but which otherwise would remain unnoticed (or little noticed). Prison riots may protest unbearable prison conditions, but in the United States, where a large proportion of the prison population is black, they may also constitute (or be self-interpreted as) part and parcel of the revolt of the "underclass." In Latin American cases of kidnapping ambassadors to be exchanged for "political prisoners," there is likewise a clear political connotation. So is there also in cases of plane highjackings by Arab Palestinians, who use this tactic to draw world attention to their "right of self-determination."

In many of these instances, the underlying situation is such as to merit sympathy and a positive policy rather than repression. One can comprehend (though surely not condone) the actions of Palestinian terrorists who will never be reconciled to the transformation of their homeland into Israel, and the frustrations of Arab refugees in their miserable camps, who have been used as political counters by regimes that one day encourage violent actions and the next day repress them. Terrorism in Latin America is more easily understood when one sees it as a reaction to economic misery and governmental oppression, frequently involving torture, in say, Guatemala or Brazil. American prison riots (such as the one at Attica) may be seen as reflections of the defeated ghetto risings of the "hot summers." The latter were the "cry for help" of the black underclass, a cry answered by suppression and inadequately fulfilled promises. Phenomena like these are in reality expressions of class or race war, which seek to engage a far wider public as allies against otherwise overwhelming odds.*

* In such "warfare," there is frequently a good deal of anarchist utopianism. See, for instance, the naive expectation of the Attica prisoners to be taken to some sympathizing foreign country. Morally, the rioters may be on a higher plane than their opponents. "If we cannot live as people, we will at least try to die like men," said one of the Attica convicts. (Tom Wicker, in the *New York Times,* September 14, 1971.) Another said, "They [the prison guards taken hostages] are sleeping on mattresses, but I ain't sleeping on no mattress. They treat us like animals, we take care of them. Well, I ask you, does animals take care of people

VIOLENCE AND ITS REPRESSION

Governments' response to violence that originates in social or economic deficiencies is usually the "gut" answer of "going in there" with their armed forces (police, "national guard," the military, or what not) and shooting. This may be called the "Neanderthal" response. The public's bad conscience resulting from ensuing atrocities is generally calmed by conspiracy theories ("outside agitators" being responsible for the unrest of prison inmates; "Communist demagogues," for large scale strikes or social outbursts; "capitalist-imperialist agents," for publicly demonstrated opposition in Communist-controlled countries). These excuses may "legitimize" repression by force for a while but do little to cope with underlying causes of unrest. For the time being, change is inhibited; but demand for reform is merely postponed thereby, and is likely to come to the fore again later, but more violently. Even where a free press draws attention to existing conditions, the public, easily aroused over glaring abuses, is likely to forget today's issue when confronted with tomorrow's, so that, in the end, all too little by way of effective reform ensues.

Thus, in the United States, France, and even Britain, one can observe a common "curve" in the development of public attitudes and official policies toward urgent reform issues, especially in cases where large-scale violence and forceful and brutal repression have directed public attention to an issue. At first, there is great concern, an outcry for "something to be done" radically and immediately. Whereupon policy makers as well as the respective elites become (or appear to become) genuinely concerned, promising or even devising more or less radical new policies and measures. There then usually follows a stage of deliberation in lawmaking bodies, which forthwith

or does people take care of animals?" (Tom Wicker, in the *New York Times,* September 13, 1971.) When subsequently attacked by the National Guard, they refrained from going through with the revenge they had threatened against their hostages. See also the fair treatment of their hostages by the highjackers of planes in autumn, 1970.

start haggling over the appropriation of necessary funds. Alternatively, there are broad investigations by commissions composed of leading elite figures and sometimes, nowadays, a sprinkling of leaders from the "underclasses," which eventually publish thousands of pages of statistics, facts, and figures invaluable for generations of scholars and students but only rarely—as with the Beveridge Report—lead to radical reform. All too often the delay gives opposing forces and interests ample time to stall action. Meanwhile, public concern ebbs or vanishes, while another concern takes the place of the former, causing the next batch of banner-headlines. The result, as far as the first issue is concerned, may be worse than nothing, for a backlash by reform-hostile groups, and thus further polarization, may ensue.

Recent American examples of situations where the purpose of enacted legislation was not fulfilled or where programs were "starved" by insufficient appropriations or diversion to other purposes of appropriated funds include: coal mine accidents and revelations of health and safety regulations sabotaged by officials of the respective mining and health authorities, the latter under pressure from mining interests; widespread undernourishment and hunger and virtual peonage among migratory farm workers exploited by corporations owning large-scale agricultural holdings, and the sabotage of federal food-stamp programs by certain officials; horrors revealed about conditions in state mental hospitals and failure to provide adequate funds for building and staffing better ones; and the failure to enact promised prison reform. One should also mention the inadequacies of the "war against poverty" launched by the Johnson Administration in the face of ghetto risings. This was a vast program that fell victim to bureaucratic ineptitude, lagging interest of the "majority" public and, consequently, among lawmakers representing it, and to the diversion of funds and attention to the Vietnam war. Parallels can be found in the initial reform programs following the so-called revolution in France in 1968 and the lack of follow-through thereafter.

THE ORGANIZATION OF PUBLIC POWER

There remains the general problem of the organization of the force of which the state has the monopoly. Nothing essentially novel seems to have happened in this respect in our century, as compared with previous eras, except that, with the increase in populations and the rise in the number of tasks in which government is involved, the categories and numbers of people directly used for the state's repressive and executionary functions have likewise increased.* To be sure, there are occasional differences in strategy and organization, such as between the unarmed British policeman on the beat and his confreres in other countries. But even the British use force when threatened by Irish or, formerly, Indian or other "outgroup" mobs. Hierarchy and discipline are necessary principles in the organization of the military, police, national guards, prison guards, body guards, private guards, and so forth. Where large numbers must be recruited, it is difficult to avoid selection of individuals predisposed to using force or to adopting an attitude of unquestioning obedience. This is increasingly so where military conscription replaces volunteer or hired forces. Social scientists might be well advised to test the incidence of violence by war veterans, or the impact of differences in the selection and training of military and police in different areas and countries. To what degree are they held to the observance of the rules for the protection of individual and group rights and liberties? Is there as much difference as we presume between constitutional regimes with limited public power and totalitarian police states when it comes to

* A recent phenomenon has been the rise, in the United States, of a vast corps of private guards, organized by private "security agencies" and hired by private business or similar establishments for the protection of persons and property. According to a recent study (see the *New York Times*, April 9, 1972), they are, for the most part, unregulated, ill-trained, and thus unequipped to protect rights and liberties in dealing with the problems they are likely to encounter. Also, according to the report, while public (local, state, and federal) law-enforcement agencies employed 395,000 security personnel, that of the private agencies amounted to 289,000. The phenomenon is virtually universal as well among the well-to-do in developing countries.

"third-degree" police interrogations and detention without immediate trial?

Recent attempts in the United States, especially decisions in the mid-1960's of the Warren Supreme Court, to provide more protection of the rights of criminal suspects against police arbitrariness and abuse met the ire and resistance of the guardians of "law and order." Very basic questions here confront societies avowedly dedicated to the individual and his basic rights. In the light of increased crime and the resulting feelings of public insecurity, does attempted burglary convey a right to kill upon the armed defender of his possessions? In riot situations, is it right to give orders to "shoot to kill" looters? During the ghetto riots of the late-1960's, California Governor Ronald Reagan and Chicago Mayor Richard Daley said yes; Attorney-General Ramsey Clark and New York Mayor John Lindsay said no. It is in such extreme situations that liberalism, in the sense of restraint in the use of force, is put to the test.

Similarly, the line between limited and unrestrained use of public force divides systems that carefully instruct their military forces in what they may and may not do in the conduct of operations and dealings with prisoners, from those that do not. Unsavory actions by French troops in Algeria, British troops in Ulster, and American troops in Vietnam have shown that even democracies fail to train their soldiers effectively in the limits to be put on their use of force.

Contrary to common assumption, the quantitatively largest use of force in our century, in terms of persons killed within countries, has been by official violence, i.e., by governments against ethnic, racial, or similarly defined groups, and not through non- or anti-governmental violence; that is, through genocide and purge, not through riot and revolution. The massacre of Armenians by the Turks at the time of World War I, the Nazis' "final solution of the Jewish question"; the slaughter of millions of alleged Kulaks by Stalin and of millions of alleged Communists in Indonesia, of East Bengalis by West Pakistani soldiers, of Hutu in Burundi, in 1972, by the minority but ruling Tutsi, are among the most devastating illustrations of this fact. All of these situations were the result of a government-controlled or -instigated action, and not a spontaneous mob action or "rising of the people." Internationally, of course, it is organized government, too, that, in resorting to war, has been the chief perpetrator of violence.

If, in this chapter, we have placed stronger emphasis on the role of force in the political affairs of men than on peaceful change and developments, we have done so because that role is often forgotten, or played down, by those (especially professionals) who study the more regular procedures of government and society. We do not deny, of course, that the ordinary, day-to-day activities of people—rulers as well as ruled —in most organized societies proceed peacefully, that the application of force is still the exception, and that even radical change is not always the result of force and violence. But it is also true that no organized society has so far been able to function without underlying compulsion or, at least, its forever present threat. Philosophical anarchism, indeed, asserts that this is not necessarily so, and that the hope for mankind lies in the realization of a force- and threat-free, peaceful, and harmonious society of freely cooperating human beings. But history seems to bear witness to the utopianism of such an expectation. What one *can* hope for is the realization that, the less the basic needs of humans are taken care of, the greater the danger of violence on the part of the neglected; that the prime challenge to organized government is to avoid provoking violence; and that this can best be done if the institutions and procedures of democracy are used in the service of liberal values, in the sense of the freedom and dignity of the individual. Where this is done, the residual apparatus of enforcement and compulsion—which, as we have seen, is inevitable for the living together of large numbers of people— can be reduced to a minimum; even more importantly, it can then itself be put under the control of the "rule of law," which is, or should be, the liberal alternative to the rule of force.

VIII

THE INTERRELATIONS OF NATIONAL AND INTERNATIONAL POLITICS

A major trend of recent times has been the growing inter-dependence and integration of states in an international system where many of them become even less independent of influence from without and where none can escape the impact of growing world integration. Despite the fact that the number of formally and legally "independent" states has been rapidly increasing, they and all others tend to be grouped into a relatively few large blocs, some dominated by super-powers and some, especially in the Third World, attempting to maintain their separateness. While technologically, eco-nomically, and otherwise all are drawing closer to each other on a shrinking globe, they tend to be deeply divided politi-cally, ideologically, and oftentimes emotionally.

The impact of this dual development is reflected not only in the foreign but, increasingly, also in the domestic affairs of even the largest and most powerful nations. Because it is a relatively new feature of government and politics, it must be analyzed with particular care, for little in the experience of the past has prepared us for the strains, but also the oppor-tunities, that it provides for weak and strong alike.

From Self-Sufficiency to Interdependence

The original and far-reaching separateness of the modern state units that emerged in the late fifteenth and early six-teenth centuries meant that the impact of international affairs on national governments and policies was relatively limited. Political institutions grew out of native soil, and changes, even revolutionary ones, were due to indigenous forces and indigenous movements. Foreign influences, to be sure, were not without effect; but they were commonly transformed and shaped to fit the needs of the respective nation. Thus, liberal democracy might change in coloring or even in meaning, when exported from one environment to another. Indeed, throughout this period, domestic political forces and movements were less influenced by foreign affairs than they were themselves influences on foreign policies, as, for example, when Britain or the United States sided with liberal-democratic forces or nations, or when Tsarist Russia backed the cause of absolutism on the Continent for its own internal political reasons.

Domestic considerations, of course, are still powerful in the policies of nations, and especially in those nations that retain the largest measure of freedom of movement in their foreign affairs. But a vital change in the impact of world affairs on internal politics and institutions has resulted from the transformation of the nation-state from a fortress into a geographical entity incapable of assured defense against modern weapons of attack.

In the past, the modern territorial state was a self-contained, closed, centralized unit that could provide its citizens with protection, both in the form of internal peace and in the form of security from outside control or interference. Fortresses lining its boundaries rendered it difficult even for stronger adversaries to penetrate by force of arms; and security was strengthened by alliances of weaker powers with stronger ones, by nations' interest in the maintenance of a balance of power, and, prior to the French Revolution, by a feeling among rulers that "legitimate" units, as such, should not be destroyed. Subsequently, when dynastic legitimacy yielded to national self-determination, the national units acquired a cohesion that made them even more integrated and permitted internal government and constitutional life to develop in accordance with the indigenous trends and inclinations of the nation's people.

With industrialization, however, economic self-sufficiency

became transformed into dependence on continued imports from abroad. World War I showed how close both Britain and Germany could come to defeat through blockade. But the still more decisive change has been in the nature of war. Air war, by opening the way to "vertical" invasion, meant that the frontier could no longer serve its traditional function of protecting legal sovereignty and political independence. Since then, and particularly since the beginning of the nuclear age, countries have had to develop their political institutions and ways of life within a milieu constantly interpenetrated by divergent influences, some supportive and enriching but others threatening. This has been, and is, true for the major as well as the small states, for no country is now immune from devastating nuclear attack.

This change from relative self-sufficiency to interdependence has led to two kinds of reactions. One, which we will discuss in detail later, has been to develop a wealth of international and intergovernmental organizations and associations. Some of these are functional, like the World Health Organization and the Food and Agriculture Organization, some are political, like the United Nations itself, and some are regional organizations for particular purposes, among which the European Economic Community is the most significant.

The other reaction, whose impact has so far been stronger, has been for states to continue to act as if they were still the sovereign, independent units of the past. The chief difference has been that, especially in the immediate post World War II period, their efforts were directed at pushing out the wall of protection to encircle entire continents or at least contiguous groups of states. This effort started from the two dominant centers of power that emerged after World War II—the United States and the Soviet Union. It led to the phenomenon of "bipolarity"—i.e., the formation of two blocs, West and East, whose antagonism, accentuated by the ideological conflict between Communism and capitalist democracy, stamped the cold war of that period. These leading, or "super-," powers tried to bring more and more countries under their influence, or at least to keep them, ideologically, politically, and economically, from going to the other side.

Subsequently, fissures appeared on either side. De-Stalinization within the Soviet Union had its reflection among the Eastern European satellites, most notably in Rumanian foreign policy, and the development of China led to the Sino-Soviet split. The self-assertion of France under de Gaulle found echoes throughout Western Europe, and Third World countries in Asia, Africa, and Latin America struck out jointly or individually along distinctive lines of policy and organization under the rubric of "nonalignment." By the 1970's, China's nuclear capacity, Japan's economic power, and the increasing unity of Western Europe meant that the bipolar system was changing to a multipower system, while other countries with large populations, notably India, Nigeria, and Brazil, were assuming increasing influence within their own regions.

Variety of State Units

The emergence of a still partly bipolar and partly multipolar world of nations points up the great variety of political units, seen not only in terms of internal structures and regimes but also in terms of their international status. And the latter, in turn, has its impact on domestic structures and developments. There is the polar opposition between superpowers, on the one hand, which, because of their power, can hardly be influenced by others in reference to domestic policies and internal institutional characteristics, and, on the other hand, units that can be called states by courtesy only. Thus, the increasing category of micro-states, some of which have scarcely enough trained manpower to represent them abroad. In between are former big powers that enjoy independence in a genuine sense, but, either because they do not yet have nuclear capacity or because they have only relatively minor nuclear equipment, are increasingly compelled to join forces regionally, in particular, economically, in order to remain competitive with the superpowers. Among the large number of still weaker units, one can single out those that owe their existence to the functioning of, first, the European, and, then, the worldwide balance of power. This balance in eighteenth-century Europe also accounted for the disappearance of a long-established sovereign country, Poland, from the international scene. In the case of so-called buffer states, in contrast, the balance of power not only may support the continued existence of viable units, such as Switzerland or Afghanistan, but occasionally has accounted for the emergence of entirely artificial and ephemeral ones (such as "Free Cities" like Danzig or Cracow).

There are, finally, states that, for a variety of reasons usually related to an international situation or constellation, are "penetrated" units. That is, they are client states, or "satellites," of others that, as a result of their victory in war or their predominance in power in a given region, exercise control over these smaller states, or at least are in a position to influence their regime and their internal developments. Thus, the two Germanies, at least initially after the defeat in World War II, came to constitute one Eastern- (Soviet-) and one Western- (especially American-) penetrated unit.

In an age of superpowers, even radical revolutions and the revampings of the internal structure of "penetrated" states may no longer be indigenous affairs, arising from the conditions and movements within the respective countries, but are imported into them by the "penetrating" foreign power whose armies powerfully assist indigenous forces of their choice in the shaping of political forms and policies. The "communization" of Eastern Europe after World War II was of this type. Which of the Eastern and Southeastern European countries then emerged as socialist or remained non-Communist was determined by the division of the area into spheres of Soviet and Western influence. This division was based on the respective positions of the Western and Soviet armies at the end of the war, and was reflected in Stalin-Churchill agreements. Greece, liberated by the British, thus remained in the

Western orbit, while Rumania, Hungary, and the others, occupied, if not liberated, by the "Red Army," fell into the Soviet orbit and, in due course, emerged as Communist-controlled. Yugoslavia, which was expected to belong to the Soviet sphere, became Communist but, in the absence of Soviet troops from its territory, was able to remain outside it—a tantalizing example to those other Eastern European countries that were less fortunate.

In Germany, the division into zones of occupation by the Soviets and the Western powers accounts to this day, not only for its partition into what by now has become firmly established as the two separate and independent Germanies (the Federal and the Democratic Republics), but for the very boundary lines that segment the two units. The same applies to Berlin, which, remaining outside the occupation zones, was divided into Western and Soviet sectors that now constitute West Berlin, a Western island within the area of East Germany, and East Berlin, now capital of the Democratic Republic.

The category of "divided," or partitioned, states is another of the many distinctions resulting from international events and relationships. Aside from Germany, divided countries resulting from international bloc-formation and ideological polarization and penetration include Korea, which was divided along the 38th parallel into Soviet and American zones of military occupation immediately after the armistice in the Far East. Subsequently, it emerged as North (People's Republic of) and South (Republic of) Korea, the two remaining separate and independent states, despite, and following upon, the Korean war. Vietnam has been divided in consequence first of French and then American intervention and support of the south against a Communist-led "war of independence" by the north. Taiwan is sharply divided from mainland China because of the continued American support of the Kuomintang after it was defeated by the Chinese Communists and fled to Formosa. Whether divided nations, particularly when they fall into the orbits of opposed superpowers and are thus endowed with opposite types of political systems, can be reunited constitutes one of the most intriguing questions on the agenda of the world of tomorrow.

The Impact of Bipolarity

We have thus seen that the impact of the bipolar split of the world following World War II has been a determining factor in the international status and domestic structures of a large number of countries. We have not yet mentioned Japan, which, owing to its conquest and occupation by the United States alone, became a member of the Western bloc of nations. Quite generally, one can say that what characterized the postwar world and still has its effects on the present balance of power has been the emergence of two major spheres of influence and two major power blocs. On the one side is the Warsaw Pact organization of Eastern-bloc countries; on the other, NATO and corresponding alliances between the United States and countries in the Pacific and the Far East. In each of these spheres, a "superpower" has been playing the role of "leading" or "protecting" unit, with the tacit understanding that each bloc, or sphere, would mutually refrain from intervening in the affairs of the other. Thus, the other superpower has been given a free hand to interfere with its own bloc members as it sees fit. As we have observed before, this had its most noticeable effects in the Eastern bloc, where the Soviet Union was left undisturbed in its control of its "satellites" and even recently felt free to take action on the basis of such principles as the Brezhnev Doctrine.

In addition to these obvious byproducts of basic bipolarity, there have been more subtle effects. Particularly, but not exclusively, in the period of the cold war, domestic issues have tended to recede before foreign affairs. This effect has been more noticeable in democracies than in totalitarian countries, whose very structure is reinforced at all times by insistence on the danger by foreign intervention. But the functioning of liberal democracy has always been favored by the existence of peace or, at least, of the "normalcy" in which wars were rare enough not to disturb their institutions radically and limited enough not to affect an underlying feeling of security. But, since World War I in Europe, and since the end of World War II for the United States, too, crisis conditions in international affairs seem to have become the normal ones. Clearly, this situation favors authoritarianism over democratic institutions; concentration of power (especially in the executive, if not the military) rather than its limitation or dispersion; broad and ill-defined mandates rather than checks and controls; and restrictions or even suspensions of individual or group rights rather than their jealous protection.

There is yet another area, that of the arms race, where competition among nuclear powers affects domestic affairs. The simple but overriding fact of strategy in the nuclear age is that, once second-strike capacity has been assured, nuclear sufficiency is adequate for maintaining the stalemate for mutual deterrence, and "superiority" (in the numbers of ICBM's and what not) is irrelevant. But the "military-industrial complex" (i.e., the sum total of the military and defense industry, with their bureaucracies) has a momentum of its own. At first created by bona-fide strategic concerns, it tends, in turn, to perpetuate this concern. So many vested interests—investments, jobs, the profits of the defense industry, or, in Communist countries, bureaucratic interests—are connected with it that the governments of the nuclear powers, regardless of type and political coloration, seem unable to transform the structure into other uses. Such a vast proportion of the GNP goes into the strategic and military sector that vitally needed domestic services are neglected. It has been queried "whether any society—the United States included—can long pay the price of competition for global political and military primacy without progressively eroding and eventually destroying the material and moral supports upon which national power and influence ultimately depend."*

---

* H. and M. Sprout, National Priorities, in *World Politics*, XXIV, no. 2 (January, 1972), 317.

The Effect of Emergencies, Actual and Potential

The bipolar split and the ultimate threat of nuclear annihilation have not had the same impact in all places and at all times. This impact has differed in different nations and tended to change with the ups and downs in great-power relationships. Thus, at times the West has been particularly concerned with the economic penetration by the Eastern bloc of areas outside of Europe. At other times, the threat of actual hostilities with the Soviet Union, or more recently with China, over clashing interests in vital areas of the Middle East, Southeast Asia, and (with Cuba) even the Western Hemisphere has deeply affected American as well as West European policies. In an era of *détente,* however, this threat appears to have receded.

Such ups and downs should not deceive us into believing that, as in former ages, emergencies will come and go. The threat that nuclear war poses is a continuous one, and the emergency is thus potentially always with us. We may hope that the "balance of terror"—the nuclear stalemate between the two blocs—will ensure permanent peace, but we cannot depend on it. Crises are apt to recur; and, while totalitarian regimes, with their concentration of power and their absence of checks and limitations, are prepared in any case to meet crises, even where they do not provoke them, democracies, if they wish to preserve their traditional values and institutions, are confronted with grave difficulties.

These dangers were illustrated by the exploitation of a degree of hysteria in the United States at the height of the cold war. The use of legislative investigation, with all its connotations and effects—a use that, for a while, was almost unlimited and unchecked—affected not only individual rights and liberties (the sphere that attracted most attention) but also such constitutional principles as the separation of powers in government itself. At one point, it threatened to render lower and intermediate levels of the executive subject to control by members of the Congress, thereby undermining the hierarchy of the executive and the authority of its chief. And it is significant that "McCarthyism" eventually declined less because of executive opposition or broad public revulsion than because a recession in international tension coincided with resistance on the part of smaller groups, in particular the federal judiciary, the leaders in the Protestant churches and some universities, and a tradition-minded group of Senator McCarthy's colleagues.

Discouraging as much of this experience was, it also demonstrated that democracy has a resilience under stress that asserts itself sometimes in unexpected ways. Likewise, it tended to show that it is less the constitutional framework that lends or denies protection to national institutions than it is the traditions of nations and the spirit in which they and their leaders act. This can be seen still better from the way in which West European nations reacted to the cold war situation. Thus, the British, whose government had made a cautious and restrained use of legally unlimited emergency powers in both world wars, proved similarly sober in their approach to postwar problems of internal security. Instead of flooding the country with loyalty investigations and subjecting the entire civil service to uniform security standards, they applied these to carefully selected sensitive agencies and only to positions where spies or subversives might do real damage. More important, they never yielded to the frenzy of fear and suspicion that leads to the invasion of vital personal concerns with far-fetched charges, "faceless" accusers, and ostracism. This experience indicates that, difficult as is the problem posed to democracies by a state of permanent emergency in world relations, the sacrifice of liberties is not inevitable.

But, just because McCarthyism has come and gone, we should not underestimate the lasting effects of potential emergencies. Especially since the involvement in the protracted Vietnam war, the American people have been deeply rent over this issue. Opposition to the involvement has led different administrations to concentrate ever more independent decision-making at the top level of the executive and to

broaden and sharpen means of repression of those suspected
of being "radicals." Confronted by crime waves and by civil
unrest created by the neglect of urgent domestic needs and
of basic liberties, authorities, using the slogan of "law and
order," have been tempted to circumvent fundamental law
and traditional constitutional order. There have been exposés
of, and protests against, "preventive detention" of suspects,
"no-knock" entry into homes, "fishing expeditions" by inves-
tigative grand juries, police surveillance of persons through
wiretapping, and maintenance of files on a wide range of
persons, including Congressmen, without legal safeguards for
the individual's reputation, not only by legitimate investigation agencies, such as the FBI, but also by numerous others,
including the Army. British authorities in Northern Ireland,
but not in England, have similarly been criticized sharply for
transgressing customary democratic safeguards.

Other democratic countries, though not immediately faced
with a war situation, have also seen fit to strengthen the
authorities. West Germany, at a time of domestic tranquillity,
enacted "emergency legislation" providing for the transfer
of vast powers to small executive parliamentary bodies during
"states of internal or international tension." This legislation
of itself contributed to the rise of an extraparliamentary opposition and to the activating of radical-leftist student groups
in the late 1960's. It should also be mentioned that virtually
all developing states have provisions for summary detention
of anyone considered a potential danger to the regime, and
South Africa has provisions for long-term detention without
trial not only for those suspected of threatening security or
order but also for persons believed to have information that
the authorities desire.

One of the most important needs of a democracy is a constant, unimpeded flow of information. Here, too, world tension is taking its toll. Witholding information for security
reasons intensified with the advent of "atomic secrets"; more
and more, government activities have been "classified," thus
all too often limiting information to predigested official news

handouts. To some degree, this is inevitable. Who among the uninitiated can judge what measures are best fitted to counter an alleged or real aggression? Dependence on nuclear weapons may make necessary quick decisions of a vital character that can hardly be arrived at through prolonged democratic discussion of issues. But an intelligence agency like the CIA may engage in activities far beyond the collection of information. And, if active citizenship is not to be excluded from the fields of defense and foreign affairs, such a development means that responsible leaders have still greater need than they did in the past to keep the public informed, not only of the reasons for such limits on information but also of the basis on which the judgments in these fields are made.

The publication of the "Pentagon Papers," owing to the courageous, though legally challenged, initiatives of former members of the executive as well as of the press, revealed that the top-level policy-makers have little feeling for the necessity of providing the public, or even Congress, with information on policies that involve the nation in far-reaching commitments affecting the initiation and escalation of a war and its extension to additional countries. On the other hand, by giving the public, however belatedly, access to what had been kept secret, a free press, protected by independent courts, has once more shown the advantages of liberal democracy vis-à-vis dictatorial regimes, under which similar revelations tend to come out decades later, if at all. Strangely enough, technological progress—in this instance, the ease of "xeroxing" classified material—has had something to do with the recent rash of making such material publicly available; technology thus has for once proved a liberalizing element.

THE TREND TOWARD CONFORMITY

We should also notice one further effect of bipolarity: what may be called the "neutralization" of politics, the trend toward avoiding strong attitudes for or against this or that policy. Bipolarity, which implies ideological cleavage, tends to render suspect unpopular or even unusual attitudes, whether held by individuals or by groups. This reaction has always been a characteristic of totalitarianism, where the essence of control consists in the suppression of deviating opinion. But it has tended to spread in nontotalitarian countries also. Such conformity opposes what Communism itself destroys: espousal of reform, protection of rights, safeguarding of liberties. In the nineteenth century, broad movements for change and reform in the major nations were often backed by large popular majorities. Today, as we have noted, most industrialized countries have "compact majorities" of the more or less affluent, which tend to be conservative. Recently, however, there has been a revival of concern for great political issues by intellectuals, the clergy, students, and other members of the elite, joining together in the interests of reform with disadvantaged minorities.

Other factors besides bipolarization have helped to create a trend toward conformity. Political indifference tends to result when vital decisions are made without the participation or even knowledge of the public. The mass media often emphasize the sensational rather than the basic issues, although their impact, as in publicizing either atrocities or new lines of policy—e.g., the Nixon visits to China and Moscow—can be great. Lastly, the rising living standard and improved social services in countries like the United States and Britain, by lessening former inequities in wealth or status, have rendered large numbers of people so satisfied that their interest in class or other social and economic issues has declined.

It is often in countries and regions afflicted by poverty or deep social strains that the political involvement and concern that we have characterized as typical of the nineteenth century still prevail. It has been in such areas that student involvement in politics has had its greatest impact, resulting in 1960, for example, in the overthrow of regimes in Turkey and Korea.

We thus arrive at the somewhat paradoxical conclusion that, although grinding poverty, economic anxiety, or class division renders the functioning of genuine democracy difficult, the very solution of these problems likewise involves difficulties to democracy. Can a society that has reached a high level of material satisfaction generate that continual concern with civic issues that is at the root of active democracy? Can it do so particularly in times when, as is bound to happen periodically, concern with domestic matters recedes behind apprehension about the international situation?

Relations Between Stronger and Lesser Powers

Let us now turn to another impact of the new power system in the world, that of the superpowers on lesser states and, in particular, on their allies. There is nothing new in unequal relationships between stronger and weaker powers. They have, in the past, accounted for dependence of all sorts, ranging all the way from mere strategic or economic influences to protectorate or colonial relationships. But, except in the latter case, where the dominant power maintained ultimate control, domestic affairs have usually stayed within the autonomous control of the weaker power. The contrast today is that similar relations tend to affect to a greater degree the internal policies and systems of the weaker states, especially those we have described as the penetrated ones. This has not meant that such dependency automatically involves control over the details of day-to-day policy-making. But it may well affect a country's fundamental decisions about social and economic structure, political constitutions and freedoms, and similar basic issues, which one expects to be settled through the actions of national parties or movements within the framework of national institutions and processes.

The issue of internal Communism provides a striking example of this trend. The Communist Party is legal and strong in France and Italy. But it is practically excluded from official positions in government coalitions. This is partly because of fear of its use of power internally, but partly also because internal alignments in our day are liable to have foreign-policy connotations. As long as Italy is in NATO, for instance, can one visualize Communist participation in a government through which Communist ministers might share the secrets of a military alliance? The Communist Party, as a French Premier once put it, is "neither Left nor Right, but East."

In the East, of course, anything other than Communism is excluded and, as proved by the Soviet Union's crushing of Czechoslovakia's liberalizing regime in 1968, even certain types of socialist deviations are not permitted. The Hungarian revolution of 1956 had already indicated the limits set on the freedom of action granted to members of the Soviet bloc. Spelled out in the "Brezhnev Doctrine" that was formulated after the Soviet-bloc invasion of Czechoslovakia, these limits are reached when the Soviets perceive a "threat to the cause of socialism" and to the "common interests of the socialist camp"; in other words, when they fear defection of a unit from the sphere of "socialism" into that of capitalism. In the Hungarian case, it was Hungary's denunciation of its membership in the Warsaw Pact organization that brought about Soviet military intervention. In the Czechoslovak case, it seems to have been the internal liberalization of the regime (especially the plan to permit intraparty "factional" opposition in the place of "democratic centralism") that proved to be the unforgivable sin.

But Western democratic states have also tried, from time to time, to make use of their influence in order to ensure what might be called the stability, "political health," or reliability of an ally. There was open use of American influence on behalf of the Christian Democrats at the time of the Italian election of 1953. In the same year, American backing of Adenauer and his Christian Democrats in West Germany was not without effect on his victory over the Social Democrats, who, though similarly Western-oriented, were at that time suspected of neutralism. Moreover, in the 1960's, the United States, under President Johnson, claimed the right to intervene in Latin American countries whenever, in its judgment, there was the threat of a Communist takeover.

But, as the Dominican case showed, attempts by democratic countries to influence too closely or too rudely the affairs of less powerful states are apt to backfire. This is why, more recently, their influence over their allies has lessened or become more subtle and indirect. Indeed, one could sometimes wish that democratic political ideals were more influential on regimes and institutions allied in foreign affairs with the West. Dictatorships, or otherwise authoritarian regimes such as those in Spain, Portugal, Greece, and in many countries of Latin America, seem sometimes even preferred and favored over democratic states with leftist leanings. The European (NATO) allies of the United States, on the other hand, are by now on a more or less equal plane with it. De Gaulle would not stand for less, and his example encouraged others. Chancellor Brandt, for instance, took bold initiatives in his *Ostpolitik* that, in former times, would not have been possible without the assurance of prior American consent.

The Major Powers and the "Uncommitted" World

We may ask how the ascendancy of the superpowers has affected those countries that so far have avoided close alignment with big-power blocs, and in this sense are uncommitted. For the most part, they belong to the category of "developing" countries, which constitute what is often called the "Third World." Many of them are newly independent and still faced with the problems of establishing their own political and constitutional systems and procedures. In most of them, previous Western influence and control determined their original governmental institutions and political processes at least in a formal way. Western-type parliamentary systems, parties, and elections initially abounded; and, occasionally, the experience of these states added significantly to our knowledge of democratic possibilities, as when elections in India demonstrated that literacy is not an indispensable requirement for genuine expression of the popular will. On the other hand, in many of these states, as we have already seen, strains and divisions have led to military rule either as a stabilizer or as a more permanent authoritarian government.

Pulls and counterpulls operating on developing states result from a wide range of competing efforts to secure influence through various forms of foreign aid. This aid is sometimes tied to military advantage, such as the American air base in Liberia, or associated with an American tracking station, as at Kagnew in Ethiopia, or associated with troop dispositions in favor of an established regime, the last of which has been characteristic, though mainly in the past, of the French in their former African territories. Still more pervasive is the French cultural influence in its former colonies, especially through its provision of teachers and control of higher education.

Sometimes great-power competition is reflected in economic and military aid programs to rival states, as with U.S. aid to Ethiopia and Soviet support for neighboring Somalia. Still more dangerous backing of rival states were Soviet support of Egypt and parallel American aid to Israel. In Asia, misguided American, as well as Chinese, backing of the military regime of West Pakistan during its attempt to maintain its control in East Pakistan (subsequently independent Bangladesh) was countered by aid to, and support of, India provided, to its own great advantage, by the Soviet Union.

Formal military arrangements like the kind the British originally had with Nigeria proved an encumbrance to the developing state and have been abrogated. During the Nigerian civil war, however, the British and the Russians both supported the federal cause, thereby acquiring kudos, while official American neutrality and lack of governmental aid to either side (although a preponderance of private American aid went to Biafra) resulted in political and popular disfavor after the federal victory. It should be noted also that, because Western countries have a relatively high standard of living, their experience may well seem to have less relevance to developing countries like Tanzania than that of a state like the Soviet Union or, more particularly, China, which has been coping with development problems more comparable to their own.

It would be a mistake, however, to underestimate the attraction of the liberal-democratic ideal to some of these newly emancipated states. It may well be true that, to the great mass of their people, it is more important to escape from grinding poverty than to secure personal liberties. But even the most poverty-stricken person has a sense of his own personal dignity, for which he desires respect. Even at this level, the right to protest and to propose is a cherished one. But more important in shaping the immediate destinies of states like India and Tanzania is the fact that their leaders have a keen feeling for democratic values and are attempting courageously in the face of great difficulties to keep them in operation in their societies.

Seen in this context, it is not the Western democracies' propaganda that will be decisive for their influence in the uncommitted countries, but what they do, for it is obvious that their activities can have a great impact when they answer the basic needs of these countries. There are two ways in which the developing nations can modernize and industrialize: largely through their own unaided efforts but at the cost of great sacrifices and authoritarian controls, or with assistance from outside. Where, as in Botswana, Western economic and technical assistance aids their development to such a degree that they can both modernize themselves and retain their Western-type institutions and freedoms, these institutions have a better chance to gain the mass backing that is essential for their continued survival. But aid and financial arrangements must be provided in such a way that countries do not become overindebted by interest and amortization payments, as happened in Ghana after Nkrumah. There are also situations, particularly in Latin America, where the profits of foreign, particulary American-owned, mining or industry are larger than the inflow of foreign aid, thereby constituting development in reverse. In the competitive struggle with the Communist powers for influence in these states, it is far more important to provide an opportunity for democratic institutions to root themselves in popular favor than to achieve any immediate backing on a particular issue.

Not only is it important to provide the kind of economic aid that can underpin democratic regimes; it is also vital for Western states to back those who struggle to keep them in operation. In this respect, the record is far from good. To back military-controlled Pakistan against democratic India, as the Nixon Administration did during the civil war on the subcontinent, or to favor the military regime in Brazil while undermining the democratically elected government of Allende in Chile, is to raise suspicions that power politics or business and mining interests are regarded as more significant than popular institutions. Moreover, in southern Africa, France's continued sale of arms to the racially oppressive Vorster regime, coupled with the active operation of British, American, French, and West German enterprises in South Africa, and the deliberate and open American break over chrome in the U.N.-sanctions front against Rhodesia, suggest a similar overriding concern for financial rather than democratic interests.

Another common form of aid is to train military and police forces of developing states. This provides a further form of foreign influence and has a domestic impact in providing support for whatever regime is in power, reactionary or reformist. The provision of military equipment serves the same purposes and may well burden the recipient with continuing expenses it can ill afford.

To support progressive, democratic forces in countries like India, Tanzania, Botswana, Colombia, and Indonesia may well be the most important way to counter the spread of Communist influence in the Third World. To some degree, the Soviet Union has been proving itself more "democratic" in its policies toward developing states than have the Western countries. It charges lower interest rates for development projects than the latter and ostentatiously maintains that there are no political strings to its aid; the Chinese, who are building the TanZam railway between Dar-es-Salaam and Lusaka with their own labor, make the same pledge. Moreover, both of the major Communist countries appear to be accepting the validity of indigenous nationalism, whether of the Communist variety, as in Yugoslavia and North Vietnam (though not for Warsaw Pact countries), or of the non-Communist variety, as in Egypt. Both the Soviet Union and the Chinese provide support to the various liberation groups challenging the Portuguese, Rhodesian, and South African regimes and doubtless to some of the so-called terrorist groups in certain Latin American countries as well. It is interesting to note that, particularly in Asia and Africa, the Chinese sometimes find it useful to exploit their color, and to oppose Soviet influence, as well as that of the West, as belonging to "white" powers.

In the face of such pressures and allurements, effective democratic influence on developing states also requires a further type of action on the part of Western countries: a convincing demonstration that they themselves are truly democratic in actions as well as words. Having long lived under colonial control and discrimination, the developing countries, or at least their leaders, not only care about improving their material conditions but also expect to be treated on a basis of equality. A major reason why the newer countries of the Commonwealth—India, Kenya, Malaysia, Nigeria, Jamaica, Swaziland, and many others—prize their membership is that, in addition to receiving material advantages, they are treated as equals in that association. To the extent that the West maintains democratic practices both in its relations with the new states and at home, it enjoys a vast advantage over its totalitarian opponents, whose words are contradicted by realities, particularly with regard to domestic practices. The degree to which democratic values, in particular racial equality and personal and group liberties, are demonstrable is likely to have a marked influence on what direction the so-called uncommitted states ultimately will take. Thus, the practice of democracy in the United States, Great Britain, and the rest

of Western Europe may turn out to be decisive for the preservation of freedom throughout the world.

THE ROLE OF INTERNATIONAL ORGANIZATION AND COOPERATION

Governments are increasingly faced with global tasks and
strains arising from the international environment in which
they must operate. We have spoken of the tremendous
changes that have transformed the relatively separate and self-
sufficient countries of the past into an integrating global society, within which all states tend to become interdependent.
Population trends and pressures affect not only particular nations but, with their byproducts of migration and (in extreme
cases) of refugee and expellee groups and stateless persons, all
the other countries, too. The "population explosion," as such
(coupled with the exhaustion of vital natural resources and
the problem of inadequate food supplies in large parts of the
world), poses as great a world problem today as does security
from aggression and nuclear annihilation. Moreover, the new
environment resulting from developments in science and technology, such as nuclear weapons. the exploration of space, the
exploitability of the ocean bed, and much besides, has itself
been changing rapidly. What this turbulent era needs for coexistence is vastly increased international cooperation, over-
all global planning, and the development of new procedures
and standards of international rule-making in place of leisurely
diplomacy and old-fashioned, complex, and slow treaty-making. Ultimately, we must move to the point where international agencies are authorized to act quickly and decisively,
and without the all too common vetoes or lack of financial
support by constituent member-states in those areas where
catastrophe threatens unless determined global action is taken.

In the area of nuclear strategy and nuclear arms races, universal agreements on arms control, nonproliferation of weapons, and so forth, have long been on the agenda, but there
are three other areas of vital need to which attention has only
recently been given: the pressures of world population, deple-
tion of resources, and the deterioration of the environment,

especially through pollution. Scarcely had the developed countries become deeply concerned about the danger of over-population when they recognized that the threats to a livable environment pose a problem of similar dimensions: The poisoning of the air, the pollution of rivers, lakes, and oceans; the exhaustion, often through waste, of vital resources; the extinction of animal species on which men have depended for their food supply—all these and other developments conjure up the possibility of an eco-catastrophe as threatening as a nu-clear holocaust. In short, the preservation of the common do-main of mankind has become a common interest of mankind. No more urgent task can be imagined than that of providing for effective international devices and institutions to protect the world from rampant deterioration or utter destruction.

For the last one hundred years, there have been attempts to bring about an ever closer integration of sovereign nations through the establishment of agencies for the pursuit of common purposes. This trend culminated first in the League of Nations and later in the United Nations, with its many af-filiated agencies in economic, cultural, and humanitarian fields. There are also multinational agencies for specific purposes and a wealth of voluntary agencies working both domestically and throughout the world. A vast number of sig-nificant activities are now coordinated or carried on through these channels.

But international organizations have not yet acquired the universal and wholehearted support called for by the growing interdependence of nations and their common needs in the interest of sheer survival. The age-old practices of power politics in the national interest and of national separatism persist. International actors still conduct international affairs as the "foreign" policies of their respective "independent" units. Domestic policy considerations often determine foreign-policy decisions—e.g., free trade versus protection, or when President Nixon apparently shapes his policies toward Viet-nam according to what the election campaign seems to dic-tate, or when a weak regime provokes foreign confrontations to rally its people. We still lack what a German has called *Weltinnenpolitik,* a "global domestic policy" of mankind. One wonders whether a world catastrophe is a precondition of a radical transformation of attitudes, but if so, the change seems likely to come too late.

Despite what seems to those fully aware of global needs a dangerous lack of willingness to transfer major functions and powers from the domain of sovereign states to that of international organizations, countries have increasingly made use of the latter for purposes that are both to their advantage and beyond their own scope. The World Health Organization has been able to do much to limit the spread of epidemics, to reduce the incidence of plagues like malaria, and to eliminate yellow fever; the Food and Agriculture Organization as well as private agencies like the Rockefeller and Ford Foundations have aided developing countries to produce new and improved crops; and the office of the U.N. High Commissioner for Refugees has stimulated and coordinated the resettlement of millions of displaced persons, over a million of them in Africa. Its predecessor, the International Refugee Organization, had settled vast numbers of homeless people through its camps, shipping facilities, and migration services, while the UNHCR subsequently coped with the sudden emergencies created by the outflow of refugees after the abortive Hungarian revolt against Soviet control in 1956. In 1971–72, it coordinated the relief for, and return of, millions of East Bengalis who had fled into neighboring India to escape the West Pakistani troops and also aided in the repatriation and resettlement of half a million Southern Sudanese following the termination in 1972 of the Sudan's seventeen-year-long civil war. Large-scale refugee waves, though caused by domestic turmoil, create serious international strains that only an international agency can ameliorate. Moreover, international organization facilitates technical and economic activities in developing countries better than any single outside state, and has lately been able to coordinate them effectively through the U.N. Development Program.

Most surprising, and perhaps ultimately most significant, may be the international force that maintains peace between Greeks and Turks on Cyprus and did so for some time within the Congo. In fact, the Congo presented an example of how, in the absence of organized internal government, international administrators could take over those functions. As in some previous instances (League of Nations administration of the Saar territory, for instance, and international plebiscite commissions), international organization has proved itself at least technically capable of providing those services that are traditionally claimed to be exclusively national ones.

It would also be a mistake to underestimate the moral and psychological influence of the United Nations, which affects state policies both by example and by expectation. The newer countries have learned much about the practices of more mature ones through contact in U.N. organizations. The principle of equality for women and the Declaration of Human Rights may not be accepted fully in some Latin American, Asian, and African countries calling themselves democratic (nor are they accepted as fully in the mature democratic states, as they should be), but it becomes more difficult for all these countries to withstand pressures at home to extend such rights when they have been promoted on the international level. From the other side, sensitivity to racial and color discrimination within countries has been intensified in Western states through the participation of Asians and Africans in international agencies. Even when nations find justification in traditional standards of self-interest for interfering forcibly in a national situation, as Great Britain and France did in the Suez crisis late in 1956, the protests in the United Nations (and, indeed, among the British people themselves) indicated new and widespread assumptions about the use of U.N. channels that hopefully will some day exert an influence on national policies. Even the Soviet Union, with its vast military strength and its rigorous insistence on its right to interfere in the Hungarian uprising and in Czechoslovakia, had to stand a fire of criticism and moral reprobation from smaller countries, while its efforts to make capital out of the Congo crisis in the early 1960's were largely thwarted through the support of U.N. action by independent African states. In a world where major power blocs strive for the support of the uncommitted countries, debates in the United Nations are far from being without influence.

It is still true, however, that operating on these traditional lines is no longer enough in our age of acceleration, where, as we have seen, problem piles upon problem of a global nature, and time is of the essence if mankind is to survive. Let us compare, for example, how international labor problems have been regulated with the devising of "ecostandards." Under the ILO system, international labor conventions are adopted not only to improve labor conditions because of humanitarian considerations but also to prevent noncooperative countries from underselling on the world market because of an interest in maintaining lower standards. Similarly, now with the wide variations in national regulations of pollution control, it is urgent to secure international agreements on comparable "ecostandards," e.g., for the regulation of sewer and industrial effluence into the oceans and of air pollution by planes, cars, and industries.

Differential regulation, or nonregulation, in some areas disadvantages the more community- or ecology-minded and also tempts interests burdened by exacting standards to migrate to nonregulated regions, which then not only suffer deterioration themselves but also spread it to others. American multinational corporations, so-called, reportedly are attracted to investing in Europe because, among other reasons, antipollution costs are "less active forces in European society" (*New York Times,* December 28, 1971). Japan's phenomenal postwar industrial boom has sacrificed the environment and, indeed, public health in certain areas like Tokyo-Yokohama in the urge to produce ever more.

Some developing states, notably Brazil, strive to industrialize and modernize without the costs and fetters of pollution regulations, claiming the right of "poor, unpolluted countries to do some polluting of their own for the sake of the benefits that industry has already brought to rich, polluted countries" (*New York Times,* February 13, 1972). This raises the question of whether those countries that are still less affected by environmental deterioration because of low levels of development and lower living standards should be permitted less exacting "ecostandards," on the argument that unbridled growth has enabled the developed countries to bring their people up to "affluence." Taking into account, however, the heavy penalties exacted internally as well as externally by pollution damage, it is questionable whether such a policy would be in their own long-range interest.

What can be done? One suggestion is that the mineral and similar resources of that "last frontier of mankind," the ocean bed, should be reserved for the benefit of developing countries. Control over the exploitation and profits from these resources would thus go to a new international agency or to the U.N. Development Program. But this is only one possible device. More generally, new ways must be found of creating speedy agreement on standards. The conclusion of international labor conventions was a slow, tedious, and not infrequently unsuccessful process. Even then, the treaties might or might not be ratified by ILO members and transformed, by domestic legislation, into national law. Current needs demand more speedy adoption of international standards and commitments to more or less automatic observance of these standards domestically.

To transform international agreement into "self-executing," i.e., automatically binding and enforceable domestic law, may require constitutional changes, particularly in countries with federal structures, or where parliamentary bodies normally share in treaty-making and similar powers. Some democracies, notably Switzerland, but also Denmark and Norway, require popular votes (plebiscites, referenda) in addition to parliamentary action in important foreign-policy decisions. Thus, the need for international regulation may well run counter to democratic tendencies. Dictatorial and totalitarian regimes are not self-hampered this way in the conduct of their foreign affairs. But everywhere the general crisis conditions in the world are forcing a greater concentration of power in the executive. If such power is used in the interest of universal regulation of environmental control or similar needs, such sacrifice of internal democratic procedures seems more justified than if it is made for the prosecution of purely "national interests."

Eventually, such internal adaptations may have to facilitate the working of genuine supranational organization or even of international government. Some postwar constitutions, notably those of France and West Germany, as well as postwar amendments to some older constitutions, notably those of the Netherlands and Denmark, already provide for a possible transfer of legislative, administrative, and judicial authority to an international organization or organizations.

Surprisingly, it has been in the area of judicial power, rather than of lawmaking or enforcement, that a trend has begun toward devolution of national jurisdiction in favor of international adjudication. The most spectacular example is in connection with war crimes, where post–World War II trials set precedents for direct jurisdiction concerning individual criminals. But, apart from defeated countries, it is not likely, as the Vietnam cases have shown, that such jurisdiction will be ceded voluntarily in situations where domestic authorities have a hard time to get convictions even under domestic standards.

More hopeful precedents are in the area of the protection of human rights; the 1950 European Convention for the Protection of Human Rights and Fundamental Freedoms, for instance, provides for a European Court of Human Rights, to which individuals can take well-authenticated cases in which a state, even their own, is charged with violating their rights. Moreover, in the field of civil relationships, the European communities are also pacemakers in providing a court that watches over the implementation of rules concerning, for instance, the relationships of business corporations to European and member-state agencies (see below).

The question arises whether a similar jurisdiction should not be created for the enforcement of international "ecostandards." Their violation, e.g., in cases of major oil spills, involves universal interests. Thus, direct imposition of damages, and perhaps even punitive measures ordered by international courts or courtlike agencies, seems justified wherever domestic prosecution cannot be expected. The fact that Britain and Canada have already claimed the right to extend their jurisdictions to ocean areas outside their territorial waters, in order to protect themselves against environment damage, points up the urgency of international regulation.

The practical significance of the constitutional provisions we have mentioned above, however, has not been in relation to international organization, in general, but to the Western European regional organizations that developed in the postwar period—the European Coal and Steel Community, Euratom, and the Common Market.

These three organizations, now merged into one, possess "supranational" agencies with limited but direct powers over individuals and corporations within the constituent nations. Although the Parliament of the European communities has so far been granted only consultative functions, and its Council of Ministers represents the "sovereignty" of the member states, nevertheless the Commission, with its own mushrooming staff organization, has grown into the role of representing the "community interest." There is also a "constitutional" court, named the Court of Justice of the European Communities, which, as we have noted, watches over the implementation of the common rules.

This example indicates that gradual development toward genuine world government is possible through a process of step-by-step devolution of national sovereignty. To be sure, even regional devolution constitutes an extremely complex and, at times, frustrating process. A decade (1961–71) of French resistance to British entry followed earlier British hesitation to join the European Economic Community, and there was a sharp parliamentary battle in Britain itself once the

Heath Conservative government overcame French opposition. Both the British and the French attitudes clearly revealed the obstacles posed by national interests to yielding their current influence in favor of playing a less predictable role within an existing or enlarged regional setup.

What has developed in Western Europe shows, however, that some nations, under certain circumstances, are willing to sacrifice their previous rights and engage in novel ventures. That the greatest success has been along regional rather than worldwide lines indicates the importance of building on common interests and common understanding. The growing speed with which the West European integration movement is developing underscores the value of patient negotiation and detailed planning.

So long as nations seek security in power blocs and similar agglomerations, i.e., in the concentration rather than the transfer of power, there is acute danger for all countries in a world of states that are split ideologically and armed with weapons of destruction. It may be optimistic, but perhaps not utopian, to anticipate that the recognition both of common dangers and of common objectives will, in the end, prove stronger than the pull of fear and the urge toward power. In that event, regional and international organization will have an impact on government and politics far greater than any other force in the world today.

IX

DEMOCRACY IN THE MODERN WORLD

Now that we have concluded this survey of some of the forces and problems that confront governments today, we are ready to return to two basic questions: What is the nature of democracy and of totalitarianism? And how valid are the charges against democracy that were raised in the beginning of this book? In reaching our conclusions on these matters, we must keep in mind that there are many states with a greater or lesser leaning toward democracy that are neither completely democratic nor totalitarian; that even liberal democracies are subject to strains of emotion, fear, and self-interest, which sometimes lead them to adopt techniques or, temporarily, even objectives more characteristic of totalitarian dictatorships than they like to realize; and that, in the world of today, both the tasks and the organization of government are at all times complex, highly demanding, and absolutely vital to the future of any "modern" society.

THE TWO PATTERNS OF DEMOCRACY AND TOTALITARIANISM

Despite the strains and tensions to which democracies are subject, there remain clear differentiations between liberal democracy and totalitarian dictatorship or totalitarian oligarchy (in the sense that we have defined these terms in the beginning of this book) that are worth reiterating. As we have seen, in a totalitarian dictatorship the power exercised by its governing group is, in principle, unrestrained, and the authority of the regime extends into every aspect of the life of the individual. In a liberal democracy, in principle, the exercise of political power is limited by a constitutional framework, or by convention, which protects certain areas of life from governmental interference and provides that the powers allowed to the government shall be exercised according to known rules and procedures. The simplest distinction to be made between these two forms of government is thus between unlimited and limited government. As someone has said: "In democracies what is not forbidden is permitted; in dictatorships it is compulsory."

Behind these differences lie two sharply contrasting conceptions of the political community. The first, endorsed by both Communist and Nazi totalitarianisms, is that this community is an entity with a specific purpose of its own, which may be something quite different from the immediate purposes and desires of its members. The community is therefore superior in claims and interests to the individual. This view is linked, in turn, to a belief in historical inevitability. Thus, the Soviet leaders, accepting the materialist conception of history, determine policy in the light of this (supposed) key to the future. In classical Marxism, of course, the state was stigmatized as an instrument of oppression used by the ruling class; Lenin envisioned it as an instrument of the working class in freeing itself from its oppressors. Stalin maintained that the Soviet state was a necessary protection of the working class against capitalist encirclement; and his successors continue to agree that it is the instrument for building the socialist society, which Marxist history maintains is the form of organization most in accord with advanced modes of economic production.

National Socialism similarly had its *Weltanschauung,* or world view, from which could be deduced the course of history. Its emphasis was on racialism, in contrast to Marxist economic determinism. But, in the general view that the purposes of the organized political community have or should be given priority over those of the individuals who compose it, there is little difference between fascism and Marxism. Consequently, they both deny that there should be any limit on the exercise of political power on behalf of such a community.

Most advocates of liberal democracy, on the other hand, are

not statists, but believe in individualism. They do not deny that there may be meaning in history, but they insist that there is no *one* meaning, and that there is no inevitability in history—because they believe men have the opportunity to shape their own future within the limits provided by their experience and their environment. Thus, they point out that Marx's prophecies about the inevitable collapse of capitalism failed to materialize because, for one thing, people were fore-warned by his prophecy and proceeded to take measures against the widening division between labor and capital that was taking place in his time. Instead of believing that the future is already determined by the conditions of the present, democratic thinkers maintain that man can use his intelligence to direct policies so as to modify, if not forestall, what may seem to be impending.

But if man can so act, it is a natural corollary that the state is controlled by its members, and not that the state has the right to control everything in their lives. And, at this point, we return to the conception of limits that has been put forward as the characteristic feature of a democracy. For it is only when there are limits on what the government may do, and on the way in which it may do it, that the citizens are in control. In a mass society, the controls should ultimately be in the hands of the whole community, but within such a framework of limitations that the rights of individuals and of minorities are protected.

It is apparent that this definition of "liberal" democracy is different from the "plebiscitary" democracy, which, grounded in the ideas of Rousseau and the practices of the French Revolution, tends to give majorities the unlimited power to determine policies. Liberal democracy implies that even majorities must respect the basic spheres of individuals and of groups, and take their interests into account. This means that the right of the individual to pursue his own spiritual and cultural life and the right of minorities to express their views freely and to influence policy are as much a part of democracy as popular control. It is for this reason that countries like

Great Britain and France as well as the United States cherish civil liberties, and that the opposition plays so vital a part in the legislative process.

It has often been said, however, that only countries reared in a tradition of constitutionalism have respect for such limitations upon government. Nor can we deny that the countries in which Marxism and fascism have had the greatest effect are those that had the weakest constitutional tradition. Thus, it seems clear that newly independent countries like India have a great initial handicap in establishing liberal democracy because of the slightness of their earlier constitutional tradition (and even India knows much more about constitutionalism because of its long contact with the British than do many other politically new countries). And, yet, if the earlier argument has been correct, the essential requirements of democracy in these new countries, as in the older democracies, will be the acceptance of restraints on the operations of government and the willingness to follow empirical methods rather than an unrestrained rule that operates in terms of some preconceived goal.

It is necessary, however, to be realistic about what is expected of a state under modern conditions. Beyond the traditional democratic demands of civil and political rights are the hopes and expectations encouraged by the material achievements of science and industrial technology as well as the requirements of modernization, made increasingly urgent by the population explosion, especially in the developing nations. And, as scientific knowledge and technological possibilities expand, so does the sphere of political activity. Whatever is capable of organization and manipulation will ultimately come, to some degree at least, within the state's purview. All the more reason, therefore, to confront the actualities of politics and world affairs with the experimental spirit. While totalitarian leaders have often been hampered by their doctrinaire approach, the students and practitioners of politics in democratic states can search for new ways to meet their problems, borrowing from others where it fits their needs and countering the dangers with which they are constantly confronted. The spread of the use of the institution of *ombudsman* to provide an impartial investigation of complaints by citizens against the operations of governmental departments is a good illustration. Each democracy can be a laboratory for others.

CAN LIBERAL DEMOCRACY WORK?

The charges against liberal democracy raised at the beginning, it may be remembered, were of two types. First are those that concern the machinery of democratic government—the instruments of information, the party and electoral systems, representative institutions, and the making and administering of policy. But there are also questions that probe more deeply and raise the issue of whether the intellectual and moral qualities necessary for the successful functioning of liberal democracy are not lacking under modern conditions; whether the enormously increased responsibilities of government are not too numerous and complex for the comprehension of the ordinary citizen; and whether the conditions of economic strain, international conflict, and racial or group hostility have not destroyed the reasonableness, patience, and tolerance necessary for voluntary and peaceful agreement.

The Machinery of Democracy Evaluated

When we look at those questions that concern the machinery of democratic governments and then reconsider the vast variety of institutional forms that exist, we realize that there is no such thing as *a* "democratic political machinery." On the contrary, one of the greatest strengths of democracy is the variety of devices that can be used to achieve free, representative, responsible, and efficient government. There may be a two-party system or a multiparty system, a system with a "dominating" party and even a more or less democratic one-party system; the parties themselves may be highly disciplined, loosely disciplined, or not disciplined at all—and the same party system may include several kinds of parties. Authority may be divided among the legislature, the cabinet, the party organizations, the civil service, the judiciary, or even extra-governmental groups in any number of possible combinations. The cabinet may be composed of one party or several, or even, as once existed in Austria, of both major parties on a cartel-like basis of "parity." The legislature may be elected in a great variety of ways, from the simple direct election of the House of Commons to undiluted PR, as in Italy, or the indirect election of the French Senate. There can be such anachronisms as the hereditary House of Lords, or the appointive system under which the Canadian Senate has traditionally operated. The legislature may have a set of specialized committees or a number of them that are unspecialized, and it may arrange its procedure so that ministers or high officials dominate the proceedings, or so that private members assume the leadership. It may be under the threat of dissolution by the executive or have secure tenure, as do American legislatures, for the entire period between fixed elections.

The government itself may be under strong one-man leadership, as in the American presidential system; or it may consist of a group of equals, among whom the prime minister is only somewhat "more equal than the others," as in the British Cabinet system; or somewhere in between these two types, as in the West German chancellorship government. The government may administer a large number of public services directly, or it may use devices like the public corporation. Different degrees of authority may be given to civil servants, who may be recruited in a variety of ways and with a variety of qualifications in mind. There is no necessary uniformity in the pattern of local government or in the division of authority between national and local governments, or, where there is a federal structure, between the federation and its components. Even the courts may follow the most divergent patterns of organization and training. No single formula is obligatory. The very lack of authoritarianism encourages experiment and inventiveness.

Every country necessarily develops its own types of political institutions in terms of its historical heritage, its social and economic institutions, and its ultimate objectives. What has been called its "political culture"—i.e., the characteristic shape its political attitudes and processes assume on the basis of its particular historical traditions—determines to a large extent how a country's political institutions function in practice. Thus, two countries may well have institutions that, to the outside observer, seem almost identical, yet the behavior patterns of their people may make them work in quite different ways. The famous study by Almond and Verba of the political cultures of various countries* showed, for instance, that parliamentary democracy functions differently in Britain and West Germany—more "democratically" in the former, more in accordance with authoritarian patterns in the latter—because Britain has a "civic culture," in which political participation on the basis of "we, the people" is high, while Germany has a "subject culture," in which the people traditionally look up to those who govern them.

Moreover, political institutions have their own coherence or inner logic. Thus, a powerful legislative committee system is not compatible with the strong executive of the British parliamentary system, which works through its control of the House of Commons, while it is compatible with the powerful American executive, because the latter has its separate sphere of action. In other words, no particular means of political action or political control can be judged apart from its historical context and national setting. Moreover, no failure of one set of democratic institutions on the mechanical level can be taken as proof of the failure of democratic machinery in general.

At the same time, there are certain tests by which we can determine the health of a democracy. Is its constitutional framework of individual rights and recognized procedures jealously safeguarded? Are its press and other media of ex-

---

* Gabriel A. Almond and Sidney Verba, *The Civic Culture: Political Attitudes in Five Nations* (Princeton, N.J.: Princeton University Press, 1963).

pression presenting as full and accurate information as possible, providing a channel for the presentation of all important political ideas, and promoting the discussion that is essential for popular participation in politics? Do its channels of political action operate to facilitate criticism, to enable minorities to differ from the majority, and to make their views heard with ease within parties, parliament, and the country at large, and to ensure that, at intervals, the general policy of a government is passed upon by the voters in a general election? And is power, whether centered in executive leadership, or parliament, or a particular party, being exercised responsibly in the interests of the common good? In any nation in which some of these questions must be answered in the negative, one may seriously question whether democratic government is genuine or can long endure.

The Assumptions of Democracy Evaluated

Underlying these tests of the working of a democratic system are certain assumptions about human beings that do not go unchallenged. Many question the capacity of people to understand the voluminous and technical problems of modern government; others suggest that war and economic strife have destroyed the qualities of character needed for peaceful agreement and compromise. Still others question whether the large-scale organization and mechanization of life allow for personal concern for, and initiatives by, the masses of the people. It is clear that no governmental device can make men more intelligent, or public-spirited, or tolerant, or reasonable than their own capacity and the conditions of modern life permit. The fundamental question for democracy today is whether, however adequate the machinery, human beings have the qualities of mind and character to make it function.

Fortunately, the attack on the capacities and character of the ordinary citizen is oversimple in some of its assumptions. The citizen does not have to be technically competent in every phase of governmental activity in order to judge whether he is well-governed. The political decisions required of him are relatively simple, and he is not ill-equipped to make them. As Aristotle noted, the person who eats a dinner is as good a judge of its quality as the cook. The citizen is concerned with purposes and results rather than the technical means of accomplishing them. It requires a technician to plan and build a bridge, but it is the citizen who knows better than anyone else his own desires and needs, and he is better equipped than anyone else to tell whether his government is satisfying them.

The Western democracies have provided us with considerable evidence that an educated and experienced electorate is not a bad judge of the important issues of modern politics. There have been encouraging signs of restraint and judgment from some of the newer Asian, African, and Caribbean states like India, Tanzania, and Jamaica. Certainly those prophets who expected the extension of the suffrage to result in a tide of reckless legislation have been disappointed. Even in foreign relations, where the judgment of the ordinary citizen would seem most badly handicapped by lack of personal knowledge and experience, the policy of the older and newer democracies has never been so disastrous as that of a Hitler or a Mussolini. Revelations of the nature of Hitler and his "court" disclose a degree of folly of which no democracy has shown itself capable. Similarly, it would be hard to think of a more devastating indictment of Soviet leadership than the revelations about Stalin made by the Soviet's own succeeding top leadership.

If one turns from the question of technical competence to that of the moral preconditions for successful democratic government—calmness, reasonableness, and patience in arriving at decisions; a desire to come to peaceful agreement or compromise, and, therefore, a willingness to make concessions; a feeling of confidence that no political group will attempt to impose its will by force, or use violent means to keep other groups from attaining power, or overthrow the constitutional system—it seems clear that such qualities are not easily and quickly acquired, but rather are fostered by long experience and by favorable economic, social, and geographical circumstances. Where such qualities and experience are lacking, the establishment of democracy is, at best, difficult; it is significant that in countries like Great Britain and the United States, where democracy has been most successful, children are taught from their earliest school days to play the game, accept defeat with good sportsmanship and victory with generosity, abide by the will of the majority, and take criticism and disagreement in good part.

In fact, the very success with which these qualities are inculcated in the democracies—the belief that any problem can be solved if only men of good will meet each other in reasonable discussion around a table—has made it difficult for their leaders to understand and deal with those representatives of authoritarian governments who, like Hitler before World War II or Communist leaders such as Stalin, think not in terms of enduring compromise but only in terms of total victory and crushing defeat; who regard concession as a sign of weakness, and a compromise not as an enduring agreement but rather as a resting place on the road to the complete achievement of their original aims; who look forward to crushing their enemies, and who cannot conceive of tolerating a "loyal opposition."

All societies, democratic, traditional, and, most of all, totalitarian, strive through political socialization to inculcate their values into the young. To a large extent, they succeed. But we must also note the extent to which, even in countries like the Soviet Union, there is a reaction against such indoctrination that may reach the dimensions of open intellectual dissent. And, in democratic states like the United States, Britain, France, and West Germany, this kind of reaction has of late taken the form of a radical turn by some of the most highly educated among the young against basic political values preferred by the "establishment." This, too, should be regarded as part of the intellectual ferment that helps to keep democracies from conformism and rigidity.

More than education is necessary for the cultivation of the

political attitudes that democratic government requires. Democracy flourishes best where there is a feeling of economic well-being and security. He who lives under conditions of civil strife or violence is likely to consider order—even when brought about by a strong man—preferable to the uncertainty and the risks of a freer existence. The man who suffers from grinding poverty and the anxieties of unemployment finds it difficult to be detached and reasonable in his judgments, to weigh judiciously the fate of the commonwealth while his children go hungry. It is here that the nations of the world face the greatest problems of the final decades of this century. The rising and rapidly growing masses of the world's "south," the "proletariat" of the present-day world, will hardly be able to achieve the maturity that liberal democracy requires without a rapid improvement in living standards; if the poor nations are not lifted out of their present low standards of development, their governments, whether now democratic or not, may fall into anarchy, or take to bellicose adventures, and the great powers may be pulled into the vortex. Therefore, it is a matter not only of moral concern but also of self-interest for the advanced nations of the "north" to lend whatever assistance they can to the development of the poor. Moreover, in their own countries, the "affluent" still possess all too many pockets of poverty, often connected with racial discrimination. But, as the example of the American black has shown so vividly, desire for human dignity does not cease, even under conditions of misery and discrimination. The same is true of the peoples of color who have recently emerged or are emerging to nationhood. And nowhere does desire for freedom flourish more glowingly than where it once was suppressed by totalitarian control. To this the Hungarian people testified when rising against oppressive rule. But the "thaw" that has since set in in Hungary, despite the outward failure of their revolution, affords reason to believe that the cause of freedom still has hope as long as people cherish a feeling of what it means and a desire to attain or retrieve it.

The democratic way of political life is not an easy one, but its rewards are great. No form of government is simpler than that of one man ruling over others; yet, history stands as a record of the abuse of power so concentrated. Democracy requires from its citizens a level of political intelligence, experience, maturity, public spirit, and self-restraint that is lacking in many parts of the world; and it also demands the exercise of ingenuity in finding solutions and developing the political machinery appropriate for a system that desires freedom and responsibility as well as efficiency. The great strength of democracy is that its way of life fosters and encourages these very qualities. It is in the democracies that no one attitude or solution is orthodox, that diversity and experiment are considered natural and desirable. And, as one looks at the great variety of devices that have, in practice, been developed for the realization of democratic aims, it would be rash to conclude that, in imaginativeness, willingness to experiment, and social idealism, the democracies yield in any way to other forms of government.